KEEPING QUIET

KEEPING QUIET

PAUL NIXON

THE AUTOBIOGRAPHY

PAUL NIXON & JON COLMAN

The
History
Press

To Jen and Isabella.
You are my heart and my soul. You're both amazing.

First published 2012

This edition published 2017 by
The History Press
The Mill, Brimscombe Port
Stroud, Gloucestershire, GL5 2QG
www.thehistorypress.co.uk

© Paul Nixon & Jon Colman, 2012, 2017

The right of Paul Nixon & Jon Colman to be identified as the Authors
of this work has been asserted in accordance with the
Copyrights, Designs and Patents Act 1988.

British Library Cataloguing in Publication Data.
A catalogue record for this book is available from the British Library.

ISBN 978 0 7509 7005 1

Typesetting and origination by The History Press
Printed in Great Britain

CONTENTS

FOREWORD

BY STEVE WAUGH

I first became aware of Paul Nixon when I walked out to bat and scratched a line indicating centre stump in the moist pitch at Grace Road, when playing for the touring Australian team versus Leicestershire.

I didn't see him, but I heard him.

It was like I had gatecrashed his party and was an unwelcome visitor. Not long into my innings I thought to myself, 'Who does this Pommie so-and-so think he is, talking with his barely recognisable accent and mimicking the way that we bloody well play the game?' But I instantly liked him and knew he was a leader of men, and one that could lift a team with his body language, enthusiasm and spirit.

More than a decade later, I had the opportunity to play alongside Nico – or, to use his more appropriate nickname, the Badger – at Kent where he was trying to kickstart the second half of his career. Nothing had changed; he was still like a tetanus injection (a pain in the backside), with the alertness of a man who had skulled half-a-dozen Red Bulls and the enthusiasm of a kid with a twenty-minute free pass in a candy store. His presence had its fingerprints all over the changing room and on the playing field, for he was always trying to keep things upbeat, striving to self-improve and desperate for the team to be competitive.

I was amazed that England never recognised his qualities until the twilight of his career. He was a batsman who lifted in pressure situations and a keeper who compared favourably to all of his compatriots, and perhaps most importantly, his combative nature and never-say-die attitude ensured that every team he was a part of had spirit and life. He was the heartbeat of the team.

Nico was from the 'old school', who loved to share his thoughts on the day's play and life in general after stumps were drawn, and it is here that perhaps his greatest legacy will be left. He was street-smart and savvy, a wolf in sheep's clothing, but above all he was a bloody good cricketer and a great bloke.

I'm sure you will enjoy his honesty and insight into what was a fascinating journey, and I look forward to catching up and hearing about what I'm sure will be the next successful phase in his life after cricket.

Always 100%.

Steve Waugh, 2012

FOREWORD

BY SIR VIVIAN RICHARDS

It is indeed a great pleasure to be asked to write a few words about Paul Nixon. I first met this young man when he was a member of the Lord's groundstaff during the 1980s. Back then, one of the duties of the groundstaff was to lend a hand to any touring team engaged in practice at the Nursery Ground. One of the young men that immediately grabbed my attention was Paul.

Why, you may ask? It was simply because he was always engaged in the game that he wanted to pursue as a profession. He was always willing to do anything for the game he loved and respected. We all know that not only was he one of the best wicketkeepers in England, but also a fierce competitor.

Paul was the best 'throw-down guy' in the business and I can remember always seeking him out for practice, because he was consistently professional in his duties. A little secret I will share with you is that whenever we played at Lord's and Paul gave me my throw-downs, I would register a century.

I am eternally grateful to him for helping me prepare for some of the best innings I played at Lord's, and that is why, when he was given his first cap for his country, I really felt the joy for something he truly deserved.

I would like to take this opportunity to wish Paul and his family the very best and God's guidance.

Sir Vivian Richards, 2012

one

HOME ALONE

Friday 3 February 2012.

> *... thanks [compère's name] ... Hello everyone ... I'm very honoured to be here tonight, but I have to say I was a bit put out that I was only second choice. You actually wanted a legend, a knight of the realm, the star of* Strictly Come Dancing *– Sir Bruce Forsyth! But sadly he couldn't make it, because he has to attend the birth of his next wife ...*

The words coming slowly together on the page in front of me will be delivered tonight to the lucky people of Coventry & North Warwickshire Cricket Club. I am writing a speech, but I'm running against the clock. And the hangover isn't helping.

> *... now, [compère's name] is such an honest bloke and I'd like to thank him for entrusting me with his problem. He's addicted to drinking brake fluid, you see, but he assures me he can stop at any time ...*

The jokes are the easy part. The first one is the property of Roger Dakin, the former England hockey player, and the second is Macca's. Macca is Paul McKeown, my brother-in-law. He has a rich supply and tells them better than me, but I'm improving all the time and – most importantly – I'm a willing learner. That isn't something I would have said thirty years ago.

Sometimes I allow myself a laugh when I think how I've changed. If someone had told me, in the beginning, that I would end up writing speeches and delivering them (and being paid for the privilege!) – I would have presumed they had the wrong man.

But I do it and I usually enjoy it, from beginning to end. As long as I can shut myself away from background noise, and create a little framework of what I want to say, I can drive to any venue and perform comfortably. It might not be so comfortable today, though; my head is still fogged up, and concentrating is hard. The words are going down, but they are landing in slow motion and I'm not even certain they are the right words, or in the right order.

Why do we do it? Why do we batter our bodies with alcohol, put ourselves through the same old cycle and then go back for more? I would love to know. Last night I went out in Leicester with some friends, gave it the big one and, as usual, it is coming back to haunt me in a big way. Hangovers absolutely ruin me. There are rashes and sores on my skin, my eyes have dried up, and I'm not feeling especially positive about the world.

This morning, after breakfast, I sat down to write an e-mail to a friend in the City of London. Any time I type something on the laptop I challenge myself to avoid the little red line that signifies a misspelt word. I think I'm getting better at that, too, but today? You couldn't move for red. It was absolute carnage on the screen, and things haven't got a great deal better this afternoon with a pen in my hand.

OK, ladies and gentlemen . . .

I put the pen down and stare at the page. The back of my neck is itching like mad. I sit up straight, give it a vigorous rub, and then, a few more blank seconds later, I reach for my phone.

Paul Nixon @Paulnico199
Minus 7!!!!!!!!!!!!!!!!!!!!! Outside now!

Jordan Carrigan @JordanCarrigan
@Paulnico199 umust be garn soft nico! It's been -9 the past few nights in gods garden Cumbria.

There is a game I often play whenever I drive back to the promised land with Jen and Izzy. It's called 'Who can be the first one back to Cumbria?', and I always win. When the sign for my home county appears beside the motorway, I wind the window down, put my right hand outside and reach forward; I then turn around to my passengers and declare my victory. It's a daft little thing, but I love it.

I've been thinking about home a lot lately. Leicester is where I live and where I call home most days of the year; it's a wonderful city whose people have embraced me. But there's no place on earth that will ever draw me back quite like Cumbria. Returning to my home county has never failed to make me feel good about life – whether as a teenage hopeful or as a veteran with dodgy knees, the warmth I received from people there during my career was priceless. When I played for England Under-15s, I would return to backslaps and 'keep goings'; when I started pushing through the ranks at Leicestershire,

I would go home to 'well done lad's and 'we're all behind you's; when I won trophies, and played for England, the same. People from Cumbria have written me countless letters over the years, even during the times when I wasn't doing so well. You have no idea how much that matters.

Jen, my wife, is a home-bird and feels the same pull. Isabella, my three-year-old daughter, seems to share in the excitement any time we point the car north and set off for Langwathby. For Izzy, Cumbria means fresh air and the chance to play with her cousins. For Jen, it is valuable time with her mum and her sister. For me, it means a living nightmare trying to get an internet signal on my iPad, and wondering why I have to do all the visiting when it's me who has just driven 200 miles ('why can't they come to me, just for once?') but mainly, it's a happy place for all of us.

Now I'm retired I should head up there more often, but I seem to be busier than at any time in my life. The other day was typical: in the morning, I spent two hours at a coaching school, and then drove home to do a radio interview over the phone. After lunch I sat through a meeting about a business interest, before embarking on an endless slog through London's charmless traffic for a charity dinner. I finally got back home shortly before 11.00 p.m., in time for a late meal – a chicken wrap with cranberry sauce – and then an hour on the phone to my ghostwriter. Jen? Not for the first time, my wife was at the back of the queue. I barely had time to catch up on her day before the yawning kicked in and it was time for bed.

But I will do it; I will visit home more frequently, now there is one fewer excuse.

Of course! I should introduce myself. My name is Paul Andrew Nixon, I am 41 years old, and if you haven't seen me by now, chances are you will have heard me. I played cricket for Leicestershire, Kent and my country; and all three – there is no point pretending otherwise – at a decent volume. That much you probably know, but there are some things you probably don't. Stories: yes; tales of a chatterbox wicketkeeper: yes; but there's more to my life than just anecdotes. Don't worry, it took me decades to learn certain things about myself – some good, some not so good, some downright strange and some I kept quiet – but we should be able to get there a little quicker.

A text arrives from Josh:
Gym tomorrow?

My reply:
Too bloody right!!

Josh is Josh Cobb, Leicestershire's 22-year-old batsman and our man of the match in last summer's Twenty20 final. Josh is a great kid. His father, Russell, was an old team-mate and a great friend, and I can remember holding baby Josh in my arms when he came to visit us on the farm. When I found myself batting with him twenty years later it made me feel very old.

At Grace Road, pre-season is under way. How do I know this? How could I ever forget? I lead a non-stop life but it's hard not to miss the thrill of a new pre-season. Even though my career was longer than many, even though I had a better swansong than most, and even though my diary is now fit to burst . . . nothing quite replaces the buzz of strapping on the pads, stuffing a box into place, pulling on the gloves and then getting down to it in the nets. The trick, I suppose, is not to miss it too much. It's one of the reasons why I refuse to sit still.

In these early days of retirement, the benefits of being an ex-cricketer are few. A little more time with the family is a blessing, and devoting my energy to different goals is exciting, but if you put a gun to my head and forced me to pick one obvious advantage above all the others, I suppose it would have to be the pain. From morning to night, things don't hurt quite as much now.

Cricket is the best game in the world but when you've played it for more than twenty years and squatted more than a million times (I've worked it out, don't worry), you find yourself creaking as you approach the end. In the final days of my career, pain was – Jen and Izzy aside – my most faithful companion. It was there when I came down the stairs in the morning and when I drove to Grace Road. It was there any time I sat down and any time I stood up. It was there when I went for a lie down, there when the temperature dropped and there when I turned around.

When I ran, when I jogged, when I walked and when I stopped – it was always there.

Let me count the aches. When I wore cricket spikes, the soles of my feet would get sore and stiff. If I went for a 2-mile run without first undertaking lengthy calf exercises, that muscle would be pulled in no time, and at night I would need to ice away the hurt. When I drove my car, my knees ached, and when I walked downstairs it felt like my legs could buckle at any time; as a result, the daily descent became a slow motion, sideways shuffle. The squatting has also taken its toll on my back, which isn't as flexible as it used to be; when I sit on the sofa for any length of time, I can only describe the resulting sensation as a kind of indigestion around the spine.

Towards the end, any time I turned my head to the side it would cause my neck to twinge badly. This obliged me to rotate like a robot, using my entire upper body, rather than just my head. And then we come to the battered old hands; during my last, unforgettable summer, any time I caught a cricket ball it felt like the force of twenty was hammering into the gloves, and in cold weather my thumbs would start to ache.

Before retirement, my life had become one of ice baths, hot water bottles, stretches, and so many other methods designed to keep pain at bay. Putting myself through the various contortions of Bikram Yoga sometimes helped, and I also bought something called a Compex machine: a piece of kit the size of an old cassette player, which you attach to yourself and allow electrodes to stimulate the muscles and get rid of lactic acid. You aren't supposed to use it while driving, but I did.

A good, old-fashioned gym workout would occasionally do some good. Lifting weights and developing a sweat seemed to balance the body and take away the aches. But only for a while, on most days, the contract had to be signed with pain. Year after year, month after month, you keep doing the deal until it finally becomes too much. Last summer, it became too much, and I knew for certain that it was time to make way.

I've not gone cold turkey since retiring – far from it. I couldn't. I still get the urge for the gym and I am a nightmare if I go for too long without a run. But it's different now; the worst of the pain has slowly subsided. The other stuff? Well, that's a little more complicated.

Outside, Leicester is Siberia for the day. Sub-zero temperatures are not exactly ideal when you haven't long been home from South Africa. The heating is on but I'm sitting here, at the table, wearing two jumpers. Jen, meanwhile, has gone to collect Izzy from playschool. Izzy, who has inherited her father's energy and was up at four o'clock yesterday morning demanding entertainment; Izzy, who has an incredible knack for finding buttons on the iPad that I didn't know existed, causing it to freeze or go dead; Izzy, who has a flower named after her in our garden (the Isabella Rose); Izzy, the apple of her old man's eye. Izzy . . . there's a story there, too.

My mobile phone trills with more tweets. I grab it, again, and run my finger across the screen to unlock it.

I love Twitter; it's right up my street. A couple of presses and you are interacting with people from all over the country and the world. When we were on holiday in Cape Town we promised ourselves one night out, Jen and me, just the two of us, so we left Izzy with the childminder, went for dinner and planned to do nothing but talk and catch up on life without any distractions. What actually happened? People started responding to my invitation to come up with a title for the book and we spent the evening roaring with laughter at some of their tweeted suggestions (*More Sledge Than Santa* was one of my favourites, and I was disappointed to learn that *The Bald Truth* had already been taken by a rugby league player).

People often ask me for a 'retweet' and I try to oblige them all. It's the simplest thing in the world, and if you can make someone happier for a few seconds just by prodding a screen, then I firmly believe you should. Mainly, though, I love it because you are never isolated with Twitter. If I am on my own for any length of time, like today, I cannot help picking up the phone and checking the latest. It's like a reflex action, as natural as anything, and sometimes it's much more preferable to being at home, alone, with just my mind for company. As I'll explain, we haven't always got along.

The speech is going nowhere fast. I gaze at the notepad and try to switch back on. If I can't finish it now I will have to write the final few lines at the dinner table.

Underlining a few words sometimes helps – that will restore my focus. The ruler, I think, is in my office room. I push my chair back, stand up and walk briskly towards the stairs.

two

THE CATCH

karl green @karlgreen3
@Paulnico199 just seen skysports catch of 2011 & your not in it???
#worldsgonemad

Aside from the trip to Cumbria, there is one journey I love to make more than any other. All it takes is a single tweet to provoke the memory and I am on my merry way again, to Edgbaston, Warwickshire County Cricket Club, on Saturday 27 August 2011. The occasion? It's the Friends Life t20 final, no less. The contest? Leicestershire Foxes versus Somerset Sabres. The significance? It's only my last competitive match in England! The problem? That would be the 6ft 5in of West Indian danger arriving at the crease.

Kieron Pollard is the kind of player who can take a game away from you in the blink of an eye. The kind of batsman so stupidly powerful he can mishit the ball for six. The kind whose wicket you want early, if at all possible.

Somerset are in reasonable shape when he comes in to bat, so it feels like a few early words are necessary.

He is walking out without a helmet. That will do for starters.

'Look at you, with no helmet!' I exclaim. 'Our quick bowlers are going to come on in a minute and we know you're scared of it, big lad.'

No response.

Pollard takes a single off Josh's off-spin and disappears to the other end. Peter Trego works another off the last ball of the over and keeps the strike.

Matthew Hoggard, our captain, then brings on Wayne White. Pollard requests his helmet and then reappears at the striker's end a couple of balls later. Ding-ding – Round Two.

'Look at you, calling for your helmet! You're shit scared of it. Are you not embarrassed about being scared of it? We're all laughing at you out here.'

Nothing, again.

Pollard sets himself for a bouncer. Chalky runs in and bowls a shade fuller than the Trinidadian expects. He gives himself room and has a waft. No contact. Into the gloves. Lovely.

'Look at you, backing away, you big girl's blouse! Do you not fancy this? What's wrong with you? Everyone's laughing, you know.'

Standard verbals, really. You're not necessarily searching for a bite; just trying to drip a little doubt into the batsman's mind – get him out of his comfort zone. Sometimes it works like a dream, sometimes it backfires. You have to pick your moments, choose your targets.

Pollard still isn't giving much away. I walk back to my position for the next ball . . . The next ball, the next ball. A wicketkeeper's life is about the next ball. It could happen at any time, so you always have to be ready. The opportunity to take your ultimate catch – your full-stretch, diving showstopper – could be around the next corner.

When I was with England, Duncan Fletcher used to love trying to give me one of those in morning practice. Eventually he would nick it in just the right place, and I'd spring to my right and keep hold. He'd do the same with Paul Collingwood at gully and Andrew Strauss in the slips. Perfectionists to a man.

When the seamers are bowling, you visualise your ultimate catch before every delivery, but the truth is you only get three or four in your entire career. It's such a rare feeling, and, by the summer of 2011, even rarer for me.

Sometimes the truth slaps you in the face, sometimes it creeps up with stealth. In our quarter-final, against Kent, Rob Key edged one of the first balls of the innings from Harry Gurney. It dipped and swung away from me at the last second, and I just hadn't been able to get there. When I viewed the video later, it looked catchable, which was strange. It hadn't felt remotely catchable at the time.

This, on reflection, had been a message from my 40-year-old limbs and muscles – it was finally getting too hard. Too much of the game was disappearing out of my reach, and the old bones were starting to let myself and the boys down. The End was knocking on my door.

White runs in for the fourth ball of the fourteenth over. Pollard, again, gives himself room and has another big whoosh.

Some edges, when they come early in an innings, can catch you out. This one I see from the moment he swings his blade. To the untrained eye such a chance passes in a flash but as soon as bat connects with ball I know I am going to get there.

The nick has taken a touch of pace off the ball. It veers away slightly, but comes through at a decent height. I dive, arm outstretched, and it slaps into the bread-basket of my right hand – just below the creases of the knuckles, so that I can wrap my fingers over the top of the ball and hold on.

Get in there! My ultimate catch! In the final! And Pollard the victim!

Before I hit the ground I feel goosepimples rise on the back of my neck.

Even now, I have barely had time to watch the footage of the best split-second of my life, so it's a good thing the film reel in my head is working.

I walk into the kitchen and prepare a protein drink. Into the mixer goes some milk, followed by a generous scoop of powder, and then a teaspoon of olive oil. I clip on the cap, give it a vigorous shake, unclip and then knock back the mixture with gusto. *How many times have I done this?*

As the good stuff slides down, I rewind and indulge myself a little further.

Finals Day . . . in the build-up, while others are outwardly nervous, I just feel hungry, keen, desperate for it. Maybe it is an age thing, but I don't harbour any butterflies or any doubt. And a sportsman free from doubt is a very dangerous animal. I should know.

In our epic, rain-affected semi-final, we beat Lancashire in a 'super-over', thanks to Will Jefferson's mammoth hitting, and when the chaos and the celebrations die down I head back to the team hotel, feeling tired and drained. I slump on the bed and lie down on my front. Texts and tweets are coming in by the bucketload but I'll look at those later. I enjoy a few precious minutes of calm, until, on cue, my left leg cramps up. Brilliant. I glug down some water, take some electrolyte drops and set off back to the ground for a massage.

One notable feature of Finals Day is that four teams occupy the ground, instead of the normal two. This means that we have to walk past Hampshire's viewing gallery on our way to the changing room. During their semi-final defeat to Somerset I see Shahid Afridi, Hants' Pakistani talisman, sitting on a chair not long after his dismissal, with his head in his hands. I leave him to his thoughts and walk past without speaking. Minutes later, I return to find him in exactly the same position. This time I offer a consoling word, but he remains motionless. Not even a flicker.

We watch the last few balls of Somerset's victory and then it is time for us to get out into the mixer for the final. The crowd is getting warmed up, the beers are clearly flowing, and we are up for it. Massively up for it. Abdul Razzaq and Will get us going, and I come in at number five, to try to work the spinners.

First rule of Twenty20: expect the unexpected. I am facing seam, not spin – Craig Meschede is the name, and I've never seen him before in my life. He bowls me a beauty first up, which I just about survive, and four balls later I hit one like a tracer bullet to Pollard at long-off. He fumbles it a few times before bringing it under control.

I shuffle off to a surge of noise and look up to see thousands of pairs of hands clapping. The lads hug me as I walk in but I quickly disentangle myself and rush into the dressing room to get some fluid on board.

We make 145-6, and when later we jog back out to begin our defence, it is my job – as usual – to start the trickling of uncertainty into a few Somerset heads – make a little mischief, if you will.

First – Marcus Trescothick, perhaps the finest batsman in county cricket. Tres is a really technical thinker. In the early stages he is struggling to get Hoggy away.

'Hey, Tres, why are your hips so open?' I enquire. 'I've never seen your hips this open.'

Drip, drip.

Craig Kieswetter, another dangerous customer. Craig has recently been working on his wicketkeeping with his England coach, Bruce French. Bruce was a fine keeper in his day but never boasted a formidable batting record.

'Hey, Craig, I didn't realise Frenchy was your batting coach these days. I thought he was supposed to be working on your keeping, not your batting?'

Drip, drip.

Those two depart for not very many. In at three – Peter Trego. A somewhat different challenge, in that he is a big, muscular, tattooed hitter whose major strength is that he always seems to play without fear. Well, we can't be having that!

'Tregs, mate, have you lost a bit of weight? You look a bit skinny. Are you not lifting weights any more? Is that bat turning in your hand because it's too heavy for you?'

He glances around, just for a split-second, but long enough for me to see him chuckling.

That means he is listening.

Drip, drip.

At the other end is James Hildreth. This is a guy we are concerned about, mainly because of his ability to sweep and reverse-sweep. But Claude Henderson rarely misses a trick, and instantly puts two men behind square. Hildreth goes up the wicket to his first ball and has to kick the ball to stop himself being stumped.

Classic.

'What are you doing, man?! That's a terrible shot on this wicket. The next ball, we know you'll want to sweep, and Claude's going to bowl a slider and get you lbw. At the most I'll give you four balls against Claude. Four balls.'

Drip, drip.

Hildreth blocks the next one. He isn't sticking to his game. The pressure builds. He hangs around for a while, but isn't hitting boundaries. He duly gets out. Then it is Pollard. And the catch.

The moment I hit the turf with the ball in my glove, it is as though someone has connected mains electricity to my body. I throw the ball as high as I can, and roar. In a flash, James Taylor rushes in and leaps on me. Team-mates are flying in from all directions.

The commotion eventually dies. Jos Buttler walks in to replace Pollard. By now I am absolutely flying . . .

'Now then big lad, it's up to you . . .'

He hits the first ball for four. Not a bad response, considering. He gets himself in and plays a few more shots, but Somerset need boundaries in bulk, and they aren't quite coming.

It is at this point that I pull out my trump card.

'Eh, Jos, all the Somerrrset farrrmerrs will be puttin' theirr comboine 'arrvesters away forr the winterr, saying, "That Buttlerr went and lost us anotherrr game".'

He declines to respond to my dreadful West Country accent, but Josh is by now bowling a great little spell, with Claude whispering wisdom into his ear. The shackles are on.

Buttler eventually goes for a big shot and is taken on the boundary by Matthew Boyce, who is on as a substitute fielder and will catch pigeons for us down there all night. The crowd erupts, and we know the job is as good as done.

Our bowlers diligently work their way through the remaining overs, but it is candy-from-a-baby time. As Andrew McDonald sends the last couple of balls down, I feel my eyes begin to well up. Somerset splutter apologetically to 127-9 and then expire. Another roar goes up. Victory!

There is no better feeling, no sweeter sensation. And no better painkiller.

On the field, with a stump in one hand and champagne bottle in the other, I walk to the boundary to share the joy. I find Dad, who is beaming, and we hug.

'Bloody hell son, what a game,' he shouts into my ear. 'It's a fairytale. A proud day.' Something like that, anyway. 'Just get this down you,' I say, extending the bottle. He takes a swig and I eventually walk on.

The cameras follow me as I come to Jen. Embracing my wife at the end of this incredible journey feels like a special moment – we've been through so much! Unfortunately for Jen, the moment loses some of its magic when she knocks back a big gulp of champagne too quickly and it surges back out of her mouth, all on live television. She won't live that one down. Around the boundary there are Leicestershire people dancing around, joining in the mayhem, supporters who have followed us through the occasional ups and considerable downs. Players like Harry Gurney, who missed out through injury, and other young lads, whose days are yet to come, as well as backroom staff who've helped us in countless ways.

After the presentation and the interviews, during which Hoggy has a nice little dig at the media for writing us off, I finally get back into the dressing room, where another pleasant surprise lies in wait. Ah, the painstaking, box-ticking monotony of the random drugs test, how I will miss you! Here, in Leicestershire's moment of glory, in the hour of my glorious swansong, I am instructed to enter a toilet cubicle, piss in a bottle under observation, and then fill out the necessary forms. The testers write down their numbers, put stickers on the bottles, note down which supplements I have taken and conduct various other little tasks. It seems to take ages, but at least it's not my worst. Once, after an attack of stage fright at Swansea, I was a prisoner of the drugs test for more than three hours – three hours of drinking pints of lager, three hours of standing under the shower, three hours of repeatedly flushing the toilet, three hours of trying anything, anything at all, to activate the waterworks. Luckily, the taps work swiftly on this occasion and after forty-five minutes I am allowed to escape.

The Hampshire players are waiting for us as we filter into the hotel bar. They greet us with a standing ovation and seem particularly chuffed that we have beaten Somerset. We sing and dance for hours, before the younger boys sneak off to a nightclub. The rest of us, umpires included, remain in the bar and proceed to get nicely lashed. It must be after 2.00 a.m. when somebody notices the highlights on TV. We form a horseshoe around the screen as my dismissal is shown. You lucky bastard, Pollard! When footage of the standing ovation follows, I notice Jen dabbing at a few tears. I pull her in for a hug.

Three hours later, or maybe longer, I am forced to admit defeat. I down my last pint, am dragged up to my room by Jen, and within seconds I am gone.

After three hours' kip we are up and away again. Our house in Leicester is on the market and some people are coming to view it at midday. So much for enjoying the spoils of victory. I greet our prospective buyers with a rotten hangover and a smell of stale ale; I don't expect them to make us an offer. Down at Grace Road, meanwhile, camera crews and journalists are waiting. On Monday we are due to host India in a Twenty20 game. I climb into the car, still fuzzy-headed, and drive to the ground. Rahul Dravid, my old Kent team-mate, is first to greet me. Lovely to see Rahul – one of the good guys.

The interviews commence. There must be thirty Asian journalists here. Thirty journalists, all with a single, favourite line.

'Just one more question . . .'

'One more question, please . . .'

'Can I just ask one more . . .'

Two hours after their umpteenth 'one more question', I am still talking. When the inquisition finally ends, somebody hands me a copy of *The Times*.

'Have you seen this?'

I accept the paper, which has been opened onto the report of Finals Day. It seems that Mike Atherton, *The Times*' chief cricket correspondent, has not been entirely keen to share in our success . . .

Any sentimentality, though, should not blind us to the unacceptable levels of sledging Nixon engaged in from behind the stumps as the match reached its climax. Buttler, a player of enormous promise, who earlier in the day gave everyone a sharp reminder of his hitting ability when taking the Hampshire attack apart, was visibly upset at the close and refused Nixon's placatory offer of a conversation . . .

Come on, Athers, you're better than that! I always thought the first rule of journalism was to present both sides of the story? If you had asked me – and what was stopping you? – I would have explained everything.

The truth is that, as we had walked off the Edgbaston outfield, removed our caps and greeted the Somerset players, Jos Buttler was sixth in line. When I made to shake his hand, he didn't look at me. I told him he was better than that, that we play hard on the pitch and have a beer off it. 'Yeah, yeah, sure,' he said, half-heartedly. Later, because of the drugs test, I had been the last out of our changing room. Coincidentally, so was Jos from theirs. I bumped into him at the bottom of the lift. We approached each other and high-fived.

'Sorry about that earlier, Nico,' he said. 'I was just gutted we didn't win.'

'Hey, don't worry bud,' I replied. 'Just make sure you go and smash it for England, yeah?'

He said well done, I said good luck. We left on decent terms.

A couple of days later, I head for Old Trafford to watch England's Twenty20 international against India. As I am being interviewed by BBC 5Live, Athers and Nasser Hussain walk past.

Athers smiles, nods, puts his hand out and I shake it. I feel like saying something, but I don't. They walk on.

Later that afternoon, I get a call from Paul Haywood, our chairman at Leicestershire.

'Nico, just to let you know, something has been picked up from the stump mic on Finals Day,' Paul says.

'What do you mean?' I enquire.

'Well, apparently you have abused Jos Buttler and said something derogatory about his mum.'

'His mum? No way. That's news to me.'

'Mike [Siddall, our chief executive] is at Lord's now and he's going to speak to the ECB.'

It is, of course, absolute rubbish. I have given out plenty from behind the stumps, but I'd never talk about someone's family like that. I ring Trescothick straight away.

'Tres, they're saying I said something about Jos's mum last night. The ECB are onto it. It's absolute bollocks. You know that's not me, bud.'

'Let me speak to Jos.'

When Marcus calls back a few minutes later, he confirms that Buttler had heard nothing derogatory. So where has all this come from? And there is more. Two days later, on 2 September, a letter lands on the mat at home. I open it and unfold the contents. At the top of the creased A4 page is the England and Wales Cricket Board (ECB) logo. I used to ache to see that logo. This time . . .

Dear Paul,

I write further to your conduct in the Friends Life t20 final last Saturday.

Your persistent verbal behaviour directed to the opposition (sledging) was totally unacceptable.

Whilst this has not, as yet, drawn any official complaint from any party, it is important that you are aware that it has been noted and placed on your record.

It continues with a fairly severe warning that 'any further misconduct' will result in 'positive action being taken', should I take up 'any role in cricket' in the future. I stare at this briefly and then my eyes shoot to the bottom of the page.

Yours sincerely,

Alan Fordham
Head of Operations, First Class Cricket
cc Mike Siddall

Well, a simple 'Happy retirement, Paul' would have sufficed. What the fuck is this? Persistent verbal behaviour? Misconduct? I know Alan from my time coaching in South Africa in the 1990s, so I call him. When I get through, he explains that 'someone' on the committee thought I had said something over the top to Buttler, and they are giving me a slap on the wrist.

'Hold on,' I say. 'So there has been no complaint from any party who was involved on the day? Somerset and the umpires have said nothing and I am still getting done? If nobody has complained, why is it an issue?'

His response is a bit woolly. I can't get to the bottom of who has actually complained. Alan repeats the line about 'persistent verbal behaviour'. I tell him that I saw Trego laugh, and I'm sure I saw Tres smirking, too – hardly the actions of people who were upset. And Buttler, the supposed target, has also exonerated me.

In the days that follow, I fish around for explanations. Had the stump mic not been very clear? Had my words sounded like something else? Had they read Athers' piece, and reacted to that?

No answers are forthcoming, and it continues to bug me. Is there somebody out there with an axe to grind? Someone who has mistakenly – or wilfully – confused a little bit of passion with unacceptable abuse? Someone in a suit who has never been out there in the arena themselves and committed the blood, the sweat and the tears to the winning cause?

I stew on this for a while, and eventually come to a satisfying conclusion. Fuck them. And, today, as I stand here in my kitchen reliving the whole experience one more time, that's still what I think. Fuck them. Leave them to it. Did this mystery individual or individuals honestly think they were going to spoil it all? Did they anticipate that my memories of Saturday 27 August 2011 were going to be tarnished by lies and smears?

Did they believe that I was going to allow the million positives – the standing ovation, the golden stump, the hug with Dad, the champagne-spewing from Jen, the singing, the dancing, the drugs test, the umpteen other things (ok, maybe not the drugs test) and, of course, the catch, that priceless moment when the body obeyed the brain and the result was almost too good for words – to be overridden by one pathetic little negative? Really?

Me?

They did not understand the half of it.

three

LITTLE MAN

Here is wicket-keeper Paul Nixon on playing in the aftermath of Friday's drinking furore: 'When I'm working my processes, my self-talk in my own mind is about my cricket and my focus, and the negativity is behind us.' Read that line again if you need to. I could be asking questions at the end of this piece.

(Martin Gough, BBC Sport website, Thursday 22 March 2007)

I did it again the other day while being interviewed about England's One-Day International prospects. I said it, and, as usual, they didn't ask.

I must have given thousands of interviews over the years. Press, radio, TV, websites, you name it. I don't like to say no, I don't see the harm in being open, I prefer to help when I can, and you might already have gathered that I am fond of talking. Sometimes I say too much, but I can't help it.

There's one thing, though, that I would like to know. Why did nobody ask?

Let me explain. When people in the media invite me to discuss my approach to batting or keeping wicket, I invariably reply by speaking about mental processes, about routines, about positive self-talk. 'It's all about keeping that little negative man out of your head,' I commonly assert.

Nobody ever dug deeper.

Nobody ever asked about the little negative man.

Pour yourself a drink and pull up a chair. This one could take a while.

1.

I am in Cumbria, preparing for a game at my first club, Edenhall. I recently played for England Under-15s, and in the pavilion they have put up a framed picture of me. I look at myself, smiling proudly in my England blazer, and think, 'That's me – I'm the man now.'

And then – 'I've got to win this game for us.'

The game, against Cockermouth, begins. I am batting nicely, totting up runs without much effort, and then all of a sudden I'm up against a bowler called Malcolm Huddart.

Malcolm is known as a tricky customer in the Cumbrian leagues. He is bowling great big away-swingers and I'm struggling to lay a bat on them. After a couple of overs of this, I come to the obvious conclusion: I simply cannot bat against Malcolm Huddart. I don't like facing him and I don't even know what I am doing out here today. I begin to over-analyse. I start thinking and worrying, thinking and worrying. Before much longer, I get myself out, badly.

Nixon, caught Nixon, bowled Nixon. All my fault.

2.

I'm playing for Cumbria Schools at Humberside. I'm our best player, capable of scoring big hundreds. I have reached fifty without any trouble, and then the next ball comes down. I grope for it, fail to connect, and it slaps into the wicketkeeper's gloves. That is all the trigger my mind needs.

Why didn't I pick that one up? Was it because of something in the background, behind the bowler? Did something get in my line of vision? Was it that red brick in the wall?

Suddenly I am fixated by the wall, in the distance. I can't take my mind off that little red brick.

That thing is going to fuck me up here. That red brick is going to get in the way. And this lad is going to get me out.

The dialogue in my head starts getting faster and faster. Then, in the corner of my eye, I see one of the cover fielders walking in.

He shouldn't be that close. What's he doing there?

I've heard something else, further away. I follow the sound – it's a train, and it draws my eye like a magnet.

I wonder where that train is going? Where could it be coming from, and heading to, at this time of day? I wonder if it's busy, if it's comfortable, if it's an enjoyable journey for the people on that train? God, I'd really like to be on that train right now.

I'm still thinking about the bloody train when the bowler is running in. You know what happens next.

3.

With Cumbria Schools again. On the bus to Christ College, Cambridge University. On tour.

I'm one of the youngest in the group and I have been subjected to the regular ritual of being dragged to the back of the bus by the older lads, and given a hearty pummelling. My shirt is ripped, my tie is frayed and I am the proud new owner of dead legs and arms. Thanks, boys!

I'm now relieved to be back in my seat, free from further treatment. Safe. But it's a long way to Cambridge from Cumbria, especially on this rickety old bus, which we have mockingly christened 'Stephenson's Rocket'.

Too long not to think.

I know I'm going to be relied upon to win the game. I don't want to let anybody down. And I want to show I can stand out. Really stand out.

So, what could possibly go wrong? Nothing, really, unless. . . .

What if my bat breaks? What if it breaks, and I can't use it? Fuck, what if that actually happened? What would I do then? And what about my pads? Imagine if they got ripped? Imagine if they got so badly torn that they weren't fit for purpose? Which pads would I wear then? Would it feel strange wearing different pads?

By the time I come to the game, my mind is littered with this nonsense. As a result I don't do myself any justice whatsoever with the bat or the gloves. Another opportunity vanishes down the drain.

4.

I'm playing for Middlesex Seconds at the Lensbury Club in Teddington, having been temporarily promoted from the MCC groundstaff at Lord's. The game, against Leicestershire, should be right up my street. It's a nice, flat pitch, brilliant to play on, easy to read and full of runs, so why am I looking at the tennis players over there?

They are the world's best, practicing for Wimbledon. One of them is Steffi Graf, the German goddess with legs to die for. I am transfixed by Graf, and the others, as they serve and as they return. I marvel at how high they throw the ball, how they fizz back returns at shoulder height, how they read the bounce and the spin, how they take pace off the ball, how they stay in control of the point, how they . . .

Once again, I want to be there, not here. In my distracted mind, it has almost become irrelevant that there is a cricket match going on, and that I am batting.

On this dream of a track, this batting Utopia, Leicestershire's spinner tosses one up. I come forward and am caught at bat-pad.

5.

The month is September 1990. I am batting at number eight for Leicestershire against Derbyshire, and have made seventeen tough runs against their useful attack.

When they bring on their top guy, the West Indies fast bowler called Bishop, I think: 'Bring it on.' Toe-to-toe with a proper Caribbean quick. I like pace on the ball and I'm up for the scrap. The adrenalin is flowing and I meet his early deliveries with a straight bat and a square jaw. It feels like I could go on for a good while.

It is as Bishop walks back to his mark that *he* chooses to rear his head.

Now, how's the field, Nico? Where are your areas? Ooh, look – there's some nice space past mid-on. What's that fielder doing there, though? Is he in the right place? Looks like he's not sure. Is he going to settle there? See him. Avoid him, if you can. Play to your areas. Where are your areas again?

Slow down, man, slow down. Let's start again. Let's . . .

Look, now he's approaching. Lovely run-up. Just look at that perfect rhythm. Hello, he's got a short-leg in now. Must be planning to bounce you. How are you going to deal with that? What are your plans?

Well, I . . .

Now, look at that short-leg. Is he going to be close enough? Have they got that one quite right? And . . . hang on, look at his head! What on earth is he wearing? A pink helmet? That can't be right! Wrong colour, surely. Shouldn't it be brown for Derbyshire? Look at him, over there – he's wearing a brown cap. So is he. Don't their batters have brown helmets? So why is the short-leg wearing pink? A pink helmet – that's crazy! Must have been a cock-up in the dressing room. Maybe . . . Ah, well. Looks odd, that's all. Sticks out a mile.

Er . . .

Shit, now Bishop's in. Forget the bloody helmet. Now, where are you? Go back and across . . . But what's he doing with it? No, wait – look for the drive. Look for the drive. Mid-on's come up. Think of your areas. Where's this going? Here it comes . . .

I am heading back to the pavilion, having played a total mess of a shot and been caught.

I march off quickly, keeping my head down as I enter the dressing room, where I kick off my pads and tear off my gloves. I put on a t-shirt and shorts, lace up my trainers and bound out of the ground in the direction of the racecourse.

6.

Grace Road, 12 August 1998. It's the NatWest Trophy semi-final against Derbyshire, and we're down to the most crucial couple of minutes of our run-chase.

We are 295-6. We need 299 to win. I am on strike and there is one ball to go. One boundary to win. One boundary for Lord's.

It's my responsibility. Forget the previous 49 overs. Forget the first five balls of this one. This is the moment that matters.

Vince Clarke is the bowler. His leg-spinners have gone, so he's sending down seamers instead. I have to watch the ball, know my areas, make a decent connection . . .

Last ball, last ball, what's he going to do? What if he bowls a leg-spinner? What if he goes back to that? If he does, smack him out of the ground. Yeah, a big, clean shot to win it. Win it, win it! Lord's is one ball away. Lord's – the dream. A Lord's final. It's all down to this ball. How did this happen, by the way? How has it all come down to this? Should it not be all over by now? Why isn't it all over? Why haven't you hit any boundaries yet? Is it not your day? Maybe it's not your day. Tough luck. But just think of Lord's, think of the crowd, think of the glory, think . . .

Clarke runs in and bowls a quick one. I take an ungainly heave but it is through me before I have even thought about my stroke. Dot ball.

I have effectively talked myself out of winning the game. Derbyshire celebrate jubilantly. I go back to the dressing room to face the music. The boys look at me. 'What was I thinking?' their expressions seem to ask.

What was I thinking?

If only they knew.

For most of my life I have been beset by negative and distracting thoughts. At the start, that's all they were – thoughts. Over time, though, the thoughts became clearer and more incessant. And the more I heard the words, the more I began to depict a person articulating them.

This little chap duly started materialising in my head or on my shoulder. From time to time, and with barely a moment's notice, he would drop by and set about sabotaging my day.

Think this sounds weird? You would be absolutely correct. I mean, how do you begin to make sense of it? How do you even start to tell people that for most of your life your mind has been invaded by an imaginary figure that appears from nowhere, chunters away and doesn't leave until you've completely derailed?

Perhaps the best way to start is with a description.

I hope he won't mind me saying, but my little negative man is an odd-looking chap. His shape is that of a skinny little gingerbread man, with thin arms and thin legs, but a big, domed head. Sometimes he has eyes, but not always. He speaks in a soft whisper, but doesn't have a mouth (don't ask me to explain that). His colour? Silver, shiny silver. Not too long ago, when I was in a department store, I passed a selection of cooking utensils and stopped in my tracks. One of the implements on the shelf looked just like my little man, with its thin body and large, spoon-like head.

I don't know why he looked like he did. I don't know where he came from. There's probably a shrink out there who could explain everything, but I never thought to delve deeper. All I know is that this strange-looking fellow would wait until I was batting or keeping wicket, and then – there he was. He would talk and talk and talk and talk until my mind was racing off in all sorts of different directions. The clutter he was able to create was extraordinary. He would tell me to do this, then think about that, then worry about something else, then question whether I should be doing the alternative, and then – Shit! – shouldn't you be thinking about what you're going to do before it's too late?

He would suggest different shots, one after another. He would divert my attention to something hundreds of yards away, or something under my nose. He would tell me it wasn't going to be my day, and I would believe him. Usually, the outcome was that I would get myself out, or miss a catch or a stumping. I don't know which bowlers have had the most success against me during my career, but there cannot be many who have dismissed me as often as my little friend, my little negative man.

When the little man wasn't there, things were different – extraordinarily different. Batting and keeping came so easily it was almost effortless. Removed of doubt, my mind would be blissfully empty and the game would slow down to a perfect pace. I have, for example, walked out in a Lord's final in front of 30,000 people and hit my first ball from Curtly Ambrose back over his head for four. He stood and stared at me; I felt amazing.

When I scored hundreds, it was precisely because of this clarity of thought. Subconsciously, I would batter myself with positivity and flood my brain with affirmative beliefs . . .

It's my day, my stage. Come on, bowl at me, bowl at me, bowl at me.

This wasn't a plan. It just happened. And the problem was, because I didn't understand how to control my mind, I would operate at extremes. When this mental pinball was at its worst, early in my career, my batting performances would go: great day, shit day, great day, shit day. All because of the way I thought, or didn't think.

The shit days would just tiptoe along behind me, and then strike. There are so many examples to relate. Try these:

I am hurriedly making breakfast and snatch the toast the second it pops. I quickly smother it with butter and get stuck in, but as I grab the last morsel from the plate it slips out of my hand and drops to the floor.

A negative day is born.

I empty my washing machine and fill a basket with my laundry. As I carry it across the room, a sock tumbles from the pile and falls onto the carpet.

A negative day is born.

I am lugging my cricket bag outside, to be loaded into the car. As I heave it up and into the boot, I lose grip of one of the handles and have to pick it up again.

A negative day is born.

I am driving to Grace Road, in dreadful traffic, and attempt to overtake the crawling motorist in front. I fail to do so and have to drop back in behind. I curse this little failure, because that's what it is: a failure.

A negative day is born.

From trivial frustrations like these, I would conclude that I was destined to miss a stumping that day, or put down a catch, or play an awful shot. The doubting thoughts would crowd in and my negativity would start causing mayhem. All of a sudden, the bat would feel like a sledgehammer in my hand and everything would be moving in fast-forward, like the classic cricketer's bad dream when you can't get your pads on quickly enough.

When my little negative man was at his most troublesome, I would work myself into a fury which could only be released by running. If it was a home game at Grace Road, and I had been avoidably dismissed, I would charge out of the gate, sprint through the terraced houses and then gallop through Aylestone Park with a cloud of doom over my head, with little regard for the fact I might be needed in the field in a matter of minutes. The consequence would sometimes be that, by the end of the day, I would be keeping wicket with legs as heavy as anvils, because I had run myself silly. But until I got older and wiser, and my knees started to niggle, and the physio told me I had to put the brakes on, that's what I would do. Run and run. And not just in the summer, either. In the winter, I would be sitting at home, with the news on TV, but I wouldn't be taking a word in, because instead I would be going over and over in my head the times I had got out the previous season. At 10.00 p.m., I would turn to Jen . . .

'I'm just going out for a quick run.'

. . . and head out into the night. At 11.30 p.m. I would be doing hill sprints under the moonlight, and really, really enjoying it. The fact it was so late didn't matter. It was something I had to do.

Before the age of enlightenment, before cricket started being flooded by analysts with laptops and before sports psychologists became the norm, an average county dressing room was divided into four categories. You were a) a drinker, b) a shagger, c) a trainer or d) a lazy bastard. I, first and foremost, was a trainer, who would run disappointment out of his system and then wake up the next day with something new on his mind.

There was no additional fifth category for thinkers, not really – not until men like James Whitaker came along. Jimmy was Leicestershire's captain in the mid- to late 1990s. To describe him as an innovator or a master of motivation is not to do the man justice . . .

The month is May 1996. Darren Maddy, the ace Foxes batsman, walks into the dressing room and greets the captain.

'Morning Jim.'

'Morning Daz, how are you this morning?'

'Ah, not too bad.'

Jimmy, visibly perturbed, glares at Maddy.

'Not too bad?'

'Yeah, you know.'

'No, I don't know. Come on then, Daz, what is "not too bad"? Not too bad? How bad is too bad? How bad is enough?'

'Ah, come on Jim . . .'

'No! If all you are is "not too bad", why don't you just fuck off home and come back when you're good?'

Maddy stands in wide-eyed silence for a moment.

'Ok, ok, I'm good, I'm good.'

'That's more like it.'

It was quite bracing, but I bought into it. His approach flooded my mind with positive thoughts, and I needed as many of those as I could get.

Jimmy's skipper-coach double-act with the calmer, more methodical Jack Birkenshaw has entered Grace Road folklore. Jack's approach was all about getting a player to relax and contemplate his game more. Jimmy would then balance this out with his more fervent leadership. He was extremely well-read and fond of slogans, and after a while began giving me some of his books to read. One author he swore by was Dan Millman, a world champion athlete, gymnast and martial arts coach who turned to writing self-help books.

One of Jimmy's many methods to galvanise his troops was to make every player write down his goals and targets and leave them on post-it notes all over the house. I followed his instructions to the letter and did not stop when he loaned me some of his books.

In no time my home was full of these yellow slips of paper carrying positive mantras. In my knife drawer . . .

Rewards in life depend on the quality and aim of the contributions you make.

In the fridge . . .

A crisis is an opportunity riding a dangerous wind.

On my bedside table . . .

The good old days are here and now.

And on the bathroom mirror . . .

Today could be the greatest day of your life.

Until this point, the average team-talk had passed through the jumble of my brain and come out the other side. When I started writing things down, reading the Millman books and chanting his wisdom to myself, it felt like I was making a commitment. It gave me clarity and helped me start the fightback against my little friend. But the battle was never going to be won overnight, for this was a war of many years . . .

four

SNAGGING

If you asked me to nominate my very earliest memory, I'm not sure what I would choose. My little yellow plastic cricket bat, maybe, or my sit-on toy Massey Ferguson tractor with pedals, or my pet lambs, Sooty and Sweep, or the day I was pushed into a paddling pool in the back garden and nearly swallowed its contents whole, or Mum's warmth, or Dad's love of sport, or the rolling fields of the farm. I don't know. But if you challenged me to declare my very first negative thought I would nail it in one go.

Let me describe, as though it was yesterday, how it felt to be curled up under my duvet, sweating and shaking with such a mortal fear that I couldn't do the one thing that would have made it all better (throwing the covers off, swinging open the front door and legging it outside). Let me explain the one thing that worried me – *I can't do it, I can't do it, I can't do it* – to the extent that I would lie in bed and fake an illness, so that Mum would tell school I'm terribly sorry, but Paul won't be in today, but fingers crossed he'll be better in the morning.

Let me tell you about my deep and dark phobia of the spelling test.

The little negative man? At 9 years old, that was me. I hated spelling tests like nothing else on earth, and with, I thought, very good reason. I mean, come on, how was I, a farmer's lad, supposed to know there were two h's in *rhythm*, or a y for that matter, or a -gh at the end of *enough*? How was I meant to realise that *unfortunately* finished with -ely and not -ly, or -lly, or -ley? How was I to understand the hidden magic of 'silent' letters? If they were silent, what the hell were they doing there in the first place? And what were these stupid rules that prevented you from writing words as they sounded, like *rithum*?

I struggled, struggled badly, and what made things worse is that I was regularly made to know that I struggled. A bad showing in a spelling test had consequences, and the consequences had a name. Mr Howarth, my teacher at Langwathby Primary School, was a clever, sarcastic type who loved taking the mickey and was programmed to nail me at any moment that I fucked up. In spelling, I was a sitting duck.

'Yes, it's another shit score for Nixon, so it must be announced to the class in all its shocking glory, and then we will rub it in by packing the poor, defenceless lad off to extra spelling lessons after school with Mrs Woods, whose marker pen smells so pungently that it will make you feel sick, but who will tell you off if you dare to complain.' OK, that's maybe not what he said, but it's what I thought he thought in my hour of humiliation.

Reading wasn't exactly a breeze, either. Whether reading silently or reading aloud, I detested it. It made me tired, hurt my head and one innocent instruction . . .

'OK, Paul, so if you can just read from . . .'

. . . is all it would take for the churning to start in my gut.

I never really talked about my fears; I didn't see the point. Mum wasn't the best academically and Dad was better with Maths – the finances of the farm – than with English. They tried to help me with homework but I don't think they knew how hard I found it. They didn't see me at school, asking so many questions that I'd end up being told off for being silly. They didn't know that what I wanted was for someone to sit down with me, on my own, and explain everything. They didn't appreciate that I steadily began to feel that I was holding the other kids back and letting them down, like the football team's dodgy goalkeeper who keeps allowing the ball to slip through his legs.

My way of coping, when running outside wasn't an option, was to find ways of creating distractions. I had tricks up my sleeve and wasn't afraid to use them. Whenever I was summoned to dictate a passage aloud in assembly, I would feel the fear and then instantly override it by pointing at someone else in the room, making a crafty quip and getting all the attention onto them, just for a few more moments. In class, the same – a joke here, an underarm fart there, an elastic band twanged against someone's ear.

I was good at that, good at making the boys and girls giggle behind the teacher's back, good at making them think I was Paul the jester, full of fun. OK, it wasn't all an act – I *was* full of fun and I *did* enjoy the banter of the classroom – but it was a useful skill to be able to create a convenient little distraction out of thin air when the need arose. And that would have been fine, perfectly fine, had it not been for my other skill – my infuriating knack of distracting *myself*.

Right next to the school, for instance, stood some dipping pens. Seriously, these dipping pens would take me into a world of distraction when Mr Howarth was talking away at the front of the room. Instead of absorbing his lesson, which might have been good or bad – it didn't matter – I would be watching the farmers leading their sheep to the pens.

In my own mind I would be out there, with them, standing by the pens and watching the farmers, watching the animals, watching, watching, watch . . .

'Paul! Are you with us today?!'

Then I would snap out of my trance and try to focus on the lesson.

Then somebody would walk through our classroom, and that would distract me.

Then the lad on the next table would swing back on his chair, and that would distract me.

Then another boy would make a silly noise, and that would distract me.

Then something else would go past the window, and I'd be gone again.

'Paul!'

I was used to a farming environment, where everything came naturally and I would just have to follow Dad's instructions. It was an instinctive way of working and thinking and concentrating didn't come into it. But could my problem really be explained so straightforwardly? Was it just the case that all farm boys were born with an appalling attention span? Sometimes I wish it was; that way, the next twenty years might have been easier to understand.

Don't get me wrong, the fear and the negativity I associated with reading wasn't there daily, or even weekly. It came in short, crashing waves and then, when the danger had passed, life was free to be happy again. And it was mainly a happy young existence. When I close my eyes and think of my home village, I first see a big wall next to a giant, ugly steel bridge. I hear the River Eden sloshing beneath. I see a group of young boys sitting on the wall, chatting happily to strangers as they stop at the traffic lights. I see one of the boys, a hyperactive five-year-old who has already mapped out his future as a crane driver.

I see a homely Cumbrian community of about 500 people. I see three village greens, a playground in front of the pub, a garage, a church, a shop and three farms. Langwathby was my universe and Langwathby Hall Farm was my own private planet. We lived at the back of the village, but Granddad and Grandma lived on the farm and that was my adventure playground. As a two-year-old I toddled around by the milking cows and marvelled at the big, lumbering beasts. When I was older, the fun was over and it became a place of work.

I can still smell all the smells, see all the sights. The best sight? That would be the shoebox on top of the Aga cooker, filled with straw and three tiny lambs, into which Granddad would gently reach down with a small, plastic pipette and watch the newborns reach up to suckle whisky from it. 'Just helping them keep warm, lad,' he would say, and I believed him, because Granddad was never wrong about his animals.

I was an only child, but it never felt that way. It was a community of friends and the Hollidays, who lived across the road on their farm, were as good as family. John, Mark, Tim and Phil were my brothers in all but name; their back garden doubled as our football or cricket pitch, and when we were not being Glenn Hoddle or Ian Botham we would grab inflatable inner tubes from the farm and sail down the river to Lazonby to explore the old lead mine. We were told it was too dangerous to mess around in places like that, but what could possibly be dangerous about the outdoors?

It was quintessential country life, with Langwathby a quintessential English village and May Day the quintessential occasion of the year. To a small boy in a big world it seemed like thousands turned up to watch the football tournaments, strong man competitions, and the sight of the village lads, including one future England wicketkeeper, dressed up and dancing around the Maypole, waving their little flags. When the Maypole came down, the other 364 days of the year would be spent playing rounders, or cricket, or British Bulldog down on that village green. Or – best of all – mass football games, contested by upwards of forty people of all ages, who would pour from the pub and the houses to get stuck in. Sometimes I would join in; sometimes I would sit on the nearby concrete steps and watch our local butcher, Duncan Fawcett, charging down the touchline in his jeans, his classic comb-over flapping in the breeze.

It was a cheerful place, where tragedy was not supposed to rear its head. At six, I was too young to comprehend what happened to Uncle David, but that was the first time I learned that the village couldn't always be an innocent domain where nothing could possibly go wrong.

Uncle David was Dad's younger brother and a regular figure in those episodes of organised chaos on the green. In a village of characters, he was one of the biggest; the sort of man you looked forward to being around. He was also a magnificent prankster. Once he slipped a toy tarantula into my glass of orange juice when my back was turned, and at the moment the horrible rubber creature crept to the surface, I leapt from my seat and shrieked with terror. David, spotting the success of his jape, roared the house down.

In Langwathby, every house was open and every home seemed like a social hub. People worked hard and liked a drink at the end of the week, and one Friday evening David threw a big party at his place, attended by everyone in the village and which did not wrap up until six in the morning. The following afternoon, Uncle David staggered off to play football for Langwathby on the field next to the cricket pitch, and most of the people who had attended his party stumbled down to watch, with bloodshot eyes and rotten heads aplenty.

The game proceeded, but by half-time Uncle David could take no more. The exertions of the night before had taken their toll and he walked off, red-faced and wheezing, to the sound of whoops and applause . . .

'Go on, lad!'

'Can't tek t' pace any more, eh!'

'Hair o' the dog, David, lad?!'

It was just another scene of fun and frivolity under the village sun, typical of the day. So why, then? Why did he do it? Why did Uncle David walk off that pitch, climb into his Mini, drive into the distance and then shoot himself?

I don't know. I have never been told. I have never established why my uncle took his own life at the age of 23. I remember the rumours – that he had been seeing someone behind my auntie's back, or that he was carrying a secret illness – but to this day I cannot explain why he borrowed a twelve-bore shotgun from the farm that afternoon, ventured down an alley and ended it all.

Jen has often asked me about it, but I have no story to share. Dad loves to chat, and can hold a room on just about any subject, but this is one topic that he has never discussed since it happened. All I have is the memory of the time – the big funeral, and a lot of sadness, and then people just seemed to dust themselves down and get on with life.

I've carried that curiosity in the back of my brain ever since, and probably always will. But as the years went by, a different curiosity gradually arose. I found myself wondering a little less about David's awful demise and a little more about the way the pain was concealed – how it was kept quiet, dealt with and then left well alone. Was this, the more I thought of it, the first lesson about the Nixon way?

Farming? Well, that was certainly the Nixon way. It wasn't just a part of life; it *was* life. When I came home from school, I would dump my bag, change my clothes, run up to the farm, jump on a tractor with one of the workers, and go up to the field where my Dad, Brian, was driving the potato harvester, while my Mum, Sylvia, helped pick the spuds. One of my first memories, now I think of it, is of climbing out of bed, pulling on some clothes, being helped up into Dad's freezing cold wagon, having a blanket placed across my knees, and heading over to Teesside to take potatoes for market, with a bacon sandwich to unwrap on arrival. Heaven!

Granddad was the head of the farm, but Dad worked as hard as any man could work, and Mum, the farmer's wife, ran the home like clockwork. She was quite a disciplinarian, and my room could never be left untidy for long, but she was a lovely, homely woman too.

When I was older, my responsibilities on the farm grew. After rising at 5.30 a.m. (the early alarm call was the first lesson of the farm) I would be instructed to sort the potatoes, feed the sheep, round up the cows and gather up the straw and the hay bales – giving myself bloody fingers in the process. There was method in Dad's madness, of course, in giving me all these rubbish jobs, as I later came to understand. But if he wanted to discourage me from a future on the farm, and remind me that a life of sport was a much better alternative, he could have left me with one particular task, no more, and the message would have been heeded.

Ladies and gentlemen, I give you the humble turnip. Actually, no, delete the humble, because that chunky root vegetable was the bane of my youth. How can such a small thing cause so much annoyance? Let me tell you.

To start the process of picking a turnip – snagging, to use the farming term – you had to squat over one, a bit like a wicketkeeper might set himself for a delivery, and then, with all your might, haul it out of the frozen ground. Then, with a big machete, you would chop the top off, and continue this process all the way down a 20-acre field. Squat, pull, pull, keep pulling, nearly there, one more pull, now it's out, chop, throw, then repeat, a million more times. It could easily take two days to get to the bottom of the field. In the middle of winter, I couldn't think of many less pleasant jobs than pulling those bloody turnips out of the rock-hard earth.

Still, I suppose it was outdoor life, and doing anything outside was better than being hunched over a desk. It's not that I didn't enjoy being at school, but I mainly lived for break-times. I had so much energy that I could barely wait to go outside, run myself silly and come back in with my shirt stuck to me with sweat. Not all schoolwork was a chore – I loved writing a story, and my Maths was serviceable – but I found that I had to do most things over and over again before they sunk in. If I was told something by the teacher, it would whiz through my head without touching the sides. If I was forced to read the page of a book and was then asked to repeat what I had learned, my mind would be blank.

Sport came so much easier. As soon as I was upwardly mobile I was displaying an aptitude with a ball that I would never possess academically. Dad recalls with a smile the moment when I went to kick a ball for the first time and went for it with the instep of my foot, not my toe, as though I had been coached in the womb. As the years went on, I would refuse to go to bed until I had, under Dad's gaze, thrown a ball at a Mr Men book which doubled as a target on the floor. At other times I would perch on my knees, roll a golf ball into our sandstone fireplace, watch it fly off at different directions and try to catch it. Sooty and Sweep would be invited to join in my football games in the yard. At Christmas I would amuse myself by doing keep-ups with balloons and when I was older I would drag my duvet downstairs, lay it across the fireplace and drive cricket balls into it.

Indoors could be fun, but it was outside where I most longed to be. Until my early teens, and even after Dad built a bigger house for us up the road, I spent more time at the Hollidays' than ours (I had a Scalextric track in the spare room at home but they had a bigger house, with a snooker table) but when they got the board games out – Scrabble was not a game designed for me – I would only be able to last for so long before I would have to make my excuses and run up the hill for home.

I was infinitely happier getting dirty knees and muddy clothes. With John, the eldest Holliday, I would be the goalkeeper, flinging myself between two trees in the garden. When we played cricket, using the same trees as stumps, the lads next door would sit in their tree house and keep score. John and me were sport-daft and like two peas in a pod. He was bigger than me and had plenty of natural talent, but I had more energy and I always thought I was a bit tougher.

Autumn, winter and spring, meanwhile, would be spent at the theatre of magic known as Brunton Park, watching Carlisle United from the C Stand, and after ninety minutes of gazing down on the Gods otherwise known as Chris Balderstone, Alan Ross and Billy Rafferty, we would visit my other grandparents, in Carlisle, for fish and chips. Mum's dad was a long-distance lorry driver who had (and still has) a wonderfully dirty sense of humour – not that he was laughing the day I accidentally shattered his bathroom window with a ball while he was in the bathroom, on the toilet. But where a ball was concerned, I couldn't be contained, and soon I had developed a strong liking for the thrill of winning in every possible discipline: drinking my milk the fastest, biking to school the quickest, running the eighty metres the fastest and throwing the cricket ball the furthest.

In rounders, too, I wanted to be the best and generally was, despite the best efforts of Mr Howarth, who would often try to catch me out by throwing the ball so high and so wide that it was difficult to hit. But each time I seemed to be able to adjust in time to smack it into the houses. True to form, he would often give me bits of stick to spur me on.

When he wasn't ridiculing my spelling, I actually quite liked Mr Howarth, because he had a sharp sense of humour and was strong in his views. But one of his little put-downs did touch a nerve with me.

'Paul,' he said one morning. 'You will never make a future out of playing sport. I hope you realise that.'

I don't know why he said that. Maybe I'd done something mischievous and it was his way of chopping me down to size. Maybe he was just in a bad mood that morning. Maybe he actually believed it.

Whatever, I knew what I believed: 'Right, you bastard, I'll prove you wrong.'

This competitive streak, which I seemed to have from the start, where did it come from? And this seemingly natural ability with a ball and a bat? I never really thought about it at the time, but many years later, when Dad showed me a dusty old photograph of his uncle Kit, something struck me. The proud figure in the whites, Dad explained, once averaged 100 in local league cricket and had rejected Warwickshire's overtures in order to stay on the farm. It was quite a tale, but it wasn't the story itself that captivated me. It was the photo. When I looked at that picture of Kit I thought I was staring at the mirror.

If I ever had to wonder whether cricket was in the blood, that image confirmed it, but all the evidence I really needed was much closer to home. When people spoke about Brian Nixon, Ernie's lad, they talked of one of the most active local sportsmen you could find in the Eden Valley. Dad was a winner on whichever field you found him and this spirit clearly rubbed off on his son. He played cricket for Penrith and then for Edenhall, which was a little closer to home, and on Tuesdays and Thursdays I would go to his practice sessions and help fetch balls. Between innings, I would venture onto the outfield with one of his friends and hit a few balls myself. Once, as a six-year-old, I hit a tennis ball onto the roof of the Penrith pavilion and thought my twenty-yard heave was the biggest shot of all time.

He was also a footballer, and set up a junior team in Langwathby which was once graced with the presence of Bobby Moncur, the Carlisle manager, who came down to present us with a new kit – an occasion more exciting than any royal visit. When I played I fantasised about being one of the flair men, like Hoddle or Michel Platini, and like most boys of my age I watched Trevor Francis win the 1979 European Cup for Nottingham Forest on TV. There really wasn't much to compare with the thought of kicking a ball around for the rest of your life. The only thing that compared was cricket.

From the beginning, it just had the edge. It was the family way, I guess. It felt more natural, and it also helped that there was already a Langwathby farmer's son showing the way. One hot summer's day Dad took me to watch Graham Monkhouse playing for Surrey against Lancashire at Southport, where I wandered among the people sat on their deckchairs until Graham's dad, Jim, introduced me to a kindly man who appeared to be involved with Surrey . . .

'Now then, son, are you going to be a cricketer when you're older?'
'Yes! Definitely!'

I doubt Micky Stewart realised the little role he played in stoking my passion for the game on that summer's day – or knew then, the effect his own son would have on my life – but his words kept me heading firmly in one direction. Even one of my earliest presents, a Pye Tube Cube, was bought with cricket in mind. This was a little black-and-white TV with a radio tuner on the top and a cassette player on the side. When England were playing the Ashes in Australia, Dad would wake me up and allow me to sneak downstairs to watch the grainy coverage with him in the kitchen, as Botham took it to the Aussies.

Every kid in that era worshipped Beefy, of course, most grown-ups seemed to as well, but I had an idol of my own.

In the living room at home, Dad had a big reclining armchair, the sort that tilted back and shot out under your feet. At lunchtimes he would come in, lie on the chair, eat his food, sleep for half an hour and then go back to work. If the cricket was on, I would then jump on the chair and sit transfixed.

I think I first fell in love in that steaming hot summer of 1979, as I watched the hero with the golden curly hair and the effortless style score a double-century against India from my prone position on Dad's chair. He was fluent and classy with his Gray-Nicolls Scoop bat. Crucially, he was also left-handed.

I would lie motionless, fearful that if I moved or twitched, England would lose a wicket. When *he* was batting, especially, I didn't want that to happen. What I wanted was to watch him carry on, for hours and hours and hours.

Dad was far from oblivious to my feelings of worship. One day, he came home and presented me with my very own Gray-Nicolls Scoop. It was only a size three, but it looked just like *his*. I held its grip and played a few swishing shots in the mirror.

In my fertile mind, I was now the run-scoring maestro myself, caressing the ball to all corners of Edgbaston, the hapless Indians scampering in forlorn pursuit as it bobbled over the boundary rope, the commentators purring at his style and grace . . .

And that's a beautiful stroke . . . four more to Gower . . .

I could not have been happier.

five

BLUES

If this is supposed to be the bit in the autobiography where I confess how one of my parents routinely struck the fear of God into me and made my life a misery, then I'm sorry, it just wasn't like that. Mum was nothing but kind and loving, and Dad? He was mainly a calm bloke with a level head, who rarely let his emotions boil over. Only once, in fact, did he tear a great big strip off me. He claims not to remember the moment but I will never forget it. It was the morning after a big night before and I could tell his mood was dark even before he erupted.

'If you think I'm going to make all these sacrifices, just so you can abuse the situation, you can think again,' he hollered. 'Don't you ever think I'm going to keep driving you all over the country to play sport so you can go out and behave like that. You can come and work for me on the farm for the rest of your life, if you want. I would have killed to have had the opportunities you've got.'

From me, only silence. It felt like I was shrivelling into myself.

Confession: I was never much of a rebel. Through my teenage years, I lived for sport, rather than for challenging authority. The most daring and dangerous music I listened to was ABBA and the clothes I longed to wear were my cricket whites, not ripped jeans or nose-studs. While other lads were causing their parents untold grief on that awkward journey from childhood to adulthood, smoking weed and drinking cans of strong lager in the bus shelter, I was going for runs with my old man.

He was always a fit bloke, who played football into his fifties, and on the farm he would issue me with challenges, like setting off a minute before me and urging me to catch him up. On other days, we would leave a tractor in a field and run home together, panting happily as we got to the front door.

These were my reasons for getting up in the morning. From my early teens, I had gym equipment in my room and pumped iron all hours of the day. And my ability with a cricket bat was starting to take me down a very obvious path. So when Dad saw something that he thought might put that voyage in jeopardy, he stepped in to intercept it.

That's why he went berserk that morning. The blood on my shirt didn't help . . .

The year is 1987 and I am dipping my toe into the wild world of east Cumbrian nightlife. With Langwathby's social scene strictly limited to the Shepherds Inn on the village green, a proper night out requires a 5-mile journey to Penrith. And Penrith means Blues Nightclub.

I am hardly a hard-drinking regular on the pub and club scene, but I enjoy a night out with the lads, and Blues is the place offering maximum enjoyment. On this particular Friday night, I comb my hair back, as usual, until I look like Simon Le Bon, and then button up my shiny blue-and-white silk shirt. When I catch sight of myself in the mirror prior to leaving the house, I pause and preen. *I am the dog's nuts.*

I am sixteen, but quite big for my age, and there is never any question of being turned away from Blues. It is always swarming with people and, for a lad like me with plenty to say for himself, prime territory for flirting with the girls. This is a new challenge, but one I am taking to with enthusiasm.

The evening proceeds heartily, one thing leads to another, and the result is a lingering, drunken embrace at 2.30 a.m. with the latest object of my affections. Sue, an older bird, is vaguely known to me as a hairdresser from Penrith and here I am, on the pavement outside Blues, with my tongue down her throat and my hands operating under their own rules. Nice work, Mr Le Bon!

Unknown to us both, our passionate clinch has led one of Sue's earrings to become snagged on my shirt. Noticing the tangle, she suddenly pulls back and yanks her head away. As she releases herself, a few drops of blood dribble from her ear and stain my silken pride and joy.

We eventually part and slur our goodnights – and they say romance is dead? – but after a few minutes' staggering I realise that I have insufficient money for a taxi, and am clearly far too pissed to contemplate driving, not that I have a car in any case. So how to get home?

There is only one thing for it. I head into a phonebox, stuff a coin into the slot and dial.

Dad answers. I explain my predicament, but before I finish talking he cuts in. He sounds weary, dismayed, and faintly furious.

'It's three o'clock,' he grunts. 'Just get yourself home.'

End of conversation.

I walk aimlessly around the streets of Penrith for a while longer, until a couple of familiar faces pull up in a car. *Nice stroke of luck.* I jump in with them and get a lift home. The rest is a haze. Unfortunately, Dad has seen the blood on my shirt by the time he confronts me the next day. I was already fighting a losing battle, but when he clocked those little splashes of scarlet it seemed to tip him over the edge.

When the tirade is over, and when my brain starts to function again, I sit down on my bed, alone, and think. After a few minutes it becomes clear enough: I don't want to put my future at risk, and I certainly don't want to see that side of the old boy again.

You can come and work for me on the farm for the rest of your life, if you want.

No, I don't want. So I concede that there must be no more veering off the straight and narrow for the foreseeable future, and, with a heavy heart, accept that there must be no more dangerous liaisons for the time being, either. Sorry, Sue.

By 1987, David Gower the Second had passed through Ullswater High School, Penrith, without great distinction. Classroom learning was still an almighty chore, information was still stubbornly refusing to stick to the inner walls of my brain, and on Fridays, there had been a new frustration – agriculture lessons.

Farming and books? Oil and water, you mean! Farming was something you did, not something you studied. Farming was rolling your sleeves up, holding down a ewe and getting on with the lambing. Farming was plunging your arm into a cow and pulling a calf out; a job I was often asked to do, because I had the smallest hands on the farm. Farming was dealing with everyday, life-or-death situations. Farming was not reading about theories of agriculture and writing stuff down. Absolute rubbish.

Who was I kidding? It wasn't just farming classes that grated. Learning across the board remained a drag. Anyway, why waste your time learning when you have sport? Mum and Dad knew where my passion lay. They knew I had a natural aptitude for ball games; they knew I much preferred the way my PE teacher, Rick Martin, encouraged and trusted me when I played cricket for the school team ('give yourself time to get in . . . make sure you look after the other lad . . . watch his running between the wickets'), rather than spoke down to me, like the others, from a seat behind a desk.

It was at the grand age of 10 when I first enjoyed the thrill of raising my bat to celebrate a half-century, and I never tired of the feeling. That titanic innings for Penrith juniors at Keswick made me want to taste it again, and again, and from that point onwards my life was more or less dominated by the little, hard red ball. When Dad went to play for Edenhall, I went with him and was soon playing for the men's seconds, and before I had left primary school I was getting picked for the County Schools Under-13 team.

That made me the youngest in the side by some distance, which brought certain pressures and maybe a little jealousy from a few of the older boys. But I always felt I was there on merit, and the averages bore tribute to my belief. One thing didn't sit quite so easily, however. As much as I enjoyed batting more than anything else in the world, I couldn't abide fielding. As the only player in the team who didn't bowl, I was obliged to spend long periods of time stationed at the fine-leg boundary, doing nothing.

Doing nothing was not my idea of fun. So, to alleviate the boredom, I filled the time by performing handstands and executing cartwheels, much to the amusement of the watching parents. Well, it was either that or stand around with my hands in my pockets. And I had far too much energy for that.

The impromptu gymnastics demonstrations, though, were brief. During a game against Northumberland, our wicketkeeper was having an absolute nightmare, letting byes through by the dozen. Eventually our coach could take no more, and asked if anybody else fancied having a go with the gloves.

Almost instinctively, I shot my hand up:

'I'll do it!'

I'd always enjoyed playing in goal in the Hollidays' back garden, so I reckoned that keeping wicket must be fairly similar. Plus, it was a way of getting involved with nearly every ball. That *was* my idea of fun.

When I tugged on the gloves and went to my position, I suddenly found myself precisely where I wanted to be: at the centre of the action, all the time. I enjoyed the ball coming to me, again and again and again. I got used to the repetition. I was a good catcher. It all felt completely natural, I had found myself a little niche.

According to Dad, my quick progress above my age group earned me some approving words in the press. One prominent local journalist, Keith Richardson, wrote that I was destined for a future in county cricket, which was a pretty big call to make about a kid, and a nice thing to write. But I didn't really take notice of things like that, I was only concerned about the action.

At thirteen, I stepped up to Edenhall's first team, biking down to nets with my kit on my back. When I played with the men I don't recall feeling nervous or overawed, partly because I was getting good scores, but also because of the nature of the club. Edenhall was a real 'together' place, where everybody socialised after games and the sound of laughter was never far away. And the teas! The teas were something else – big plates, stacked high with cream cakes, which were absolutely irresistible to visiting teams. Our rivals never seemed quite as keen or athletic when they went out to field after tucking in. Against more than one such overfed opposition I took happy advantage, and on one memorable occasion joined Dad in a fifty partnership, as we knocked off the runs to seal a handsome victory against BAE Systems.

Most of the time it felt easy, as though hitting the ball and running was something I was born to do. From an early stage people seemed happy to help me, too; Dickie Spruce, who played for Penrith and Cumberland, gave me some quality coaching with the county's top wicketkeepers and

I kept improving at a sharp rate. At thirteen, I was confident enough to stand up to quick bowlers; at fourteen I was named Edenhall's young player of the year; and at fifteen I topped the Cumbria League's batting averages and even had a bat contract (again, thanks to Dickie).

Then I was picked for Cumbria Under-15s, went on tour to Denmark and filled my boots with more runs and catches.

Then I graduated to the North of England Under-15s, carried on as before and did not pause for a moment to consider how fast things were moving. Then I played my way into the England Schools Under-15s, and finally reached a point where I had to accept that the spotlight could no longer be on me alone.

This was my first time on a national stage, where expectations were high and competition was considerable. In all honesty, I didn't feel out of place when I slipped into my England blazer and posed for photos, though I knew people back home thought a lot of the achievement. When I got my kit on and started playing, things came as naturally as they always had, and when we played against Scotland and Wales I did OK, as did many of the other young lads (Chris Adams, the future Sussex captain, among them).

But it was another who ruled the roost.

Mark Ramprakash was barely out of short trousers when he became one of the most talked-about boys in English cricket, and he had the game to go with the reputation. He had scored a heap of hundreds by the time he was sixteen – even a double-ton, which was amazing – and had a huge, 3lb Gunn & Moore bat, which seemed four times as large as mine.

He already resembled a man in a boy's world, but was also quite a carefree and fun-loving lad who had an enviable repertoire of impersonations. When he knew a game was won, for example, he would take the ball for one of the final overs and bowl in the style of Gladstone Small, running in with his shoulders raised and his head tucked in.

We all laughed along, barely disguising our admiration of this multi-talented prodigy who seemed to have a glittering international career in front of him. Me? I was just enjoying the ride. Mum and Dad were encouraging me all the way, chauffeuring me the length and breadth of the country and sacrificing all their time and money so I could follow my path.

I wouldn't be the first sportsman to salute his parents for the things they did, but there were times when mine seemed to go above and beyond. Dad, for example, would think nothing of driving from Langwathby to Truro (approximate distance: one million miles) for an England junior festival, watching me play, and then ferrying me home again in his old

Triumph 2.5 Overdrive. Those occasions in Cornwall were a big deal in the calendar and a decent measure of a young cricketer's progress, and I performed pretty well at the festival I remember. But it is not for the cricket that the day comes to mind.

The journey home was a ten-hour slog and the will to live had just about drained from my body by the time Dad whipped around the last corner into Langwathby and accelerated for home. The moment we cleared the bend, however, a problem quickly arose. Another car was hurtling towards us, on our side of the road, having plainly overtaken in a stupid place.

There is nothing like the prospect of impending death to jolt you out of your sloth. Collision was inevitable and would, I am absolutely certain, have been lethal, had the old man not then shown reactions that would have put Nigel Mansell to shame. With a flick of the steering wheel, the Triumph shot to the left, ploughed through the grass on the roadside, avoided impact by a whisker and then, in the blink of an eye, Dad had us back on the Tarmac and chugging towards home, as though we had never been in a moment's danger. The old man didn't seem to think much of his skilful manoeuvring . . .

'Bit close, that. Anyway . . .'

. . . but I struggled to sleep that night.

Christ, imagine if . . .

I was amazed we were still alive.

I woke up the next morning with the same thought as the previous morning, and all the others: *I am going to play for England.* The full, grown-up England, that was. The England of Beefy and Gower and the rest. It felt like my destiny and I was determined to make it happen.

But this wasn't an era when a boy had to pigeon-hole himself too early; I was still free, mainly, to enjoy any game I pleased.

If it happened outside, I was there with bells on. I was always decent at rugby, capable of slotting the winning kick for Cumbria Schools against Lancashire (an act which guaranteed me some local brownie points), but that was third in the list of my sporting loves. Second, and a high second, was football, and in certain corners of Cumbria I swear there are people who still talk in hushed tones of the energetic central midfielder for Penrith who went into battle with the Carlisle teams like Denton Holme and locked horns with players like Steve Harkness, later of Liverpool.

I must have been useful, because I also played for Carlisle United's reserves for a couple of years. This might sound like I was close to wearing the hallowed blue shirt at Brunton Park. I wasn't – not really. The reserve team was basically a group of decent local lads, and however much I enjoyed the training, the weights, the running around the athletics track at the Sheepmount in Carlisle and being a kid among men, at no point did I ever really feel like I was going to make it as a footballer. I didn't seem streets ahead of other lads in the way I was in my chosen pursuit.

Cricket was beyond doubt where I was headed. I knew this for certain by the time I was invited to Nottingham for England Under-16 school football trials, but I went along anyway. It sounded like fun and I didn't see any reason not to go.

The trials were held at Nottingham Polytechnic, and began with a speech from Brendon Batson, the former West Bromwich Albion star and Professional Footballers' Association secretary.

We all filed into the lecture hall and sat down, and then Batson, standing at his lectern, cleared his throat.

'Now, everybody in this room wants to be a footballer, don't they?' he said, looking expectantly at the room, but not really anticipating an answer.

'OK, I'll put it another way,' he continued. 'Does anybody here *not* want to be a footballer?'

He was smiling by now, and, again, not expecting a response from the audience. I put my hand up.

Sixty heads swivelled in my direction. Sixty pairs of eyes looked upon me as though I was the village idiot. Batson looked mightily puzzled.

'OK, well . . . what do you want to do?' he asked, addressing me.

'Oh, me, well, I want to play cricket.'

A few of the boys sniggered.

'So what on earth are you doing here, then?' Batson enquired.

'Oh, I just came down to see what it was like.'

'Oh. Right . . .'

Everybody in the room fell about laughing, but I just thought I was being honest.

I had travelled to Nottingham with another gifted lad from Ullswater School. John Scott was without question one of the most talented footballers in that lecture theatre – he was like a little Peter Beardsley, full of skill and fizz, but he never made it. His parents, unlike mine, used to shout at him a lot when he played, and he ended up rebelling. I think it was too much pressure for him, in the end – pressure I was grateful never to feel.

Back on home territory – cricket, not football – my next step forward was to be given a brief taste of Minor Counties action with Cumberland. But this was a time memorable more for the presence of our most celebrated player than my performances with bat or gloves. David

'Bumble' Lloyd was an absolute crackerjack, the life and soul, a man who taught me more about my ability to withstand ale than how to play a correct forward-defensive.

My first involvement with Cumberland was as twelfth man for an away game against Cambridgeshire, and Bumble's way of initiating me into the team was to take me out for a red-hot curry and then get me royally pissed, which in those days probably meant a couple of lager shandies. Lancashire and Cumbria did not always mix happily but that night Accrington's finest played a significant part in my development. I went in as a raw, inexperienced young lad, and came out as a raw, inexperienced young lad with a sore head.

On the field, meanwhile, my first proper game was a nine-wicket win against Bedfordshire, at Carlisle's Edenside ground. Graham Monkhouse, now back in his home county at the end of his distinguished career, rolled them over and enabled me to nab a couple of catches off his bowling – the old farmers' union, strong to the last. My second outing, against Cambridgeshire, on a horrible, wet wicket at Penrith, was less notable, as one of their bowlers, Turner, took 9 for 11 off 12 overs before adding me as his tenth victim, when I went back for a pull shot and felt the ball skid off the wet turf and rap my ankle in front of the stumps.

I didn't have much chance to atone. A couple of weeks and one more contest (against Scotland B) later, and my illustrious Cumberland career was over, almost as quickly as it had begun. And the stats were truly mouthwatering: three games, five dismissals, eleven golden runs. The big time beckoned.

That cameo for my county might not suggest it, but I had by now outgrown Edenhall. Before the start of the 1987 season, it was decided – by me and by Dad – that it was time for me to take the next step, to join a bigger club in a bigger league in order to push me further. The obvious move would have been up the road to Penrith, but they only wanted me to bat, not keep wicket. Dad also thought them a closed shop with a drinking culture, so instead he made a few calls and got me a place with Vickers Sports Club in Barrow. They played in the North Lancashire and Cumbria League and were short of a wicketkeeper. 'It'll be good for you,' Dad said. 'An education.' He wasn't wrong.

Because Barrow was such a hike from Penrith, I would stay with a team-mate during the week and then go home on the train at weekends. This meant that, for the first time, I was responsible for getting myself up in the morning, for sorting my kit, for turning up to nets on time. It was a reality check in the fundamentals of growing up, and also in cricket, because the standard of player in the North Lancs League was noticeably better than anything I had confronted before. Opponents were less forgiving and team-mates were more gifted, such as Steve Wall, a quick bowler who had played for Warwickshire, and our Pakistani genius, Ijaz Faqih.

Ijaz had played internationally a handful of times, but nowhere near as often as he should have. The result of his rejection by Pakistan was that a club like Vickers could reap the benefit of his skills. He could turn the ball sideways and you could actually hear it fizzing as it came through the air. I had never kept to such a masterful bowler before. To me, still a naïve teenager, the guy was an absolute professor of pace, spin and bounce. I studied his action, scrutinised his variations, and gradually became a better wicketkeeper for the experience.

There were other things to absorb, too. The North Lancs League was a serious scene.

The bars were full, hundreds of people came to watch, opposing professionals went toe-to-toe and the rest of us worked like demons – this was what cricket was meant to be. There seemed to be strong rivalry in every game between teams and players, all of whom seemed to be out for the other lot's blood. A lot of abuse was traded on the field, and more than once I saw a bowler square up to a batsman after a decision hadn't gone his way. Things never actually came to blows, but it was a more hard-nosed approach to cricket than I was accustomed to.

There was a lot of chat on the pitch, as a rule, and as I settled into the Vickers team I started throwing my piece in. I don't actually recall my first bit of chirp to a batsman, but what I do know is that the North Lancs League did not reward a player who could not stand up for himself.

I learned a lot about mental toughness and weakness from that time. Older players would often pick on me as the so-called rising star with a big local reputation. They saw it as their duty to bring me down to size . . .

'Come on then, golden boy, let's see what you've got. Are you gonna win this game today?'

. . . and it felt natural to give a bit back.

But I was still a boy, still feeling my way in, and there were times when I would dwell on the doubting comments. And other times when the distractions would start to crowd in. And other times when I would, without warning, keep wicket like a total idiot.

The reason? Something stirring in the crowd. Some tennis coaching going on to the right. A little commotion, somewhere, anywhere. Something that would begin in the corner of my eye and very quickly dominate my consciousness.

One of the worst things that could happen was for another game to be taking place on the top pitch at Vickers. I am there now, in my mind, thumping my gloves together, urging the team on, readying myself for Steve Wall's next delivery, hungry as hell for the next Barrow wicket, and then, hello . . .

Look over there! What's the score in that game? What does that say on the scoreboard? Wonder what the ball's doing? Oh – good shot, pal. Now, wonder what . . .

In a flash, Steve has sent one down, and it has vanished for four byes before I realise what has happened. Really poor.

This, I suppose, is where the negativity really kicked in. Every so often there would be a fuck-up around the corner and there wasn't much I could do to explain it. Fortunately, though, the good days came along more often than the bad. I was mostly able to perform to a reasonable standard, I got myself into the League's Under-16 representative team without much difficulty, and anyway – it wasn't as though *all* the distractions were unpleasant. The distraction in the catsuit who took it upon herself to teach me a few essential non-cricketing skills during my stay in Barrow could not have been any more pleasant, for example. But that's another story.

In essence my one summer at Vickers felt like a wonderful summer. And why wouldn't it? I was suddenly getting a few quid in my pocket for playing cricket, I was honing my craft in a hard and competitive league, I was adjusting seamlessly (I thought) to life as a grown-up, and if my mind was starting to play one or two strange tricks – what was that little voice all about? – I was hardly going to dwell on that when an incredibly sexy older woman was, for a short but glorious while, shagging my sixteen-year-old brains out.

Good times.

I had no idea how much I still had to learn.

six

WHITEWASH

July 1988.

'You'll have to run faster than this, son.'
  I am fucking petrified.
  'I'm getting closer.'
  Absolutely shitting myself.
  'You can't keep running, you posh wanker.'
  I'm going to try. I don't have much choice.
  My MCC jacket is flapping as I tear up Hampstead High Street. I'm a good runner, but so is he – decent feet for a big man, as they say. He is laughing and snarling as his galloping footsteps draw nearer, and I am almost out of breath when my legs are finally whacked from under me.
  As I try to get to my feet, the first firm kick connects with my side. Fuck! Then another. After a couple more blows I try to scramble away. For a few seconds I don't know where I am, then, clarity – I swerve the next incoming blow and make a frantic dash towards the hostel door. I flail for the handle and miss. I continue grasping and grabbing when another of the pursuers makes a lunge for me. Finally, I have a firm hold of the handle. As I yank the door open, another boot hammers into the back of my hand, tearing off half the skin.
  Jesus! Why me?
  At last I manage to hurl myself inside, slamming the door behind me. I stand with my back against it, wheezing deeply, and the next thing I hear is the sound of laughing outside. Then . . . Nothing. Silence. Now what? I chance a look over my shoulder.
  They are leaving! Thank Christ!
  A few more seconds to catch my breath, and then I stumble up to my room and inspect the damage in the mirror. Staring back is not Simon Le Bon but a shambolic figure in dusty clothes, with a stinging nose, a scarlet lip and a swollen eye. I remove my shirt, twist my neck and see a group of angry red bumps on my back. One of my hands is raw with pain, and bleeding. In the other is my Rolex watch – my precious Rolex, my symbol of flash – in several shattered pieces. I flop down on a chair, still panting.
  This didn't happen in Langwathby!

In 1988 I was offered the chance of a week's coaching at Lord's by a cricket writers' committee which supposedly had a Cumbrian spy in their ranks. I travelled down to the smoke with Dad, hit some balls in the shadow of the world's most famous ground, and must have done something that impressed them, because by the end of the week I was invited back, this time for a year.

Joining the MCC Young Cricketers on the Lord's groundstaff was an exciting prospect laced with worry. I was a naïve farmer's lad from Langwathby who thought London was a different planet, with its flash city boys and yuppies and bright lights and traffic. In the months that followed, the capital would never really feel like home, but when I was first shown to my digs (a massive hostel up the hill from Lord's) and introduced to my room-mates (a pair of solid northern boys, Rob Gofton and Tim Chadwick), the first wave of homesickness began to ease.

What also helped was that the hostel was full of young people from different walks of life – performers and dancers, musicians and chefs, males and females – and a permanent party atmosphere prevailed. Soon, Rob, Tim and me adjusted to a standard nightly routine: go to bed early, get up again at 11.00 p.m. in time for the performers to come home from the shows, then pile into somebody's room for that evening's carousing. This close proximity to roomfuls of girls had its obvious benefits, and after not very long in my big new abode I hit it off with Claire, an aspiring dancer.

Claire was fun, but different. On one of our early dates she revealed, with great excitement, news of her big break in the performing world . . .

'Guess what – I'm going to be a tap-dancing lemon!'

Well, you didn't get that in Langwathby either, but Claire insisted I watch the TV advert in question. I don't quite remember what it was selling but I do recall its content: bloody hundreds of lemons with legs, all tap-dancing in time . . .

'Which one are you?'

'Honestly, I'm on there somewhere.'

. . . we didn't go out for long.

When not working my charms on gyrating fruit, I would catch the bus or the tube to the home of cricket, walk through the gates, puff my chest out and visualise the days when I would be doing it for real, in my England blazer. Once there, I would join my fellow young cricketers in practice, under the eye of the head coach Don Wilson, and carry out the traditional groundstaff duties, which ranged from cleaning the windows of the famous Long Room, to pulling on the covers and selling scorecards. The latter offered a princely dividend of 2p for every sale, resulting in a nice few quid being added to my whopping £63.50 per week wages after a Test match; a bonus which would then be blown at the Hammersmith Apollo in an attempt to be flash and pull the capital's glamorous birds. Another job I always volunteered for was helping Tony the chocolate-loving scoreboard man pull the levers to change the numbers, because it gave me the perfect vantage point when a Test was under way and allowed for some serious daydreaming . . .

That will be me, one day.

One of the less chilled but more unusual tasks was to bat or bowl against MCC members whenever the old boys fancied a go. At the time, the secretary was a cheerful old soldier called Lieutenant-Colonel John Stephenson, and on one occasion it fell upon me to face him in the nets. I padded up and was then met by a Brylcreemed figure who bore a passing resemblance to Penfold from *Danger Mouse*. His best cricketing days were far behind him and what he proceeded to send down can generously be described as rubbish. He, of course, was loving it.

'Right then, my last one,' he announced in his polite voice at the end of his session.

'OK, Colonel,' I replied. 'But just so you know, I'm going to hit this one as far as I can. Then I'll go and fetch it.'

He smiled, then creaked through his action one last time. As I opened myself up for the big shot, the ball held up on the pitch, and the result was an ugly top-edge which cannoned into my face, bursting my lip and smashing a tooth. The Colonel was aghast as I reeled away. 'I'm terribly sorry,' he spluttered. 'I seem to have pinned you!' The rest of the MCC lads fell about themselves, and then queued up to hammer me for apparently kissing the arse of one of the big cheeses.

These pointless (and dangerous!) interludes aside, Lord's was mainly an inspiring place to go to work, and Don Wilson was a decent coach. But there was also a lot of sitting around and doing nothing, especially if it rained. Instead of finding something useful to occupy time, we would muck around playing stump cricket in the dressing room. It didn't feel like we were receiving enough attention and for a lot of the time I felt like I was stagnating – and stagnation, as the world knows, can do strange things to a bunch of teenage boys.

Outside, around the back of our dressing room, was a huge, old oil drum. On first viewing there was nothing remarkable about this. But a few steps closer and you quickly learned why it was kept out of sight. The drum, as the summer progressed, would be used as a vessel for the most unpleasant cocktail known to man, and the thought of which still makes me gag.

Shit? Piss? Dog turds? Creosote? Grass cuttings? Petrol? Rain-water? Certainly, sir. And would you like some white emulsion with that, as well? Into the pot it all went, to be stirred around from time to time, and resulting in a stench that words simply cannot describe.

This happy concoction was destined at the end of the summer for the Wanker of the Year, a title handed down by a kangaroo court whose proceedings were more stringent than the Old Bailey. A typical hearing would see the older lads, wearing their helmets and gloves and gripping their bats, take up position at the head of the dressing room and order the rest of us to sit in silence. One by one, we would then be summoned forward and subjected to a prolonged burst of screaming and hollering, tickling and leg-whacking. Any sign of mirth or discomfort, and punishment would be soon to follow.

I managed to hold myself together under severe cross-examination but the same could not be said for Roger Twose, the young New Zealander and future Warwickshire star. Roger was a bright boy, and a big talent, but had something of an arrogant streak and was incapable of sitting in silence during his own interrogation. He couldn't stop himself from saying something back and in no time at all it became apparent that the Wanker of the Year crown, with all the horrors it entailed, was destined for his head.

'Get him!'

Very sensibly, Roger responded to his impending doom by bolting out of Lord's at the speed of light. He ran and ran through the streets of London, managing to evade the older lads who gave chase for a while but then lost him, and gave up. The end of the courtroom drama? No chance. They simply returned to Lord's to seize another victim.

Poor Bradley Donelan. Unlike Roger, Brad was quite a sensitive lad, but that didn't earn him a pardon from the 'whitewashing' treatment. He was duly dragged out to the Nursery End, stripped naked and laid flat on his back, and smothered from head to toe in the evil juice. He was then staked out and left to bake in the sun for two hours, as the office girls walked past and had a good, cruel laugh at his expense.

'When a man is tired of London, he's tired of life.' Whoever said that clearly never experienced a whitewashing, nor can he have spent much time in the Three Horseshoes pub at Hampstead. That was the regular meeting point for many of the groundstaff lads at the end of a hard day's training. As a rule we mixed happily together and if the Three Horseshoes wasn't known as the world's most wholesome public house, it had two major benefits. It was nearby, and it was a more than willing recipient of our wages when we felt like a change from the hostel bar.

One evening we were in there, a group of us, standing in a circle with ale in hand, talking and laughing and braying about the events of the day, as you do – one of us may have been brandishing his Rolex – and all was fine until the big bloke by the bar started taking a close interest in our little gathering.

Among a bunch of like-minded monsters, he was Goliath. His head was shaved to the bone, a huge tattoo of a spider's web spread all the way down his face and neck, and it soon became apparent that this charmer and his friends were not taking very kindly to the collection of blazer-wearing teenage sportsmen in their pub of choice. The words 'posh wankers' were in the air, so we made a quick, discreet decision to head back to the hostel.

As we made for the door, they also rose from their stools.

They wanted a piece of us. This was abundantly clear. So we decided to make a run for it.

What followed was a desperate footrace through the streets of Hampstead, and it was just my luck that Spiderman had chosen me as his intended target. The other lads split in all directions – Ian Salisbury, later of Surrey and England, has probably never moved as fast again in his life, and Alan Van Lint, the pretty Essex boy, protected his golden looks by hiding under a parked ice-cream van – but my own athletic ability did not hold up too well under the influence, as I discovered when Spiderman's foot eventually made its acquaintance with my ribcage.

The only lasting damage, once the hiding ended, was to my Rolex, but that encounter scared the shit out of me, and the fear was still in the air a couple of weeks later when I stepped off the tube at Hampstead station, looked to my left and saw him – Spiderman – leaving the very same train from another door. Gulp.

Fortunately, he hadn't seen me. I dashed out of his line of vision, whipped off my jacket and tie, stuffed them in my bag, bounded up the station's steep steps, and then legged it towards the hostel, as fast as I could. A few deep breaths and all was fine.

And that, rather abruptly, was the end of Spiderman. A few weeks later, the *Evening Standard* ran a story about a Hampstead man who had been sentenced to life for killing someone. Murder or manslaughter, I don't recall, and I don't much care; the only detail that mattered was the identity of the villain. None other than my tattooed friend!

I put the paper down, blew out my cheeks and walked the streets a little more confidently from then on. A little.

One May morning, Don Wilson pulled us all together for an announcement.

'. . . are going to be based here at Lord's before the Test matches start. They want us to do some fielding with them, give them throw-downs, that sort of thing. So you're all going to be needed.'

That's roughly what he said, but I had stopped listening after his first few words.

The West Indies were coming!

These were the megastars of the day, the legends of the 1980s, the players I had grown up watching on TV, so I made sure I was at Lord's extra early for their first day.

The first Caribbean hero to emerge in the morning was Wayne Daniel, the veteran fast bowler. Wayne was not actually in the West Indies squad but was on the books at Middlesex and was naturally keen to be around to greet his countrymen. At the time, he was fighting his way back from an injury and invited me to join him for a run around the ground before the icons arrived.

I didn't need to be asked twice to go for a run, but it must have been an amusing sight: me, the wiry young lad, and Wayne, the big, muscular unit with a towel around his neck and his nostrils flaring. He had the look of a heavyweight boxer preparing for a big fight, and as we jogged along he started shaking his head and chuckling.

'Nico, I tell you,' he said in his deep voice. 'What a night I had. This American girl . . . oh, man.'

'Yeah, right,' I said, laughing along.

'I swear to you man, she was beeeeautiful. And I'm gonna prove it. At nine o'clock she's gonna give me a wave.'

Sure enough, 9.00 a.m. came around, and Wayne drew to a halt, before looking up at one of the flats overlooking Lord's. On cue, a gorgeous blonde appeared at the window and waved down to the big fast bowler, who flashed the world's biggest, toothiest grin and waved back. 'Beeeeautiful, man,' he said, still shaking his head when we eventually resumed. Must stick with Wayne, I thought.

Back at base, there was a noticeable buzz as we stood on the outfield awaiting our instructions. The West Indies players had by now turned up and were setting a few things up, chatting among themselves and sorting various items of kit when one broke away from his gathering and walked across with his gloves on and a bat in his hand.

'Right boys,' he said, casually. 'Anybody fancy throwing a few for me?'

There was no mistaking the face or the voice. My hand was in the air before he had finished asking the question.

He caught my eye. 'OK, come with me.'

He led, I followed.

'Just a few outside off stump first, yeah?'

I threw, and he stroked effortlessly through the offside.

'Now try a few on my legs.'

I threw, and he unrolled a series of perfectly timed shots through midwicket.

'Now a few shorter ones.'

I threw, and he dropped onto his back foot to cut and pull with majestic style.

Throwing to Viv Richards – I had to pinch myself.

The most remarkable thing was my lack of nerves. I was suddenly practicing with one of the greatest, but I knew I was a good thrower and wouldn't embarrass myself.

For the rest of the week, he came to me every morning for his throws, and as time went on I plucked up the courage to return a few words to him. 'Well played. . . . Nice shot skip . . .'

He got 80 in the drawn First Test at Trent Bridge, and soon they were back at Lord's for the Second Test. Viv appeared from the changing rooms, jogged down to the pitch, summoned me straight away and the ritual resumed.

After helping the West Indies open a 1–0 series lead, he came and found me one last time before the squad left for Manchester. 'I want you to come to Antigua with me when we go home,' he said. 'Come and be my throwdown man.' He was joking, but I rose to about eight feet tall at that moment. I would have been perfectly prepared to sprint to Heathrow, beg and steal to pay for a flight, and greet him at Antigua airport with a bag of cricket balls and my throwing arm ready.

Watching the West Indies at work was fascinating. Their practice was intense, they appeared to relish each other's company, and they had that aura that the best teams always carry. They were also magnificent specimens to a man: Haynes, Greenidge, Logie, Viv and a pair of lanky young hopefuls called Ambrose and Walsh. I wanted to be around them all the time. I wanted to be like them. I wanted to *be* them. But there was one thing about them that unsettled me.

When I had been on scoreboard duty in the Second Test, I had not been able to take my eyes off Jeff Dujon, the wicketkeeper. He was standing so far back that he was nearly halfway into the pavilion. Patrick Patterson was banging it in with menace, Graham Gooch was dodging and weaving, and I was staring down in awe at a game being played at a speed I struggled to comprehend. When Gower came in, peeled off 46 elegant runs but was then sent packing by Walsh, I found myself wrestling with an uneasy thought: Would I ever be good enough to cope with *that*?

When my mind was right, my game was right. This was true of my career from beginning to end. By the time I was on the groundstaff, playing for the Young Cricketers team against county second XIs, the little man had announced himself in no uncertain terms, but, as at Vickers, I had enough decent days to convince people (and myself) that I had a decent future ahead of me.

When it was bad, it was horrible, but when it was good, it was good enough. And often enough.

It helped that a useful opportunity quickly arose thanks to Paul Downton's call-up into the England squad for the West Indies series. Paul was Middlesex's main wicketkeeper, and when Martin Olley moved up from the seconds to fill the gap, he left behind a vacancy. Middlesex duly reached into the groundstaff and plucked me out.

Linking up with the county's second team for a month and a half was another small advance, and it also landed me with some immediate perks. No longer would I catch the bus to work, for instance; instead, I would be collected from the hostel by Alex Barnett or Neil MacLaurin, two of the Middlesex boys from wealthy backgrounds. If it was Alex, my chariot would be his dad's Rolls-Royce; if it was Neil, I would be conveyed to Lord's in a Bentley. Second-XI cricket had its appeal, it's fair to say. It also helped that an extra £80 suddenly started appearing in my wage packet.

The cricket was of a high standard, as decent young players mixed with the older, established heads who would step down from the first team any time they needed to get back into the run-scoring or wicket-taking habit. It wasn't uncommon for Mike Gatting to be among those dipping into the seconds to feed on some gentler bowling until his form returned, and with the likes of Gatt around I was never going to get too many knocks. But it was a good period to keep wicket, all the same. When Norman Cowans thundered deliveries into my gloves I learned exactly why he was nicknamed Flash, and then there was the beautiful, slow left-arm bowler with a twinkle in his eye, name of Tufnell.

That long, hot summer put more fuel in my tank, but I never felt completely at one with London life. I was a social animal, but the jungle was just too big. And so, when Middlesex, contrary to the rumours at the time, declined to offer me a contract, Don Wilson wasn't impressed, but I was secretly pleased. Matches for the MCC gave the boys the opportunity to impress counties – I had the pleasure of keeping to Salisbury's masterful leg-spin in a game against Sussex, when he made mincemeat of their top players and earned himself a contract there and then – but I was just as bothered about getting out of the capital as I was about securing my cricketing future.

Fortunately, the cards fell in my favour. If you had asked me at the time what I knew about Leicestershire, the list would have been short:

1.   It's north of London.
2.   David Gower plays for them.
3.   Their logo is a fox, like Carlisle United's.

. . . but an opportunity was an opportunity, a trial was a trial, and what did I have to lose? Leicester was a city, but a much less chaotic (and slightly more northern) one than London, I reasoned, as I hopped onto the train at St Pancras, hopped off it a couple of hours later, threw myself and my kitbag into a taxi and asked for the cricket ground.

Not so fast, destiny. First, the taxi driver had to negotiate his way to Grace Road. People without local knowledge have sometimes been stumped by the fact that the main entrance to the cricket ground is not actually on Grace Road, but on Park Hill Drive. A taxi driver is generally supposed to have local knowledge, but mine must have landed from Mars that day. We drove and drove, turning the same corners over and over again, with the cricket ground in sight but infuriatingly unreachable beyond a wall. Eventually, I gave up and ordered him to stop. I paid up, jumped out, and after a hopeless attempt to find the entrance on foot, I opted to leap over the wall.

As I landed on the other side, I looked up to see a game in progress.

My trial game, against Warwickshire's second XI.

I hurried towards the pavilion to make my introductions, pausing to watch a tall, wiry, fair-haired bowler sending down a thunderbolt which reared up at the batsman, forcing him to glove it to the keeper thirty yards back.

Within twenty minutes I was out there in the middle myself, facing this young speed demon. He was South African, and more aggressive than many bowlers I had faced before, but his snarls and stares didn't bother me, and nor did fast bowling as a rule. I loved the buzz of facing the quick stuff, and, usefully, I found that I could play this bloke pretty well. He was zipping the ball across me, allowing me to leave anything that landed on off stump, meaning I just had to focus on playing the straight ones.

I was fine – operating on adrenalin, but with a clear head. I made a decent 35 on a difficult track and in the next innings scored 38. Unlike Russell Cobb, who had gloved that early snorter to Keith Piper behind the stumps, I had gone up against Allan Donald for the first time and survived. I felt so at home in the heat of battle that I can recall nearly every ball, but what happened next is a blur.

I do remember being invited into an office and shaking someone's hand (that someone being Mike Turner, the Leicestershire chief executive). I do remember the words 'you've done very well,' 'we're impressed,' and 'two-year contract'. I do remember the man pushing a piece of paper towards me, I do remember glancing down and seeing the figure £3,200, and I do remember scrawling my name on the bottom of the page and handing it back.

The rest of the conversation, though, is lost in time. Someone else will have to fill the gaps. In what seemed like the blink of an eye, I had entered a room as a wandering young hopeful, and left it as a professional cricketer with a brand new home.

seven

SHIT PIT

July 1992.

The ball thumps into the gloves. I toss it to first slip. As the bowler walks back, I look up to the crowd, just to make sure he is there.

Of course he is there. You could set your watch by him.

He's there, in his regular seat, with his old raincoat zipped up to his chin and his binoculars raised to his eyes. Nobody recognises him, which is perfect.

That means it is just me, and him.

I am, as usual, observing our secret code. The code? Of course, I should explain. It goes like this. If he raises his arm high in the air, it is good. If he brings it down a little, at an angle, it's OK. Horizontal means average, just below horizontal is just below average, and when the arm really dips down – perish the thought! – I have messed it up. It's my job to make sure that arm gets nowhere near his knee.

I'm desperate to impress him, in case you hadn't guessed. He is looking to see how cleanly I take the ball. Is it going in nicely? Does it catch my thumb on the way in? How do I respond to its deviation? How are my feet moving?

In the morning, he hit balls to me and identified a couple of flaws in my diving technique like Sherlock Holmes arriving at the killer clue. He also offered some tips on my hand positions, which I'll try to remember. Then, when play began, he retired to the stand, zipped up that coat, fished out the binoculars, and away we went.

The code again.

High – good.

Down a bit – OK.

Horizontal – average.

Below horizontal – below average.

Right down – poor.

For the following six hours, for as long as the ball is coming to me, I am in the careful hands of Alan Knott. There cannot be many safer places to be.

The other code, the first rule, was spelled out the moment I walked into Grace Road as a new recruit. 'Know your place' was the unspoken law and it could not have been clearer had it been pinned up on every noticeboard. Joining Leicestershire was to be pitched into a world of stars, but these stars preferred to exist in their own galaxy. Not for me the chance to lace up my boots next to a Peter Willey, a Jonathan Agnew, a Winston Benjamin or – I could scarcely believe it! – a David Gower. While these senior players enjoyed the luxury of a large, comfortable dressing room, the second XI hopefuls were immediately dispatched to a tiny, windowless, brick enclosure downstairs, near the kitchens. Its floorspace seemed little more than ten square feet and was strewn with a dirty, great mass of bags and kit.

'The Shit Pit', as it became known by its inhabitants, was the most obvious symbol of the great divide. And the divide was always there, from the day I saw Gower's sponsored Audi Quattro in the players' car park, to the time I was instructed on the etiquette of approaching any of the first-teamers (knock politely on the dressing-room door and await the captain's permission to enter).

I went to Leicestershire full of beans and eager for everything they could throw at me. The pre-season trip to the Isle of Wight – so cold there was ice on the swimming pool – was my first proper chance to see the greats at close quarters, and offered the first big surprise of my new life: if these were the hard-bitten professionals, why did I seem to be fitter than them when we did the running drills up the hills? There was no answer, because when we came back to Grace Road it counted for nothing.

Throwing, throwing, throwing . . . That's pretty much how it was to begin with. Not to Gower, who had the England captaincy on his mind and claimed nets got him into bad habits (and who was I to argue with my hero?), but to the others? Only all the bloody time! I enjoyed throwing, as a rule, but the monotony was a killer. After a while I would deliberately start sending down garbage, just so it would get smacked and I could run after it.

There were few benefits to the divide, but one big plus did emerge, over time. The distance between Us and Them helped to create a great solidarity among the residents of the Shit Pit. In the seconds there was a core of young players who were coming into the game at the same time – top lads like Lloyd Tennant, Martyn Gidley, Peter Hepworth, Ben Smith and Justin Benson – which served to foster a special atmosphere both in practice and in the pub at the end of the day. We burned the candle at both ends, certainly, but there was a lot of cricket talk over the beers, and our coach, Ken Higgs, was nothing if not unique. Ken was a straight-talking ex-bowler from Staffordshire who, if I missed one down the leg-side, would simply holler: 'Hey, come on kid, do you want my bloody raincoat to throw on it?!'

It was a strange blend in some ways, but it must have worked, because in no time at all this tightly-knit team had won the Bain Clarkson Second XI Trophy, a triumph we celebrated by piling into two cars – all fifteen of us – and embarking on a victory parade through Leicester with some players on the roof and others hanging out of windows, brandishing the trophy to bemused pedestrians.

Did I spend those early months pining for a place in the first team? No, I wouldn't say so – none of the seconds did. To the casual observer that might seem an unforgivable attitude but the atmosphere and the division at the club was such that if you got called up, you would simply do your duty and then desperately look forward to the time when you'd be back with your mates.

When my summons did come, on 1 July 1989, I didn't feel remotely ready or, in all honesty, massively keen for it, but when news emerged of an injury to Phil Whitticase, the senior wicketkeeper, it could only mean one thing – my County Championship debut. Well, what else can you do when you're green and nervous and unsure of your lot but get stuck in and see how it goes?

The game, against Warwickshire, was at our outground at Hinckley, not at Grace Road. This in itself was a bit of an anti-climax; I had always imagined myself walking out in front of the members at our home ground. Maybe, though, that helped. Maybe, thinking back, it kept the pressure off, because the upshot was a Leicestershire bow which went better than I dared imagine. The highlight? That's obvious – not the diving catch I made to dismiss Keith Piper off Gordon Parsons, but what happened immediately afterwards. As I hurled the ball into the sky, Gower dashed straight towards me with a broad smile, wrapped his arms around my waist and hoisted me into the air.

I felt on top of the world, like a footballer who had just scored the winner at Wembley.

I took eight catches in total and the game faded out as a rain-affected draw, but not before Dermot Reeve, Warwickshire's chirpy all-rounder, had managed to get under Benjamin's skin with some choice remarks, earning for himself a full-blooded beamer from our Antiguan fast bowler. Reeve got his gloves up to protect his face and if he took the bite out of the delivery, he hadn't drawn Benji's sting.

As the ball dropped, the big man took a stride, angrily swung his right leg and kicked it from the toe of his boot to within a foot of the boundary rope. Reeve duly ran four, and for this he was rewarded with another beamer, next ball. The rest of us didn't really know what to say, or do.

Once this show was finally over and I could kick off my pads, I had two new things to add to the memory bank. The first, which I would never forget, was that Championship cricket was tougher and more enjoyable than anything I knew. The second, which I didn't retain for quite so long, was that Benji did not seem a difficult man to wind up.

So began my life with the Foxes, a rollercoaster of educational highs and strange lows.

The ups? The professional coaching and the slow but steady progress with bat and gloves. The downs? The divide, and the way dissent was routinely gunned down.

It did not take long for me to rub some of the older players up the wrong way when I started complaining about the pointlessness of a split squad, where nobody seemed to bother sharing their knowledge. Why were the senior stars not giving more to kids like me who were desperate to learn? I may as well have informed them I was sleeping with their wives.

At best, they were stand-offish. At worst, they were Peter Willey. He is without question the most miserable bugger I have ever played with, and not just when I missed a stumping off his bowling. Yes, I knew he'd played twenty-odd Tests for England and yes, I knew he was never reputed to be the sunniest of blokes, but Christ, he was a grump. I don't know if it was the daily drive from Northampton to Leicester which blackened his mood, but it seemed that every time I opened my mouth he couldn't wait to tell me to shut up and get on with my game. When I spoke up in team meetings, someone would invariably shout me down, often Willey. The attitude seemed to be, 'What do you know? You've done nothing in the game yet. We'll tell you when to talk.'

A winning mentality? A team ethic? Sorry, you've come to the wrong place.

The best part of it was watching the elder statesmen from a distance, and leaping on any other chances you had to learn. In 1989, an unmissable opportunity for education presented itself when Australia came to Grace Road, shortly before the Fifth Test of a victorious Ashes series. To my delight, I was picked. This was the hard-nosed Australia of Allan Border and Merv Hughes, and when I went in to bat, the flak started coming from all angles. 'Fantastic,' I thought. 'Real cricket.'

My first task was to deal with Tim May's spin. I tried to sweep his first ball, without much success. His next one, the same. Quick as a flash, a harsh voice broke the sudden silence . . .

'Fuck me, mate, what time does the cricket start?'

Steve Waugh. We would meet again.

The worst part was being made mincemeat of by the Aussies, but the learning process was still entertaining in certain ways. Jonathan Agnew was a bowler of the first order, and he could also bat – provided you were giving him throwdowns. Against serious pace in the middle he had a heart the size of a caraway seed and on this occasion he infuriated Geoff Lawson by constantly backing away, waving out his bat and nicking the ball over the slips. When Lawson then bowled one in his slot, he hit it with beautifully correct style for four, and received for his troubles some ripe verbals. To his eternal credit, Aggers simply sat on his bat and replied: 'I say, is that Shakespeare, Mr Lawson?' A rare triumph for the quintessential Englishman against the Aussie juggernaut.

Those times at Leicestershire were certainly a mixture of ups and downs; the daily excitement about where the journey might go next, then learning with awful suddenness that there was no such thing as the invincibility of youth. Richard Edmunds was a fantastic lad and a player with a very promising future. He was a tall, left-arm seamer who had already earned young England honours and seemed destined for more. On 22 November that year, he was pulled from his car after a crash near Oakham and later died from his injuries. It was a tragic waste which hit the club hard and spread disbelief through the squad. How could he be taken away, just like that? Numb – that's what I felt. He was only 19 years old; the same as me.

The divide was going to take some closing but things began to change for the better when Bobby Simpson arrived. To date, the Australians were the most fiercely competitive team I had encountered, and when Simmo joined Leicestershire as coach from that very same Aussie set-up, he brought a new intensity which the older players, inevitably, didn't particularly like.

Simmo's attention to detail in practice was phenomenal. His mantra was 'train hard, play easy', and he seemed intent on creating a new breed of cricketer. In 1991 he brought over a young Aussie batter called Damien Martyn, who ran like a demon between the wickets and began totting up the hundreds. With the more attentive Nigel Briers taking over the captaincy from Gower (who had too much on his plate with England), it was a regime I quickly took to.

Nigel gave me time and attention, constantly talking to and encouraging me. For the first time I felt I had a captain who believed in me, while Simmo was keen to make sure we clicked as a team both on and off the field. Barbecues and social drinks were now the order of the day, usually hosted by the coach at his house in Leicester, which was brave new ground for the club and also a red rag to a bunch of young cricketers who had a certain concept of what 'social drinks' meant, and for whom the no-alcohol rule meant that you just had to disguise your vodka by pouring it into a bottle of cola instead.

Before one of these gatherings, the secret mixture was prepared, carried around to Simmo's place and set on a table while we got stuck into the food. I don't know how much time had passed before the pointing and the laughing started . . .

'Look at the boy!'

'Have you seen him?!'

'The lad can't stay on his feet!'

. . . but it soon became obvious that Simmo's three-year-old grandson had a problem. He would run with his little football, fall over, get up, run again, stagger and fall, up again, run – Bam! – and hit the deck once more. It was hilarious, and Simmo himself laughed along, just too loudly to hear the whispering which then broke out.

'Shit – have you seen the bottle?'

'No, why . . . Fucking hell!'

The bottle was half empty. The boy had been returning to the table for regular refills and none of us had given a moment's thought to what he had been knocking back. No harm was done, thankfully, but I don't think anyone dared confess to Simmo that we had got his grandson intoxicated by accident.

If that was a forgivable distraction (just about), the next one gave my learning curve a sharp upward jerk. For a while, I lived with Benji in a club house in Countesthorpe, a village just outside Leicester. He was sometimes a bit distant with the younger guys, but I got on with him OK, although not as well as his partner in crime, George Ferris. The two Antiguan pacemen made for quite a double-act; one would regularly turn up at the other's house to shave his countryman's head, before getting bored and failing to finish, leaving half a head short and sharp but the other half still covered with hair. They weren't so relaxed when it came to the day job, however, as the bumps and bruises would usually confirm after you had spent a few minutes facing them on our new green net surfaces.

Like all the West Indies pros of the time, there was nothing Winston and George enjoyed quite as much as getting one over on their own. Around the house, Benji was particularly animated in the build-up to a Championship game against Middlesex at Lord's. Why? Because he was hankering for the scalp of the great Desmond Haynes.

Well, this was one mental note I must have written using invisible ink, because when the match came around I had a proper bad day, a self-inflicted stinker. Instead of focusing on the task in hand, I jogged onto the field and immediately distracted myself by yakking away to the slips. Benji was steaming in from ball one and soon enticed Haynes into a nick.

Had I been set, and ready, I would have taken it without a problem, but my feet and my brain were all over the place. The ball shot between me and Laurie Potter at first slip and was skimming away for four before either of us had been able to react.

Fuck.

Benji stopped dead, shot me a glare, kicked the ground and then emitted the loudest four-letter expletive I have ever heard on a cricket pitch. Haynes, predictably, glided onto a big score without offering another chance.

When we got home after the game, Benji was still incandescent and spent the rest of the night in silence. The next morning, when I entered the kitchen for breakfast, he lifted up his bowl of cereal, rose from his seat and moved into the living room without a word. At the club that day he gave me nothing and at night he blanked me again.

The next day, the same.

The day after, the same.

The day after that, nothing again.

Let me tell you – if there is one thing more intimidating than a big West Indian quick running in to bowl at you, it is a big West Indian quick giving you the quiet treatment. It was a full week, in fact, before Benji finally ended his vow of silence, and when he did speak it was not exactly sweetness and light.

'Listen, gabby,' he spat. 'You can chat all you want and do all the press-ups and sit-ups you want. You can run around the ground a thousand times and be the fittest guy in the club. I'm not interested. Your job is to catch the fucking ball. Catch the fucking ball and get some fucking runs.'

He stared at me. I swallowed hard. 'OK, Benji.'

The ups, and the downs . . . For my first couple of years after joining Leicestershire, I was free and single. There were plenty of girls around who were keen to associate themselves with the cricket set, and plenty of the cricket set, it's safe to say, who were more than willing to indulge them.

Girlfriends came and went. I was married to the good life and to cricket in equal measure and was in no particular hurry to divorce either when I went home at the end of the 1991 season. One night in October, shortly before my twenty-first birthday, I drove to a hotel in Penrith to greet the parents of my friend and team-mate, Andrew Roseberry. By this time I had spent a couple of winters in Australia with Rosey, whose old cricket master at Durham School had been Mike Hersch, a proper, fair dinkum Aussie who also coached at Melville Cricket Club in Perth. We lived in Hersch's back garden, slept in a shed which doubled as a sauna once the sun blazed down onto its corrugated iron roof, worked on his garden and then went off to play cricket in the furiously competitive Aussie leagues. We got involved in throwing to the touring England team during the Fifth Ashes Test at the WACA, and off the field we got pissed together and chased birds.

After all this, it was clearly time for me to do Rosey a good turn, so, offering local knowledge and the assumption that Langwathby's new sporting hero might be able to haggle a better deal for his folks, I sidled up to the hotel reception to begin my bartering. But I soon got sidetracked by the pretty, tanned, blonde girl behind the desk. Jennifer Young was her name, and if she was a vaguely familiar face from school, who I'd seen in Blues with her sister, I didn't know much else about her other than the rumour that her dad was a tough ex-rugby player who it didn't pay to mess with. I lingered at the desk for a chat and, to my great astonishment, she wasn't put off by my repartee. We hit it off straight away, started dating, and from the start there seemed to be something special about Jen, something that set her apart.

If only life could always be so perfect. If only the laws of physics – for every up, there's a down – didn't exist. Shortly before returning from my next Australia trip that winter, I rang Mum and told her I was looking forward to seeing her when I got home. This was a ritual of my travels and we would normally chat for a while, but on this occasion she didn't want to talk much. The conversation was brief – I found that odd.

I later learned why Mum had been so short. When Dad met me at the airport, he broke the news that they had split up and he had moved out. I was gobsmacked. Split up? Moved out? The rest of the journey was mostly spent in a stunned silence, and when Dad then dropped me off at home I went through the door to find Mum in tears. What the fuck had happened? I could not get my head around it and the news crushed me.

I ran around to the Hollidays' house and bawled my eyes out, and then started to think back for any signs I had missed. Then it hit me. Before I had set off for Australia, the Holliday lads had pulled me to one side and told me that a rumour was spreading around Langwathby that my old man was playing away from home with a girl who did a bit of work for us on the farm. One day I had seen his van not far away from her house, but I didn't think much of that, and anyway, this was my old man! A load of bollocks, surely?

Not so. Dad subsequently moved into a flat with this woman – a flat which, as chance would have it, was on the same road in Penrith as Jen's parents. Wordsworth Street was one of six steep streets in the same area of town which I found ideal for hill sprinting. But from that point onwards I felt my heart quicken along with my pace when I saw Dad's van on the roadside. As I belted past I felt a sadness and an emptiness, and also a rage I had never known before. And the questions, always the questions . . .

How? Why?

How, and why, could he leave Mum, who had always assured me, in that warm way of Cumbrian women, that everything would always be 'alright'? And leave her on her own? There was so much I couldn't understand.

The rage hadn't subsided by the time of their divorce. I spent most of the intervening period becoming Mr Angry, driving around aggressively, snapping at people and avoiding Penrith like the plague. Dad was no longer my favourite person and I didn't want to spend any more time with him than I had to.

Mum eventually sold the house, moved into a smaller place in Langwathby and tried to rebuild her life. But Rome was not built in a day, and for the next couple of summers I drove home from every match, every weekend, from wherever I played, for however long it took – to make sure she was OK. It was draining and put me on intimate terms with every bend and curve of the A1 but at the time it was the only thing that felt more important than the next catch, or the next adventure.

Benji was right. I always had a lot to say for myself, but I had not yet learned how to get my thoughts under control, and how to switch on and off at the right times. Nor had I learned the important skill of choosing your targets carefully when it was time to give the opposition some chat.

One man who it was not advisable to wind up at the crease was David Smith, the enormous Sussex opener who was known for his volatile temper, and at whom I went hard from the outset in a game at Grace Road in 1992:

'Yeah, you're fucking useless mate.'

'That was a load of rubbish.'

'Fucking lucky bastard.'

Really intellectual stuff, and I thought I had done the team a favour when he departed early for seven. Smith looked at me before stalking off. It wasn't an affectionate glance.

As the game resumed, the lads made clear their opinion that I had really needled him:

'Fucking hell, Nico, what have you done here?'

They were in my ear at regular intervals thereafter, gleefully reminding me that I had poked the beast and would probably have to pay for it before the day was done. I spent the rest of the day getting more and more anxious, then started to panic when Smith was seen putting his fist through our dressing-room door. By the time I walked unscathed to my car after the close of play, I was seriously relieved to be getting out of there.

He was in the car park, waiting for me.

I more or less shat my pants on the spot.

'Hey, come here you,' he barked.

I dropped my bag, and steeled myself for what would surely be a fairly one-sided rumble.

'You were a fucking little weasel today,' Smith said, jabbing a finger at me. 'You overstepped the mark . . .'

I was trembling. Was this it how it ended, then? My last day on earth? Then . . .

Was that half a smile?

Incredibly, it was!

'. . . but I quite like it. I let myself get upset and I shouldn't have done. You did me there.'

Then . . . Nothing. That was the extent of my confrontation with the fearsome giant. Those closing words were better than any Christmas present. He walked away and I drove home, with all my bones surprisingly intact, but resolving to tone things down a little when I next encountered David Smith.

It was true – sometimes it really did pay to say nothing. One of my first away trips was against Glamorgan at Cardiff, on a real turning pitch, and when I was caught at bat-pad for ten, convinced I'd hit the ball, I walked off without a murmur. At the end of the day, the umpire, Dickie Bird, came up to me with an admiring smile on his face. 'Hey, lad, that was a brilliant walk,' he said. 'I didn't see that one, so I appreciate you doing that.' It went down as one of my best-ever investments, since Dickie never gave me out bat-pad for the next ten years, even when I knocked the cover off the ball.

As for Benji, I was relieved that he didn't hold a grudge over the Haynes disaster. Had he extended the feud, I might not have scored my first Championship hundred.

By 1992, Whitticase's injuries were giving me more opportunities in the team, and this led to a Championship contest at home against Hampshire, whose main weapon was the great Malcolm Marshall. I had by now faced faster bowlers than Marshall, but no finer craftsman. Before going in to bat, Benji took me to one side and explained how I should tackle his illustrious countryman:

'Just hang back and watch the ball,' he said. 'If you come forward to his natural length, you will nick it. You don't need to come forward.'

'OK, Benji.'

I followed his advice to the letter and by the end of the day I had made my way to 96 not out. The next morning, I walked out with an attack of the butterflies and hoped for a couple of looseners to help me to my maiden ton. Marshall ambled in and sent his first ball fizzing over my shoulder like a rocket. A similar missile followed, next ball.

Christ, he's making me work for this!

Somehow, I survived the longest over of my life, running a leg-bye off the last delivery to get to the other end. Then, from the first ball of the next over, Cardigan Connor sent down a nice, floaty leg-side half-volley, which I clipped away. *Phew!* I whipped off my helmet, raised my bat and was treated to a vigorous handshake from Parsons.

First of many, Nico!
The lesson this time? The value of paying attention, of course!

These lessons, and the counsel of the legendary Alan Knott, who Leicestershire enlisted from the ECB to give me some one-to-one tuition, got my mind in its best shape yet as time passed. There was much work still to be done, but progress is progress, and when Leicestershire reached the NatWest Trophy final at Lord's in 1992, I was in a decent place.

The same, sadly, couldn't be said for the team. This was the day I strode out with my chest puffed out and gave Curtly Ambrose the heave-ho from ball one – the nerve of the boy! – but we didn't get enough runs across the board and the Northants batsmen Alan Fordham and Rob Bailey took us apart. On the bus trip home we consoled ourselves with a few beers, and by the time we got back to Grace Road at night the collective decision was made to drown our sorrows even further. I volunteered to drive some of the lads into town, and then motor back home in order to get changed and hire a taxi to rejoin them, but a couple of minutes after dropping my team-mates off I was stopped in my tracks by a member of the local constabulary.

I had been thinking of so many things on the journey home that I had not considered the pitfalls. Had I had a bit too much to drink? Maybe. Maybe not. *Maybe is bad news.* This was just what I didn't need.

The copper appeared at my window as I rolled it down.

'Do you know why I've pulled you over, sir?' he enquired.

'Er . . . No, I've no idea . . . I was doing the right speed, wasn't I?'

That sounded convincing.

'You haven't had a very good day, have you Paul?'

Not if you're about to nab me and give the local paper a gift of a headline: COUNTY STAR IN DRINK-DRIVE SHAME.

He recognised me, though. Maybe I could use this to my advantage.

'No mate, I've had a shit day,' I said. 'In fact, you might as well have this.'

I don't know why, but I thought the best thing to do at that precise moment was to delve into my jacket for my loser's medal and hold it out for the policeman.

'No, no, I don't want that,' he replied, brushing it aside.

This is it, then. I'm done for.

'Now listen,' the cop continued. 'You need to get yourself home, and if you do, we'll say no more about this. But before you set off, would you mind doing me a favour and turning your lights on?'

eight

SURGERY

Broadly speaking, the university of life was a good place to be. Not only was Grace Road a fine home for a young cricketer's studies, it also helped him broaden horizons and go through certain doors that were open only to a select few.

In the winter of 1992, another opened. The Northamptonshire batsman Nigel Felton had made it known that he was looking for a group of English county players to join him on a trip to South Africa. Guildford-born Nigel was of Cape Coloured heritage, and a man with a plan. South Africa was undergoing historic change during the dying days of apartheid, and Nigel's intention was to sign some English cricketers to some local non-white clubs, to play, coach and, in the process, establish whether there was enough talent in the areas to encourage the Western Province Cricket Union – who were sponsoring the trip – to invest in new facilities.

I knew next to nothing about the country, and even less about international affairs, but when Nigel called, I couldn't think of a reason to say no. I signed up with six fellow players – James Boiling, Wayne Noon, Karl Krikken, Keith Piper, Dougie Brown and Alan Fordham – and was assigned to a club called Mitchell's Plain.

There was no brochure for this adventure. How could there have been? Imagine the blurb:

'Come to South Africa, a place of contrasts! Your journey from Cape Town airport to Mitchell's Plain will allow you to witness the full majesty of our country's rich and varied heritage. One minute, it is skyscrapers and affluence as far as the eye can see; the next, you will pass Gugulethu, one of the area's biggest townships, where naked children can often be spotted by the roadside with their mothers close behind, begging with their babies in their arms. Then, a minute later, affluence again, as though the township had all been a trick of the mind! Do enjoy your stay . . .'

Sunny, sporty, wholesome Australia it was not. South Africa appeared a more complicated place from day one and at the age of 22 I hardly felt qualified to be sharing my expertise in such a troubled land, but when I arrived at Mitchell's Plain to see concrete practice pitches covered in holes, wire nets with sagging roofs and not a great deal of hope other than the forty or so eager children who had turned up to greet their new English visitor, I began to appreciate Nigel's thinking.

I emptied my car boot of kit and oversaw a session which saw the youngsters go full throttle at a range of drills and games, helped by a group of willing adults. I concluded that as long as they remained as keen for the duration of my stay we wouldn't go far wrong, and by the end I was daring to reflect on a job well done as I lingered to chat to a couple of the club's senior players.

When I then returned to my car to find that most of the kit had suddenly disappeared into the night, I realised things might not be so straightforward. After starting with twenty balls, ten pairs of pads, ten boxes, ten pairs of gloves, ten bats and ten of everything else, I was left with two boxes, one glove and one thigh pad to show for my first session of a six-month assignment.

I brought some of the kids together and explained that I was here for the duration, not just one night, and could they please pass the message on to whoever had ran off with the gear? 'We want to make this place brilliant,' I said. 'But we need your help.'

Two days later, every single piece of kit had been returned, as if by magic. Also out of thin air, for that next session, had appeared twice as many kids. One lad had run four miles with his boots tied around his neck, and would later run home at the end of the session. Another was as inquisitive as they came and showed a real enthusiasm for keeping wicket. The rest could not have been keener.

So began life at Mitchell's Plain. Once I started to earn their trust, the place took off. The coaching sessions were a joy, and I also had the distinction of being the club's first ever white player. This being 1992 in South Africa it would have been natural to expect a bit of hostility, or suspicion, but I encountered none. It was a happy and welcoming place, where the resentment seemed to be reserved only for certain opponents.

When poorer teams such as ours confronted the affluent, white clubs whose players had been to private schools, the spirit of rivalry was fierce, and not always pleasant. The attitudes were quite startling to begin with, but what is the saying about walking a mile in another man's shoes before judging him? The more I laced up my boots with my new friends, the more it sunk in.

Put yourself in their position for a moment: you basically have nothing apart from your love of cricket and your mates. You turn up and you change into your tatty old whites in the car park, before heading out to play. You do your best with what you have, but the other lot have the smartest kit and the finest equipment money can buy. When, a few weeks later, you go to their plush ground and watch them strutting around with their private school arrogance and haughty accents, is it any wonder that you eventually start to ask yourself why they have so much, and why you have so little? When you think about all this, what else can you see except Them and Us? And what else, given the circumstances, would offer you as much pleasure as knocking off one of their pretty, posh heads with the quickest bouncer you could possibly bowl?

For venom, it was the North Lancs League multiplied many times over, but the gap was hard to bridge and with the grass on our outfield six inches long, our facilities lifeless and the standard of player not brilliant, we struggled to win many games. The upside was that winning was not everything and it seemed more important that the place was full of fun and enjoyment along the way. At the end of the season one of the batsmen, a former Navy chef called Greg, threw a party in his garage. It was an absolute hoot and I laughed all night, until someone stepped forward, hushed the gathering and launched into an announcement.

'Paul, we are all grateful for everything you have done here . . . and we would like to give you this.'

When I walked forward and accepted the tracksuit, I saw that it was embroidered with a Mitchell's Plain logo, and my name was also stitched into the fabric.

'Nobody else has one of those,' Greg added.

I returned to England feeling enriched by the whole experience and with a sense of perspective on the world and on cricket which I didn't previously possess. I also felt I had learned something new about generosity. I wasn't sure whether I had given them enough in return, but I had tried to make a difference. I hoped I had helped.

One winter in South Africa was never going to be enough. The Mitchell's Plain experience whetted my appetite and a few years later I joined Nigel's old club, Primrose, which was also on the edge of Cape Town. I shared a house – owned by the Primrose player Rushdie Magiet – with a student called Sofia: a lovely, hard-working girl with the patience of a saint any time I rolled back in three sheets to the wind.

There was an eventful party scene around Cape Town if you knew where to find it. Jason Smith knew where to find it and was happy to lead me there. Jason was a sports agent whose brother and father had played county cricket, and who was married to a shrinking violet called Jacqui De La Cruz, the first ever Cape Coloured girl to pose for *Penthouse* magazine. Jacqui was absolutely barmy. She would go out wearing next to nothing, frequently unveil her boobs, and take over any bar she entered.

On one night out I saw her find the biggest geek in the pub, drag him by his tie to the front, lay him on the bar, get on top and then pretend to ride the poor, embarrassed nerd. The locals loved it, whooping and hollering, but Jason just shook his head.

This was the beautiful side of South Africa, with its stunning women and plush nightspots. The English cricketers spent most evenings around the Waterfront – the new, cosmopolitan development with shops, restaurants and clubs as far as the eye could see. We were paid 2,500 rand a month, the equivalent of about £500, and more than enough for us to live like kings.

It was a very pretty world, but the other side of the country was never too far from your door. All the whites still had maids (some were treated better than others) and a sharp contrast to the flash bars, flash cars and flash women was the sight of little, rickety buses, chugging uncertainly down the road, full to the rafters with blacks on their way to work. There weren't supposed to be white-only and black-only bars in the cities any more, but they were there. In certain places at night you would quicken your step when walking for a taxi. Prostitutes were everywhere, drugs seemed to be plentiful and a lot of black guys were milling around with drink on board and a sense of grievance against the world.

When I close my eyes and think of Cape Town in this period, it is not always the cricket that first comes to mind. Sometimes it's the adventure, and sometimes it's the fear. Things were going well with Jen, who had been to Australia with me the previous winter and had also come out to stay in South Africa. When her sister Clare and her future husband Paul (Macca) were over for a later visit, I took them out for a knees-up. All was going fine until, on the journey home, I hit the kerb while rounding a corner and felt the car immediately slump to one side. The front left tyre hissed and was soon as flat as a pancake. And if there was one thing that wasn't recommended in South Africa, it was breaking down and then standing by your vehicle, scratching your head and changing a tyre, especially in the dark and especially near a township. So I pulled the car into the side of the road, got out, felt the fear and announced the only course of action open to the three of us – we would have to make a run for it.

An hour-and-a-half later – ninety minutes of galloping through gardens and hurdling fences – we eventually made it back home. As soon as we got in, Paul and Clare stumbled off to bed, as did I, but I then had the sudden impulse to leap back out again and call Jen. I ran through the kitchen and into the lounge, making a ham-fisted grab for the phone, but I was so pissed and confused that my fingers refused to connect with the right buttons. As I continued jabbing incoherently at the handset I suddenly felt myself tottering off balance, and I duly landed with a humiliating thump on the sofa.

I hauled myself up, slurring a few quiet curses, and then sat upright, giving it just enough time for the room to stop spinning. I closed my eyes for what felt like seconds, but my next sensation was a sharp throbbing inside my skull. Argh! My tongue also felt like sandpaper. Argh! And the light, tearing through the window. It was excruciatingly bright. Argh! I was curled up in a ball and . . . what was this? A towel draped across me? I looked up to see my future sister-in-law stood over me, laughing her head off. What the fuck?

I blinked a couple of times, then pulled myself into a seated position. Of course! I had obviously passed out and been gone for hours. Clare then went on to explain that my poor housemate had woken her several hours earlier in order to help retrieve her university folders from underneath my steaming, snoring frame. To complete the scene, I had, Clare said, munched on some of the food Sofia had prepared and laid out for the next day.

What a performance from Nixon! I shook my head and chuckled ashamedly. 'Well, at least I had this towel over me, eh?'

'Oh, no, you were starkers,' Clare replied. 'Everything was out. It was me who put the towel on you.'

If I had been living with Jacqui De La Cruz it might not have been worthy of mention, but Sofia was a strict Muslim girl. The food she had prepared was for Ramadan, to be eaten outside of daylight hours, and there was presumably nothing in the Koran to prepare her for the sight she saw that morning.

I gingerly got to my feet and went straight back to bed.

The cricket remained hard, and the nightlife remained, well, different. At all times it paid to remember the golden rule, which stated that in South Africa, there were nights out, and then there were nights out. Towards the end of another big gathering in Cape Town, with a friend, Amanda Biddle, and a host of other cricketers, I again took advantage of the slack local attitudes towards drink-driving and ferried some of us to a pub called the Green Man: a cracking place at the end of a shopping centre which specialised in playing old English songs. We had a rare old time, singing 'Knees Up Mother Brown' until closing time, at which point I strode out of the pub and declared confidently that it was someone else's turn to drive.

I tossed the car keys into the air, but this time the laws of physics failed me. They went up but failed to come down, having got stuck on a ledge above the pub. Observing my mistake, a doorman disappeared into the building and reappeared a few seconds later with a wiry-looking chap in Doc Marten boots who, with remarkable dexterity, shinned up some steps, clambered up the side of the pub, mounted the ledge and flicked the keys down to me. I was only beginning to shout my gratitude when our saviour suddenly lost his balance, staggered backwards and tumbled straight off the ledge. He landed, feet together, with an almighty slap on the concrete, and then crumpled into a heap. His wailing and moaning indicated his agony and, feeling responsible, I volunteered to take him to the hospital straight away.

In South Africa, 'the hospital' could mean one of two things; 1) a plush, well-equipped private facility with the finest equipment money could buy, or 2) a run-down public infirmary. Needless to say, this guy did not have private insurance. Accepting directions from the doorman, I drove the patient to the hospital where he was helped into a wheelchair and taken away. As I sat in the waiting area, still half-cut and wondering what on earth was going on, I became aware of another man standing over me. He was wearing a t-shirt, a pair of old jeans, and an urgent expression.

'Excuse me,' he said. 'Would you mind helping me in this cubicle over here?' He tilted his head in the direction of a drawn curtain.

'Er . . . Yeah, ok, no problem.'

Well, they certainly didn't do nights like this in Cumbria, or Leicester for that matter, and when he then opened the curtain the smell of booze hit me like a train. On the bed in front of me was a huge black man, face-down and with half the back of his head open.

'This man has either fallen out of a train or been pushed out of one,' announced the casually dressed surgeon as he began to organise equipment. Then, without a word, he placed a host of implements onto a silver tray and held it out in my direction.

So began my temporary, one-night-only job as a surgeon's assistant; standing by the bed and holding the doctor's instruments while he stitched his patient's head up. When the procedure was done, I was thanked and ushered back out into the waiting room, still in a state of mild confusion.

I never learned whether the big guy survived, but our key-finder certainly did, because a few weeks later I bumped into him again in the Green Man, where he told me, from his wheelchair, that he had broken both his ankles when he had fallen. All I could do was apologise profusely and keep a closer grip on my car keys from then on.

You know how it is when you live anywhere for a period of time. Soon enough you locate your comfort zone, and after a while I found myself getting quite blasé about the harsh contrasts of South African life. But no matter how many evenings at the Waterfront I embarked upon, no matter how many glamorous encounters with the beautiful people I enjoyed, and no matter how much disposable wealth I seemed to have, the fear would never completely shift.

At the house in Primrose, the windows had bars to protect against any unwanted intruders. One night I heard a rustling outside my bedroom window and the fear properly kicked in. Someone from the township with dark intentions? Or just an animal rummaging in the bushes? I wasn't brave enough to find out. Another area where I later lived, Pinelands, was a more exclusive development but its suburb stood practically side-by-side with the Langa township, and nearby was another – Khayelitsha. On no account, very obviously, was it considered safe for the well-off white man to venture away from his comfortable habitat and into these places, so my future career as a tour guide was ruined for good when Jen flew out for another visit with her parents, David and Christine, in tow.

This was towards the end of my latest six-month stint and I was so knackered from weeks of cricket and partying that I just wanted to stay in and chill out. Jen let me know in no uncertain terms that she had not travelled to South Africa to stay indoors sipping tea, and added that David had conquered his fear of flying especially to make the trip. They were all keen to explore the place, so I got my act together and took them out for a drive around my old haunts, sporting and social. When the grand tour was over we set off for home, and I chatted all the way back, until the road started turning into wood chippings. When the wood chippings turned into grass, a little further on, it became clear that I had driven us right into the heart of Khayelitsha.

We were lost and not especially welcome, judging by the hordes of people who appeared from nowhere to regard the vehicle that had just invaded their community. Just picture the scene: one confused, red-faced white man at the wheel; another perplexed, slightly older white guy in the passenger seat; a young, attractive blonde woman in the back seats and her glamorous mother alongside, wearing fine jewellery and Gucci glasses. If you had been asked to design a perfect target for the disaffected, impoverished black population of South Africa, you would have drawn up something similar to this. And the best thing? I couldn't see a way out.

I was absolutely bricking it as I tried driving on further down the narrowing track, but all this achieved was to take us further into the township. I was by now dripping with sweat as I slowed down again. When I stopped and tried to regain my bearings, I looked out of my window to see a hollow-cheeked, irate-looking black man leaning over and staring back at me. With a sharp, jabbing movement, he made a violent hand gesture and mouthed the words: 'Get out.'

It wasn't a polite suggestion. I held my hands up in apology and then attempted an improbable three-point turn. Miraculously, I crunched the car around 180 degrees in the tightest space imaginable and sped out the way we came in. The sight of tarmac was like a rainbow on the horizon. I put my foot down and kept it down until we were back on recognisable ground. Later, when the sweating had stopped, I tried to make light of it, but it was not an experience to be repeated. And it's safe to say that Jen and her folks were not in any hurry to return for another look.

For a few more years, I kept going back to play in South Africa. The cricket was competitive, with strapping, raw meat-eating fast bowlers testing your courage as a batsman. Plenty of English guys were out there for company and the challenge of cricket in a new country gave me something fresh to occupy the mind – I thrived on the responsibility of being the overseas pro.

I came up against some of the best South African players in their own back yard (a teenage Graeme Smith, I'm certain, was among them) and gave it everything I had. Overall the experience helped me grow as a player and a man but maybe the best memory of all was provided by the young buck I often encountered in the gym at Cape Town.

Herschelle Gibbs was a boy megastar who could have played for his country at football, rugby, athletics, or anything else he wanted, but had chosen cricket and was by now making magic with a bat in his hand. He was also a talkative lad and a good storyteller, and one morning after a strong session on the treadmill we sat down together to cool off. We were sharing tales about life, the universe and everything, as you do, when he pulled out an absolute classic.

Herschelle, like me, had not found schoolwork a breeze and described how a teacher had once suggested he spend some time with the brainiest kid in the class – the chess champ, the maths expert – just to see how he went about his work and his life.

Herschelle dutifully followed the suggestion, and reported back a week later.

'So what do you think?' asked the teacher.

'You're right,' Gibbs replied. 'He seems to be quite bright.'

'Only quite bright?' enquired Sir.

'Yeah, quite bright,' said Gibbs. 'But not *really* bright.'

'Can you explain that?'

'Well,' Herschelle said. 'Look at it this way. When he plays chess, he gets thirty seconds, or a minute, or . . . basically, he gets as long as he needs to make his move, but when I play cricket, and a bowler bowls a ball at me, I have to think about all sorts of things. I have to decide whether to go forward or back. I have to decide whether to hit it on the legside or the offside. I have to decide whether to hit it in the air or on the ground.'

'OK . . .'

'. . . I also have to decide which of nine fielders, plus the bowler and the wicketkeeper, I should try to beat. And when I beat him, do I want to run one, two or three? Or do I hit it for four, or smash it for six? And when I run, will it be my call, or my partner's at the other end? The thing is, Sir, I have to make all these decisions in one-third of a second. So I think I'm quite bright after all. And that kid is not as bright as I thought he was.'

I would have paid money to have seen the teacher's response to that work of genius. I also wished I had thought of something similar when I was at Ullswater High School.

nine

DOPE

By 1994, Leicestershire's culture of selfishness was on its last legs. Many of the older guard had moved on, replaced by a younger wave of players who had been schooled by Simmo and forged together during the Shit Pit years. I was feeling more contented with my lot, and with my first-team chances coming more frequently, I was finding myself increasingly able to take them.

From coming in at eight or nine in the batting order, I began creeping up to six and seven. I took on nightwatchman duties and clocked up a few not outs, which improved my average. Over time, I came to be regarded as a decent batsman who had a bit of natural ability with the gloves. And there were certain games when I had managed to find a little bit extra, such as Durham's visit to Grace Road in June 1993, when Potter bowled, Botham top-edged and I elbowed my way past a swarm of fielders and dived forward to take the catch.

The trappings of being a first XI player were also, at last, appearing. The sponsored BMW. The wage rise. The extra days off after a game. All welcome signs of personal progress. We also had the makings of a decent side, bringing in good, experienced players like Vince Wells from Kent and then making the inspired move for Phil Simmons. The arrival of the Trinidadian Simmons to replace Benji as our overseas player for the 1994 season marked a deliberate change of approach from the club. Instead of temperamental fast bowling, the Leicestershire public was going to be treated to several summers of calypso batting. On his debut against Northamptonshire at Grace Road, Simmons made an eye-watering 261 with a display of the most ferocious hitting I had ever seen. Strangely, he never made it to 1,000 runs that summer, but he remained a hugely positive addition to the team; catching pigeons in the slips, bowling at serious speeds when he wanted, mentoring the younger players in the nets and winning matches with his flashing blade.

I had a dream of a year, meanwhile, scoring 1,000 Championship runs for the first and only time in my career.

It helped that I was now at the centre of the new team spirit, rather than on the outside, tapping nervously on the dressing room door. I was channelling my energy better, rounding everyone up on the social front, and Grace Road was steadily starting to resemble a united camp. I had contributed centuries against Northants, Essex and Hampshire and was feeling like a more important cog in the wheel by the time Alan Knott quietly slipped the idea into my head that England were taking an interest in my progress. 'Keep scoring runs,' he said. 'They like you. And I like you – you're doing well. Just keep going.'

No elaborate promises or over-the-top statements – that wasn't Knotty's way. But then other things started happening which seemed to confirm his idea. One day, for example, Graham Gooch rolled up at our game at Hampshire, and during a period when I wasn't batting or keeping he beckoned me over.

'Come on Nico,' he barked. 'Get your fackin' bat and gear on and let's get in those nets.'

The former England captain began sending me throwdowns from close range. And not just your average throwdowns. I liked facing fast bowling, but Gooch in throwing mode was something else. He peppered me relentlessly and I almost had to ask him to slow down, and move back a bit, so I could catch my breath. But you couldn't say that to Graham Gooch.

He had, I later learned, been sent by the ECB to have a look at my technique. Knotty was right – they *were* interested – and at the end of the summer my name was included in the England A squad to tour India and Bangladesh. My selection was a thrill, but I didn't regard it as a massive surprise. That wasn't an arrogant thought; simply a reflection of how good I was feeling. All of a sudden I was in a fantastic place, with the best season of my life tucked safely under my belt. It seemed nothing more than one more stride towards destiny.

The tour was to be my first taste of the subcontinent – another big adventure – but began with a four-day camp in Malaga by way of preparation. I was one of two wicketkeepers (Keith Piper was the other) with a third assigned to work with us in Portugal. When I was informed that Jack Russell was joining us for the trip, I was equally thrilled and terrified. From the first day I had seen Jack in county cricket, I hadn't been able to take my eyes off him. Once you looked past his famous idiosyncrasies – I knew about his Weetabix-soaking habits, and had observed his tatty old kit – it wasn't hard to realise how good he was. His foot placement, his hand movements, his body rotations, his diving techniques; the man was an absolute Rolls-Royce. I hated it if I didn't play well against him, and had not been able to avoid treating matches against Gloucestershire as personal auditions to impress Jack. Never mind the team.

In the event, we got on fine in Malaga and I felt better for the experience. Piper, meanwhile, was regarded as a rising star by everyone in county cricket and a serious rival to my England ambitions by me. He had God-given ability with the gloves in his favour, but my batting was coming on better than his. He was also, quite openly, a worrier. 'What are people saying about me?' was one of his regular refrains, while I was keeping my occasional demons to myself; not that I much understood them, of course.

The England A squad was of a high calibre. Alan Wells from Sussex was our captain and the touring party was filled with emerging talent: Michael Vaughan, Jason Gallian, Nick Knight, Glen Chapple, David Hemp, Dominic Cork, Min Patel, Mark Ramprakash, Mark Ilott, Richard Johnson, Paul Weekes and Richard Stemp, with the ex-Sussex captain John Barclay as our coach. Life on tour was a different experience from the domestic scene. For one thing, you see players at closer quarters than is possible at your respective counties. In India I started to get to know Michael Vaughan for the first time, and found him to be a really deep thinker who enjoyed analysing what made people tick. I also enjoyed the company of Jason Gallian, the Lancashire batsman, who reminded me of a younger Mike Gatting in build, ability and appetite. A little less friendly was Richard Stemp, the Yorkshire slow left-arm bowler, who seemed quite highly strung and not always at ease with the rest of the group.

India, the first leg, was like nowhere I had been before – so busy and noisy and smelly! – but we were a group of young lads together on tour and determined to have a great time. The games went well enough (despite the Indians boasting a couple of rising stars named Dravid and Ganguly, we won the series) and I played in two of the three Tests; not scoring as many runs as I had hoped, but keeping fine on the low, dusty pitches.

But the trip was not without its surprises. In the early days of the tour, whispers started spreading that drugs were going around one or two members of the squad. I didn't see any of this for myself, but the rumours were strong, and I did learn very quickly how easily a player could pick up some illicit substances if he was that way inclined. You didn't have to look very hard.

You didn't even need to leave the hotel. A common feature of our daily life in India was to be approached by cricket-mad locals who thought nothing of walking off the street, strolling into your hotel, sidling up to you and attempting conversation. Mostly it was harmless, but there was one bloke who was a little harder to shake off. He made his presence felt by following me into the hotel lift, tugging my sleeve and embarking on a hurried sales pitch as the elevator rose.

'Oh, Mister Nixon, wicketkeeper Mister Nixon, very good player,' he said. 'I am big fan of yours, I am huge cricket fan.'

He then reached into his pocket and produced a little tin box. He opened it to reveal some dope.

'You want some of this, you have it. Maybe you have gloves we can swap? Or maybe a bat? We do a deal Mister Nixon. You interested, Mister Nixon . . . ?'

'Sorry bud, not interested.'

'It is very good Mister Nixon, very good my friend.'

'Sorry bud, not interested.'

Eventually my personal salesman got the message, and he scurried off. It clearly wouldn't have been the wisest of career moves, and in any case, I knew cannabis didn't agree with me. I had tried it once – on a New Year's Eve in Australia – and the results had been alarming; I had spent the rest of the night clambering on the roof of the house next door, and then I coughed for a week afterwards.

If that winter did nothing for my future as an international drugs baron, it certainly sharpened up my wicketkeeping. Until now, I had spent most of my short career standing back to high-quality seamers like Benji, Aggers, Les Taylor and Gordon Parsons, but I was less experienced keeping to spinners, so standing up to the likes of Patel and Stemp on the slow Indian tracks did my game the world of good.

While India were predictably competitive, Bangladesh didn't provide the same kind of opposition. My abiding memory of the trip's second leg is of Nick Knight and David Hemp batting for so long in Dhaka that I took to sunbathing on the roof of the stand, despite holding a high position in the batting order. It wasn't the greatest of challenges, and by the time our last game was brought to an early end by a ferocious downpour we were keen to get back to our hotel to round off the tour in style. Wayne Morton, our physio, had organised a fancy dress party and this rapidly descended into carnage with Paul Weekes being hurled into the hotel's freezing cold swimming pool . . .

'Look at Weekesy!'

'He's all over the place!'

'Fucking brilliant!'

'Christ, maybe he's actually struggling . . .'

. . . but the subsequent eruption of thrashing arms and legs told us that the one guy in the touring party who couldn't swim was the Middlesex all-rounder who had ended up in the water. So Weekesy was quickly fished out, red-faced and panting, and the party resumed.

If anything I felt even more confident about my prospects as I flew home from my first international trip. I had not done myself any harm with bat or gloves, and I felt part of a new and exciting scene which offered an obvious path to even bigger things. After all, if they could pluck Ramps off an A tour and drop him into the full England side, as they had done two years earlier, it showed there was a route for the rest of us.

I hopped off the plane and prepared to take the next step, but it didn't exactly go to plan.

The season of 1995 was notable for many things at Leicestershire, not least the shy, slip of a lad who started appearing at our net sessions. Jack Birkenshaw confided that this naïve-looking Asian spin bowler had been taking wickets galore for Leicester Ivanhoe in the local league, and had accepted an invitation to come and practice against the county players. The boy had an unusual action, with a strange flexibility in his wrist and the ability to put phenomenal revs on the ball. Soon he had our batsmen groping in the dark on our damp, spinner-unfriendly surfaces.

I don't think the club fully realised how good he was, otherwise they would have moved heaven and earth to get him on the books. Alas, he was soon on his way back to his home country of Sri Lanka, and by July 2010 Muttiah Muralitharan had retired as Test cricket's all-time leading wicket-taker.

I had returned for pre-season aiming for a big target of my own. England's wicketkeeping position was bang up for grabs – Steve Rhodes of Worcestershire had barely got a run on the winter Ashes tour – and there seemed to be a void. Why couldn't I be the man to fill it?

England! Just imagine! The achievement of a dream! The chance to repay everyone who had supported me! The chance to stick it up people who had doubted me! Mr Howarth, are you listening?! And Justin Benson – remember when you very casually told me, before a South Africa trip, that there was 'no way' I would play for England?! I will show you all!

My first game of the season was not for Leicestershire but for England A again; a four-day match against Warwickshire. They were the newly crowned county champions and domestic cricket's major force, inspired by Dermot Reeve's captaincy, Bob Woolmer's coaching and the skills of players like Brian Lara, Gladstone Small, Dougie Brown, Keith Piper, Trevor Penney and Roger Twose, who was avoiding dismissals as successfully as he had avoided being whitewashed a few years back. They also had my old friend, Allan Donald.

We rolled up at Edgbaston to be confronted with the greenest track of all time. When the game began, the ball started seaming here, there and everywhere, with Donald pumped up and in his element. 'Just the kind of battle for me,' I thought, when it was my turn to join Alan Wells in the middle. I ducked and dived my way to 47 and was enjoying myself under the barrage, but then Donald got one to lift sharply off the pitch. Before I could adjust, the ball reared up and smashed into my thumb.

I got through the last over of the day, working a four off my hip to fine leg to reach my half-century, but my thumb had instantly gone numb and the moment I got back in the dressing room it was obvious something was wrong. When I took my glove off, I saw that one of my bones had popped clean through the skin. I was immediately retired hurt and sent away for an operation.

What I thought might be a short spell on the sidelines then became a six-week absence, just at the stage when I was ready to press home my case for that England call-up. It couldn't have happened at a worse time. Then, in my desperation to impress, I came back too soon and couldn't produce the goods.

Watch the ball . . . Hold on, you're not picking this guy up . . . What's he doing? Why can't you get him away? Where are you? You're nowhere today, that's where.

It was infuriating. At the very time the selectors were starting to pay Grace Road a few extra visits, my luck had deserted me and the little man had returned with interest. I knew the window of opportunity would never be open for long and, sure enough, England turned back to Alec Stewart, with Jack Russell still in the wings. The rest was history. So, it seemed, was I.

It annoyed me that Donald had bowled the ball that fucked up my chances of a Test cap. It wasn't anything personal, but I always prided myself on my ability to take on the quickest and the best. I don't know why, but from day one I never had a moment's fear when the ball was whistling around my head at extreme speeds. It always got my adrenalin pumping and sharpened my focus. Not many of the leading fast bowlers of the time took me to the cleaners (one notable exception was Courtney Walsh, whose bouncer I simply couldn't read) but the rest I tackled pretty well.

One of the greats I particularly enjoyed facing was Wasim Akram. The Pakistani legend was so keen to get you out that he would set attacking fields from ball one, practically giving you runs. Most of the time I found I could pick his bouncer and read his swing. The only time he properly nailed me was late in his career, when I got a little too big for my boots. Before going into bat, Alan Mullally told me Wasim was feeling sore and wasn't the force of old. I went out to the middle and began sharing this opinion with Wasim in no uncertain terms. He came charging in and I nailed him for four.

'Come on Was,' I taunted. 'Five years ago you were amazing. What's happened to you?'

He responded as only a great international bowler could: by knocking my middle pole out of the ground with his very next delivery. Unfortunately for him, the umpire then signalled a no-ball. Unfortunately for me, Wasim wiped his brow, bustled back in and detonated my middle stump again, next ball. 'Whatever you think, Nixy,' he grinned, wagging his finger as I walked off to take my medicine.

Some you lose, some you win. The main thing was to be out there, jousting with the best. These were the sort of battles I was missing as I sat at home after my Edgbaston mishap, miserably nursing my broken thumb and tending to my smashed-up dreams.

Not that it was all misery that year. At Leicestershire we had a new overseas player with a formidable reputation. Having recently been appointed South Africa's captain, we knew we were getting a first-class operator in Hansie Cronje but we didn't realise how much of an example he would prove to be. As with Phil Simmons, our recruitment of Hansie was another departure from the habit of going all-out for big West Indian fast bowlers, who were often inconsistent, frequently got injured and didn't always work wonders on flat pitches. Hansie was a different specimen altogether – he was a high-class batsman, an amazing player of spin, and a tactical genius in any given situation.

He appeared as disciplined a sportsman and as decent a man as you could wish to meet, but it was his approach to fitness that impressed me the most. I had always been regarded as the fitness king at Leicestershire, but Hansie offered serious competition for the crown. He had apparently trained with Zola Budd, the Olympic middle-distance athlete, in South Africa, and his appetite for running was clear as soon as he arrived at Grace Road. Every evening, after a day's play, he would pull on his trainers, sprint around the boundary edge from one sightscreen to another, walk to the next, and then sprint again. He would repeat this gruelling routine six times, while the rest of the players were nursing their aches and pains in the dressing room.

I loved the challenge of testing myself against Hansie. We competed against each other every day and pushed ourselves to the absolute limit. As much as anything, it gave me something new to tackle instead of just moping around after the broken thumb episode, but I still only got the better of him once, when we went for a 5-mile run and followed it with a series of bunny-hops – a routine which rendered his legs so stiff the next day that he had to pull out of our next Sunday League game. Otherwise, he was a physical machine who brought a new intensity to our training and nets and never flagged. Around the club, he commanded natural authority with his 1,300 Championship runs, his mastery of run-chases, and his helpful attitude towards the younger batsmen.

He was the perfect man to have around, really – in a few short months he had got me feeling better about life – and it seemed innocuous when the jokes started flying around about his legendary love of money. As quickly as he earned admiration for his approach to cricket, Hansie attracted a reputation as the tightest man at the club. Early into his stay he latched onto Gordon Parsons, his brother-in-law (Gordon was married to Hansie's sister, Hester) and began heading to his house every night for dinner. This, we concluded, was mainly because he was too stingy to buy his own food. We hammered him relentlessly, branding him Scrooge, but this never seemed to bother him, apart from one memorable occasion.

Hansie was very well-paid, drove a sponsored BMW and had all the trappings, but was notorious for never buying a drink. And so, before a game in London against Middlesex, we resolved to stitch him up. Prior to the trip, a few of us devised a rule whereby the first person who reached the hotel bar would have to get the first round in. This information was then shared with the rest of the team, with only one man left in the dark. We finally informed Hansie of the new directive seconds before we rocked up to our expensive London base, and as we walked into the foyer we surrounded him, shoved him to the front of the group and threatened to pile on him and remove his clothes if he didn't break the habit of a lifetime.

'Ah, no, come on guys . . .'

He pleaded and protested, but eventually gave in and the resulting round relieved him of about £200. Judging by his expression, he would have preferred to have handed over one of his limbs than the money.

Joking apart, he was as sharp as a tack when it came to financial matters. Whenever he was dismissed in a game, he would briefly disappear into the dressing room, to get his frustrations out of his system, and would then reappear on the balcony with some paperwork, or a laptop. He was doing his accountancy qualifications, he explained – another string to his impressive bow. The only time I saw a different side to him, in all honesty, was when he invited me on his stag do in Bloemfontein during one of Leicestershire's pre-season trips to South Africa. Many of the details are vague but one image is clear: Hansie, chained to a bar stool, talking nonsense and the great man well and truly away with the fairies.

For some reason, probably because I was somehow more sober than the others, it fell to me to take him back to his house at the end of the night. This was an experience in itself, for Hansie's residence was a huge, lavish place the size of a hotel. Its front gate was operated by remote control and it took me ages to figure out which buttons to press in order to gain entry. Finally, after ten minutes of garage doors flying up and down, and lights coming on and off, the gate at last flew open.

Once inside, I somehow had to get Hansie into a prone position, where he would hopefully sink into a quick and safe sleep. Again, easier said than done. As he entered the house, he swiftly careered into the dining room, bashing against furniture and then veering shambolically towards a table. On the table stood a big, shiny trophy – his international player of the year award – and it was about to hit the floor.

I lunged in front of Hansie and grabbed the silverware just in time. I put it somewhere safe and then returned to the job at hand. Eventually I brought Cronje under control, directed him through to his lounge and helped him down onto the sofa. I whipped a bin out of the kitchen, placed it next to his head, and departed to the sound of a country's greatest sporting icon throwing up.

If you had told me then that this would be the last time I would see Hansie Cronje in the flesh, and that a few years later I would be watching the news and learning about his involvement in one of cricket's most appalling match-fixing scandals, with his eyes no longer sparkling as they used to, but sunken and hollow in a televised courtroom scene, I wouldn't have believed you. If you had then predicted I would wake up a couple of years further on to reports of his death in a plane crash in the Outeniqua Mountains, I would have chased you out of town. Not just because he hated flying and always preferred to drive from Bloemfontein to Cape Town for two days rather than make the trip by plane, but because of who and what he was.

Back then, he just seemed like the rest of us at Leicestershire during those mainly exciting, formative times – so young, so fit, so full of vitality, so skilful, so hungry, and . . . well, just so bloody *good*.

ten

BRANDY TIME

My old friend John Holliday once said something profound: 'The human body is a tough old sod, in the end.' He was talking about something more serious than a broken thumb but I can recognise the principle now. By 1996, my Donald-inflicted war wound had healed, and so had my more lasting scars with Dad, who had since split up with the woman he left Mum for, and met Irene, who would become his second wife. I was slowly learning to remove my sainted old man from his pedestal and see him as a bloke, living his life, instead of the villain who had walked out on my mother.

Another happy development that year was the appointment of Jimmy Whitaker as Leicestershire's captain. If Bobby Simpson had been the first man to change the tired old environment at Grace Road, Jimmy cranked things up further. From day one, our new skipper made it his business to create a constructive atmosphere. He regularly took us out for team meals and in no time the talk was all about cricket – our plans, our ideas, our ambitions – rather than who had been shagging who, and who had been the most drunk the previous weekend.

He was also a man of many phrases – little nuggets of wisdom which I found blissfully simple to understand:

'It's not about if, it's about when.'

'We're all a bike-chain – we're all in this together.'

One thing Jimmy hated was the idea that the dressing room should fall silent the moment the captain or coach came through the door. He wiped away the remaining 'Them and Us' feeling at a stroke, encouraged us to share our opinions, and insisted that we were honest and mature with each other. If someone was batting like a bag of rubbish in the nets, we now had licence to tell them. If a bowler disagreed with the skipper's field placings, he would now be invited to say so. It made perfect sense and was empowering.

With his books and his mantras to back all this up, he was basically Mr Positive. The ideal captain for me, in other words, and someone with whom I would develop an unbelievable rapport as the years went on.

Another innovation was Jimmy's request that we should form a huddle before the start of a day's play, and any time a wicket fell. This was unusual in county cricket at the time, and it drew a lot of curiosity from around the game, but we knew what we were doing. It helped to create an outward show of togetherness and was our symbol of unity. It was also another helping of positivity for me, keeping the little man locked away in his box and helping me forget about my England woes. Linked with Jack Birkenshaw's calmer, trusting approach to coaching – 'Come on Nico, keep playing straight, keep hitting the back wall of the net' – it made for a potent formula.

We were deeply unfancied at the start of the season, as distant as 40/1 with some bookmakers for the County Championship, but I was so confident in the environment Jimmy and Jack had created that I told anyone who was listening around Leicester to stick a few quid on us. We had a small, tight core of men who loved each other's company, and as players we were surely reaching our peaks together: Simmons was in magnificent order, Maddy was making an impact with the bat, Aftab Habib and Ben Smith were pushing through, Wells was a match-turning all-rounder, Alan Mullally was a serious weapon with the ball, and David Millns was an effective bowler who was also capable of scoring hundreds at eight or nine.

Millnsy was something else. He seemed to spend most of pre-season out on the tiles until all hours, an approach which led him to bowl a heap of shit in most of our warm-up games. On the way to Grace Road one morning in April I stopped at a set of traffic lights, glanced in my rear-view mirror and saw a big 4x4 pull up behind me. Inside, at the wheel, was Millnsy, clutching a bacon sandwich with one hand, cradling a bucket of coffee with the other, and operating the steering wheel with his knees.

A finely-honed athlete he was not. And yet, when the season started, he clicked into gear, got himself super-fit, and produced the goods. That summer, we all did.

It is hard to describe the feeling when you are involved in a team at the top of its game; things just seem to work. In 1996 we won a ridiculous number of Championship games by an innings, batting once on ten occasions. In our game against Yorkshire, for instance, we amassed 681-7 in our first innings on a billiard table at Bradford Park Avenue in June, eventually declaring after tea on the second day. As Jimmy and Vince made their respective way to double hundreds, I heard a lone, plaintive Yorkshire voice shout out from the crowd: 'Whitaker, you're killing the bloody game!' Then we rolled them over and won with a day to spare. It was that sort of season.

When Essex came to Grace Road on 4 July, we soon got into another dominant position. Millns' four wickets helped dispatch them for 163 and then he teamed up with Vince to bat them out of sight. By the time both had completed centuries, Jimmy declared on 454, leaving our guests from Chelmsford an uphill climb to save the game.

This was far from an unusual predicament for an opposing team at Grace Road that summer, but in Graham Gooch Essex at least had the ideal man to lead a fightback. Even in the later part of his career, to keep wicket to Gooch was often to be cast as a spare part. At 42 he was still one of the finest groove machines in English cricket, and whenever he remained at the crease for longer than an hour it was time to start worrying.

This was one such occasion. As he played himself in at the start of Essex's second dig and then began to purr, Jimmy started looking for some alternative solutions.

'Come on Nico,' the skipper said, between overs. 'Let's try something different. Let's see what we can do.'

It was clear what he meant.

I am often asked when I became an expert in the art of sledging, and I find it difficult to answer. For one thing, I'm not a huge fan of the word. It implies abuse and derision, not the more subtle art of trying a little banter to get someone off his game, which to me is well within the boundaries of acceptability. For another, I'm not really able to put a date on it; I just had the nerve to try anything if I thought it was going to get the team an advantage. Jimmy was always happy to encourage me, and it still seemed more profitable to get inside other people's heads than my own. You live and learn, basically, and by the time Gooch was gliding through the gears I had learned quite a bit.

In order to get up the nose of a player, you have to be a few things. One is confident – no problem there – and another is observant. I watched Gooch closely for anything I could use to my advantage and it did not take long for me to spot his little habits. The moment the ball was dead, he took a couple of strides back towards square leg. At this point he plopped his bat in the ground, had a little kick at something on the floor, and then spat.

The same routine, without fail.

Walk, kick, spit.

Next ball.

Walk, kick, spit.

I committed this to memory, and then began to copy him. Between deliveries, I shuffled forward a few steps and acted out his little superstition myself.

Walk, kick, spit.

I was his shadow, and there wasn't anything he could do except try to ignore me. He walked, I walked. He spat, I spat. He spat again, I spat again. After I had copied him a few times, Gooch looked over his shoulder at me and raised an eyebrow. That was the first sign that I had got inside his bubble.

I had also noticed something about his gait. He seemed a little knock-kneed. Something else to throw into the mix? Why not.

'Have you got your top strap mixed up there, big lad?' I asked. 'You're walking a bit funny today.'

He grunted under his breath. A couple of balls later, he started to nibble.

'You need to concentrate on your own fackin' game, son.'

Just what I wanted to hear.

'What have you done in the game?'

Music to my ears.

'You haven't fackin' made it yet, son.'

Bingo.

Gordon Parsons was bowling and I was standing up to the stumps. Gordon thought it a challenge to his pride whenever I stood up to him during his latter years, and would sometimes bowl a bouncer or a legside wide, as if to say, 'You – get back to where you should be.' He thought he was a bit quicker than he actually was towards the end, but Jimmy was clear in his strategy. We thought there was a chance of getting Gooch lbw if we kept him back in his crease. 'Come on Gordy,' I encouraged Parsons. 'I think I'm getting under his skin here.'

Eventually, Parsons ran in and got one to hit the seam like a dream. Gooch came half-forward, missed, and his bails went flying. After his departure for 72, Essex's remaining six wickets went down cheaply and we wrapped up the innings victory.

That day has since been described as a cricketing rarity: the time Graham Gooch got angry while batting. Little victories against a player of his calibre were few and far between, but to me it just confirmed what was possible if you were strong and bold with your words and your actions. If, as a wicketkeeper, a batsman turns around and gives you grief, I don't believe he is completely on his game. Some players can click back into their mindsets, but others can't.

Gooch was an amazing player, one of the very best. But that day he gave me a bit of shit in return. And I knew we had him.

The Championship was within reach when we lined up against Durham at Chester-le-Street on 12 September. It was here that I teamed up with Simmons for a sixth-wicket partnership of 284 that still stands as a club record. Despite the home team handing a debut to a big, gangly lad called Harmison who sent down a mixture of the unplayable and the unreachable, Phil utterly pulverised the bowling and I nurdled my way to a hundred in his shadow. As usual, we cruised to a handsome victory, this one inside two days.

If Simmons often provided the magic, he was far from being a lone star. A lot of our rivals that year were often depleted by England call-ups, but we made it through the season using just thirteen players, which helped keep the unit tight and the juggernaut rolling on.

We clinched the title during the tea interval at Grace Road as we were putting Middlesex to the sword. Mullally, nicknamed Audi because of his habit of getting four ducks in a row, resembling the car logo, smashed a barely believable 75 and then bowled like a dream, and once it was confirmed that Surrey, our nearest challengers, were out of range, the ground went ballistic. We sprayed champagne from the balcony and the final session went past in a blur. I then led a conga of fans and players around the outfield, watched one well-refreshed spectator mark the occasion by climbing up one of the sightscreens and refusing to come down for hours, and later flopped down in the dressing room with a bottle of something strong and let the achievement sink in.

What does it feel like? I will tell you. Relief, mainly. Relief that it's over and you have your reward for all the heartache, all the training, all the miles on the treadmill, all the catches, all the claps, all the previous days in the dirt, all the niggles and all the pain. When you come out of it all as champions, and when you know you have contributed in a serious way, the feeling is unsurpassable.

That summer I got a lot of runs when we were in the shit. I would come in at 40-4, get a hundred and set us off again. At the start of the season, I had resolved that the best way to get my England disappointment out of my system was to get fit and fired up, and to produce the goods for Leicestershire. I was back in a good place, and the results showed.

We were never a fashionable club or a big-money bunch like Surrey – we were just humble lads who wanted to win cricket matches, whose management believed in us, drove us, educated us and trusted us. The old saying, 'You can choose your friends, but you can't choose your family' is also true of cricket. You don't get to sit down and select your team-mates and, if you're unlucky, you won't get along. That summer, we were like the closest family you could imagine. It's the best team environment I have ever known. We leapt out of bed every morning and galloped into work and the outcome was Leicestershire's first County Championship for twenty-one years.

Once the conga line had dispersed, we had the mother and grandmother of all parties. The next morning we came back and cleaned up the last five Middlesex wickets in the space of half an hour. We were on top of the world, feeling completely untouchable, and by the end of the season I had almost managed to forget that I nearly didn't live to see it.

I first encountered Alan Mullally during my winter jaunts to Perth with Rosey. He was a left-arm seamer with bags of talent, who had gone back to Australia after a brief time with Hampshire. After learning he had English parents, I had nagged and nagged him to come and sign for Leicestershire, which he eventually did.

I don't know why, but I just seemed to click with Alan. We were both mad as hatters, certainly, and as well as being a serious player he possessed the worst singing voice I have ever heard. There are only so many times you can hear Mullally belting out Bob Marley numbers during a car journey before you want to open the door and jump out, but we often travelled around together in our sponsored BMWs and talked the hind legs off each other.

My car was one of the first to have a CD player, which fascinated Alan. One horrible wet night on the way home from a friend's house in Great Glen, a village near Leicester, saw him sifting through a bunch of CDs in search of some suitable songs for his tuneless vocals. As he did so, a disc came bouncing across to the driver's side.

I leant down to retrieve it, but suddenly lost control of the car and veered across the road, skimming the edge of a ditch. Immediately, I rounded a sharp corner and careered onto the other side of the road. I then overcompensated wildly, swerving back across. The car was by now all over the place, and before we knew it we were skidding back into the ditch and hurtling unstoppably towards a telegraph pole and a tree. In the half-second before impact I did something I had never done before. Well, there was no time like the present . . .

'Please God, we can't die now,' I said, out loud. 'You've got to look after us here, God.'

My very next memory is of being upside down in the ditch, with a snapped pole next to us. A few seconds passed as I scrambled to get my bearings. I was OK. So, thankfully, was Alan. We stumbled groggily out of the twisted mess of the car without any obvious injuries, called for assistance, and let out a little laugh of relief. A few days later, I was watching Alan playing for England and smiling to myself when I saw him rubbing his neck after taking a catch. If only the rest of the crowd had known the cause of his stiff joints that day.

Later, the crash made its way into the papers, and gave me the once-in-a-lifetime experience of being on the front and back pages of the same edition. On the back was a routine cricket story, while the front-page splash told the tale of how a fox had bolted across the road and caused two of Leicestershire's top players to swerve into a ditch, writing off their car but miraculously escaping unscathed.

That version of events wasn't entirely correct. We *had* encountered a fox, but much earlier in the journey. It certainly hadn't caused our crash. It was our own silly fault, fiddling with CDs, but there was no way we were admitting that at the time.

When the title was won, we were the toast of Leicester. And I mean literally – people around the city couldn't stop themselves buying us drink after drink. Jen was often flying abroad with her job with British Airways, so I was left to my own devices for long stretches of time. The city now had a road called Championship Way but at best I could only stagger down it. With a big win bonus in my pocket and a feel-good atmosphere prevailing, I was effectively pissed until Christmas.

A more civilised celebration took place at Buckingham Palace, when we travelled to London on a special train hauled by an engine christened *Leicestershire County Cricket Club* in order to collect the County Championship trophy from Prince Philip, the Patron of the Lord's Taverners. He met us all in a line and seemed in jovial spirits as he congratulated us on our achievement, and seemed to perk up even further when he came to the wives and girlfriends. As he arrived at Jen, who was sporting a nice tan having just returned from South Africa, he leaned in for a chat. The resulting dialogue has since entered Nixon legend:

'Tell me,' the Duke enquired. 'Are you that colour all over?'

'Well,' Jen replied, 'I have got a couple of white bits.'

The 1997 season was a washout. We missed more than twenty days of cricket and it wrecked our chances of repeating the previous summer's glory; not that it curtailed our appetite for the good life whenever the opportunity arose.

Our philosophy under Jimmy had always been to play hard and make no apologies for celebrating hard. Any victory had to be toasted, and we generally took up the challenge, but nothing compared to the bash that was thrown towards the end of the summer of '97. Maybe it was the fact we weren't playing so often that explains why we really went for it on that night, but whatever the motivation, it was the outcome that set it apart.

The theme was 1920s fancy dress, with gangsters aplenty and one old-fashioned footballer with outrageously long shorts, lace-up shirt collar, a football taped to his heavy-soled boot and a comedy moustache for good measure. At a glance I could have passed for a hero from Carlisle United's early years but I doubt my next act was a common feature of life in the '20s.

One of my most popular party pieces of the time was to pour nail varnish remover over my clothes, flick off the lights in a room, and set myself on fire. It never failed to impress, and I was always confident I could quickly bring the flames under control. Not so on this particular night. As a group of us continued the party back at Jimmy's house, I was a little too liberal with the liquid. I doused myself with the stuff, walked into the darkened room, struck a light, and . . . wumph! My hands were up like fireballs and I couldn't put them out. I rushed around, desperately trying to shake out the mini-infernos at the end of my arms. The lads were crying with laughter, and by the time I had finally succeeded in extinguishing the blazes, half of Jimmy's coffee table had become a black and charred mess.

The two main tools of my trade, meanwhile, were left in such a state that I spent the next few days with them wrapped up in clingfilm, with a pair of frozen fillets of fish pressed against my palms. They were red raw and almost unbearably tender to the touch. Dressing myself became a painful ordeal. Going to the toilet . . . well, you can imagine. And when I kept wicket in our penultimate Championship game, against Northamptonshire, I had to get hold of some strips of artificial fat tissue from the club's medical staff to stuff inside my inner glove, just to help avoid the sheer agony that I knew would come the next time a ball slapped into my hands.

Despite my best efforts, the pain was still absolutely searing when the first few deliveries from Millns and Jimmy Ormond thumped into the mitts. The most basic part of my job was bringing me out in goosepimples and making me wince. As early as the third over I was in the skipper's ear, trying to persuade our new captain to bring a slow bowler on:

'Come on, Jimmy, let's have a look and see if it turns.'

But Jimmy was having none of it. Our two opening bowlers got through 46 overs between them. It was excruciating from the first ball to the last, and when we finally knocked Northants over for 332 in their first innings I was relieved beyond words.

Everyone found my mishap amusing – apart from Jack, who never found out – but it was mainly a frustrating summer. There wasn't much we could do but stand under our brollies and watch as Glamorgan took our crown. In 1998 we then responded to this minor setback by winning another Championship.

It wasn't quite as comprehensive as the first, but it was close, and it was also notable for the most insane game of cricket I have ever been involved in. *Wisden*, not known for exaggeration, called it 'one of the most remarkable run-chases in Championship history' and even now I can hardly believe it happened.

The month was July, the venue was Grace Road and the opponents, Northants, had put up a second-innings rearguard battle to frustrate the life out of us. By the time we finished them off, we needed an unlikely 201 to win from just 21 overs. As we quietly regrouped, a voice broke the silence.

'Fuck it, let's have a go.'

As a man capable of scoring hundreds before lunch and who had the nickname Superman, Vince Wells could never be accused of lacking confidence. But even this mission appeared beyond his powers. Nobody seriously believed it was possible except, it seemed, Vince, who marched out to bat with Maddy with a spring in his step. Before our innings started I kicked off my wicketkeeping pads and went upstairs for a chat with Craig Mortimer, our physio, but within seconds I heard a big burst of applause. Three more ovations swiftly followed – what was happening? – and another noise, as regular as clockwork, only just audible above each outbreak of clapping . . .

'BRANDY TIME!'

Leicestershire have always had many magnificent supporters but few more distinctive than Lewis Springett, a West Indian regular who had a steady stream of amusing catchphrases:

'Brandy time!' (any time a Leicestershire player hit a four).

'That's my boy!' (any time a Leicestershire player played a successful shot).

'Keep the gate open!' (as a rival batsman made his way to the middle).

'Close the gate now!' (as a Leicestershire hero took guard).

'Nico . . . I've been to church this morning . . . We're gonna be aaall-right!' (on any given Sunday).

If you wanted to know how things were going for Leicestershire, it was possible to listen to Lewis and the picture would soon become clear. On this occasion it was brandy time every few seconds, so I wandered down to the dressing room and peered outside at the scoreboard. We were 60 without loss from five overs. Vince was actually going for it. 'What the fuck are you doing?!' someone hollered. 'Get straight back up there!' In my eagerness, I had breached the oldest superstition of the dressing room – don't move an inch when things are going well.

Back up to the physio's room I scurried, as the boundaries kept coming. Lewis was hollering so much he was starting to go hoarse.

'BRANDY TIME! THAT'S MY BOY!'

Vince eventually perished for a brutal 58 and by the time I made it out to bat we were 114-4 and still needed ten an over. I lasted a matter of minutes before being run out for two, and cursed my way back to the pavilion as Iain Sutcliffe trotted out to take my place.

But I need not have worried, for Chris Lewis was still at the crease.

Chris was a fearsome hitter when he was on his game, but what he proceeded to do that afternoon defied belief. He smashed Northants' best offerings to high heaven, including one six to cow corner off Paul Taylor which might still be travelling now. All Northants needed to do was get a spinner on and take some pace off the ball, but they were rabbits in the headlights, sticking with their seam attack and watching quality bowlers like Taylor and Devon Malcolm go around the park.

Lewis ended with a ridiculous 71 from 28 balls and ran off to a hero's reception. *Wisden* got it about right, I think.

Winning that game felt like winning the title itself, with champagne in the dressing room, music pumping, people dancing and eleven Leicestershire players delirious at what had just happened. It made us feel unstoppable, as though nothing was beyond us.

Chris Lewis was not so bulletproof. His fall from grace was quick and hard. One quality Jimmy demanded of his players was maturity, which explained why he came down so hard on Chris when he was late for a training session before our Championship game against Notts at Worksop in August.

In the early days, Lewis was one of the most gifted athletes you could imagine. He was a workaholic, could bowl 90mph from a ten-yard run-up, and was capable of hitting it for miles. It was no surprise to anyone that he got into the England scene so quickly, but it was alarming then to see him lose his way.

When he came back to Leicestershire as an established international player, after spells at Nottinghamshire and Surrey, it was as though he couldn't handle being the main man any more. He got more nervous and began to behave increasingly strangely, to the point where none of the boys would travel with him in his sponsored Lexus.

When Jimmy dropped him for the Notts game it gave him a kick up the arse, but he then seemed to continue to spiral downwards. By the end, he was so anxious about playing that he would shut himself in his car during a game, and we would have to ring him to tell him he was due in to bat next.

I sometimes wonder how modern-day sports psychologists would have handled Lewis, who is now serving a thirteen-year jail sentence for smuggling liquid cocaine. Part of me still thinks he could come out of prison and score a First-Class hundred, but he was a troubled man, and Jimmy's belief back then was simple: if you abused his trust, he reckoned that somebody else would come to the party. In Lewis' absence, Wells and Mullally shared a heap of Notts wickets and Simmons and Smith made 194 and 159 respectively as we won at a canter.

Our next challenge, to widespread surprise, proved beyond us. In the Benson & Hedges Cup final against Essex we were wiped out for a measly 76. In the Championship, though, we kept rumbling on and the season culminated in a winner-takes-all decider at the Oval. Surrey had a ridiculously strong cast-list – Stewart, Thorpe, Butcher, Bicknell, the Hollioakes – and we were missing our injured captain. But, cometh the hour, cometh the men: Smith batted them out of sight with a brilliant 200, Habib and me added very satisfying hundreds and then we ruthlessly set about the legendary home batting order.

Towards the end of the third day we had Surrey nine down in their second innings and were one scalp from clinching the title. Their last man was the slow left-arm bowler Rupesh Amin, who was blocking and blocking and not looking in any mood to venture a stroke. There was a risk that we might not get the job done and would have to come back the next day; a real anti-climax for us and our busloads of supporters.

A few balls later, the picture changed. Against Matthew Brimson's left-arm spin, Rupesh came careering down the wicket and had a whoosh. I whipped off the bails to finish things off and the party could start after all. But one question lingered as the bubbly was passed around. Why, all of a sudden, had Rupesh done it? Adam Hollioake, the Surrey captain, later explained. With the day drifting to a close, Adam had watched his team-mate prodding back our final few deliveries and then met him in the middle for a chat. The discussion was one-way and had gone something like this:

'They've beaten us, mate. This is their time. It's not going to tomorrow. One of us is going to get out. It's important these boys have their night and enjoy what they have done. We will have our day, but this is theirs.'

He knew the game was up, and was happy for us to have our moment. Nobody competed longer and harder than Adam Hollioake, but he allowed it to happen. That was unbelievable sportsmanship. Top class.

Two Championships in three years made us feel unbreakable, but empires will crumble. No sooner had we enjoyed some of the best years in the club's history, the plates started drifting apart. Mullally left for Hampshire, Millnsy went back to Nottinghamshire, Jimmy hung up his boots and winning suddenly became harder.

Sure, we retained the knack for making headlines and doing memorable things, but no longer always for the best reasons. Before the 1999 season, for instance, Matthew Brimson got into hot water for revealing a delicate part of his anatomy on the team photograph.

I had heard a story a few weeks earlier about an old mate who had rested his manhood on the shoulder of his headmaster when a school photo was being taken. For this he had been expelled, but during the cold, shivering tedium of team photo day, I persistently suggested Brimmo do something similar . . .

'Go on, lad!'

'No, no, I can't.'

He could, and he did, and the offending photo duly made it into *Wisden*, and then, inevitably, the press. At the time I hadn't realised that Brimmo was preparing to quit cricket and become a teacher at a top public school, and after his misdemeanour was exposed (so to speak) the club had to write a letter to the school and defend his character. Fortunately, he got the job and the fuss died down.

There was more end-of-season, fancy dress carnage involving the unforgettable sight of the Mad Hatter (me) swinging on an expensive chandelier and crashing down in a cloud of dust and glass (the repairs cost me £300), but the fun couldn't last. By the end of that summer, after we had finished a distant third to Surrey in the Championship, Leicestershire offered me a year's contract. I was a bit put out by that – I felt I was worth a little more. I had become a catalyst of a winning side and it didn't feel unreasonable to request an additional year.

Was it really too much to ask? Apparently so – the club wanted nothing to do with my request. For some reason they were not prepared even to discuss it. I wasn't a million miles from a benefit year, but all of a sudden I was in limbo. After so many good times, their stance was hard to take. I couldn't get my head around why and spent days and weeks trying to get them to talk. But the club was not for budging and it did not take long for word to spread that I had reached an impasse at Grace Road.

Matthew Fleming, the Kent captain, was first on the phone, offering to double my money if I agreed to move to Canterbury. This, straight away, was a tempting scenario: Kent was a big club, and I was so disillusioned with Leicestershire that I gave Fleming a verbal agreement there and then.

Shortly after, I received another call, this one from Chris Adams at Sussex. He invited me to meet Peter Moores, the coach, and Don Trangmar, their Cumbrian chairman, at Hove, where they sold me their long-term vision of how they would turn one of the Championship's whipping boys into contenders. It was a nice idea, but Kent were contenders *now*. I was 29 and wanted to play for a county who could help me get back on the England scene. And, in any case, I had given Fleming my word.

Sussex then made me an offer worth more than £80,000, and then upped it to £100,000 when I demurred again. 'We really want you here, Nico,' Adams said. 'Please think about it'.

It all seemed to be happening at the speed of light. One moment I was an established part of the county I knew as home, the next I was at the centre of a bidding war!

Well, what would you do if someone offered you more than two-and-a-half times your current wage? So I thought about it some more, and then some more, and then, finally, I committed myself to Kent, and this time there was no going back. The first person I told? My bride-to-be.

eleven

DAVID MAY

Before travelling to Buckingham Palace to collect the Championship trophy in 1996, I had the brainwave of my life: why not propose to Jen, there and then, in front of the Duke? It was a stroke of genius, but by the time we boarded the train at Leicester I had abandoned the scheme. Deep down, I knew Jen would have crucified me for making her the centre of attention like that. So instead I popped the question when we were on holiday in Langkawi, and we got married on 9 October 1999 at St Peter's Church in Langwathby, with Jimmy Whitaker as my best man, the Holliday boys as ushers, reception at the North Lakes Hotel (where we had met) and a honeymoon in Barbados.

Perfect? It was. Everything was, in fact, right up to the moment when I first strapped on my pads and embarked on my new life as a Kent player.

If Jen took a while to settle in Canterbury, it being so far from home, I was no quicker to adjust to my new working environment. My first indoor net session put me in opposition to the meaty Martin McCague, and very quickly he had me struggling. His second ball hammered into my elbow and caused me to spend the rest of the session hopping around in pain. I played, missed and had my stumps rearranged with uncomfortable regularity.

The truth? I was a nervous wreck. I felt like I was on trial again. The old confidence was gone, the negativity and worries were back, and if someone had then told me where my opening summer at Canterbury was going to lead, I would have laughed.

In my favour, as I tried desperately to shake off new-club syndrome, was the fact that I was joining a county that was renowned for its wicketkeepers. How could I not take inspiration from a club which boasted names like Godfrey Evans and Alan Knott in its history books? And how could I not see the positive omens when I went for a run around the St Lawrence Ground, stopped to do some stretches under the famous lime tree and then returned to a host of puzzled looks in the dressing room?

'What's all that on your back?' somebody asked. 'You're absolutely covered in it.'

I found a mirror, looked over my shoulder and saw that my kit was smothered in a white, powdery substance. When I explained what I had just been doing, laughter broke out, and then I was informed that I had been rolling around in the ashes of a certain T.G. Evans, who had died recently.

I always felt I carried a bit of Godfrey with me after that. This was a useful thought, because in my first season I needed more help than usual to get by.

The atmosphere at Kent was noticeably different to that at Leicestershire. They had a lot of players with England experience, like Dean Headley, Mark Ealham and Matthew Fleming, and this seemed to create a more relaxed environment. Many of the players also had private school backgrounds and carried themselves with a natural self-confidence. They did their best to make me feel at home and the man I had been signed to replace, Steve Marsh, could not have been more welcoming.

Another major difference was John Wright, the coach and one of the toughest men I have ever met. On one occasion early in the season he was reading the riot act to the team about a sloppy fielding performance, with his trademark baseball cap pulled so far down his face that he could hardly see. As he spoke, a cricket ball flew through the air, catching him flush in the face and splitting his chin wide open, causing blood to gush everywhere. 'Ah, it'll be alright,' said John, dismissively, before carrying on as if he had just nicked himself while shaving.

The overseas players were different animals, too. Rahul Dravid was a humble professor of cricket, who lived close to the ground so that he could practice on his days off. Andrew Symonds, it's safe to say, was built from alternative materials. On *his* days off, Symo would arm himself with a few cans, climb into his Vauxhall Vectra and chug off down Kent's country lanes on a shooting or fishing trip. Sometimes I'd go with him to pot a few rabbits, and the outcome was always the same: anything Symo caught, he ate, and he routinely used the back seat of his car to gut his prey (I inherited the Vectra when he left, and nearly passed out when I opened the door for the first time; the stench was mind-blowing).

He was Crocodile Dundee in whites, the most dyed-in-the-wool Aussie you could ever imagine, and also a classic grump who did not carry a hangover well until he had played a vigorous game of touch rugby in the morning. By about 10.30 a.m. his eyes would start to open and Symo would finally be back in the room. On the field, he was an amazing talent, capable of hitting the ball miles and winning matches on his own. He was far from the only high-class batsman at Kent, and this meant my own opportunities at the crease were restricted. Coupled with my nerves and the inevitable return of the little man, it left me grasping for form for most of the summer, and the result was my lowest Championship runs tally for five years.

But there was still an important moral to the tale – even when you are some distance below your best, there are still ways of getting noticed.

That summer was Shane Warne's first in his long association with Hampshire. The great leg-spinner was at the stage of his career when he could take wickets just by being Shane Warne. When he arrived at Canterbury for a Championship game in August, my approach in our first innings was simply to be positive, and see what transpired. If he pitched it up, I would go over the top. Anything loose would have to be dispatched, anything else would be a bonus, and if there was a magic ball with my name on it, well, so be it.

We were struggling on 102-5 when I walked to the wicket, with Warne and Mullally having made a mess of our top and middle order on a belter of a pitch. The pressure was on, and Warne was spewing out a lot of hot air between deliveries, but that kept me nice and sharp, and things somehow just clicked into place. I made a career-best 134 not out – easily my best knock of an average summer – to help us to a tight fifteen-run victory, and then, to his credit, Warne invited me into the Hampshire dressing room afterwards for a beer and a chat.

A couple of days later, I opened a newspaper to find him singing my praises in his column, generously suggesting that I should be in the England selectors' thoughts for the upcoming Pakistan tour.

That was a pleasant surprise. I hadn't honestly thought I was anywhere near. But maybe Warne's words would carry some weight?

A few weeks later I hit upon a stranger way of getting noticed when we went to Headingley for a day/night Sunday League game. I wasn't the greatest fan of floodlit cricket that summer, because my eyes were starting to give me serious grief. They were getting cloudy and painfully dry, and when I had tried contact lenses they stuck to my eyes, leaving me in need of an optometrist to remove them. I had them lasered a few years later, which was the best thing I ever did, but before the Yorkshire game the problem had got so bad that I approached Fleming, our captain, and asked if I could be excused from combat:

'Mate, I'm in a bit of trouble here. I don't think I can play.'

'You've got to play, Nico. There's nobody else.'

Necessity being the mother of invention, I somehow found a way of coping. When the bowler was running in, I actually couldn't see the ball in his hand, so I had to stand up to the stumps for everything, just to allow my dodgy eyes a glimpse of what was going on.

As the game went on, I developed a bizarre routine:

1. Look down at the floor during the bowler's run-up; 2. Look up and squint in his direction when I sense he is close to delivery; 3. Look down again; 4. Look up once more in time to catch the ball; 5. Hope for the best.

I was playing more or less from memory, and yet – excuse the pun – I had a blinder. Every nick stayed in the gloves, I carried out a successful stumping, and also made a quick 30 with the bat to help us win the game.

Televised games always carried a bit of extra weight with county players. You felt a touch more likely to be noticed when you were performing in front of the cameras. You imagined an ECB big cheese watching at home and thinking, 'This lad can play'. To a casual observer – and a selector – it probably looked like I was on top of my game that day in Leeds, but all the while I had barely been able to see what was happening, and was completely terrified of mucking it up.

Sometimes life grabs hold of you and pulls you along at a crazy speed. The day David Graveney called to inform me that I had been named in the England Test squad to tour Pakistan and Sri Lanka, I was on the way to John-Paul Getty's sprawling estate at Wormsley Park in Buckinghamshire. Kent had a day off and I had been invited, along with a bunch of Hampshire players, to feature for the Getty team against the touring West Indies. As chairman of selectors Graveney relayed the news; my father-in-law, David, who was driving, cried tears of pride and punched the air.

I barely had time to let the news sink in, to reflect that the dream hadn't been killed by Allan Donald after all, because in no time I had my pads and gloves on and was keeping to Shane Warne, who was bowling to Brian Lara. The great Warne versus the great Lara, plus me: it was like a scene from a dream. In the slips next to me, meanwhile, Hampshire's Robin Smith was engaged in a little game of his own with Lara.

'Over extra cover for four, Brian,' Smith chirped.

Warne bowled, and Lara obliged.

'OK, run the next one down to third man for four,' Smith suggested.

Warne bowled, and Lara obliged.

This went on for ball after ball after ball. Smith would nominate an area of the field, and Lara would dispatch Warne's bowling to that precise point. Eventually he retired on 103 before lunch. And don't think Warne wasn't trying.

When that entertaining episode was over, I got changed and wrapped my mind around the idea that I was going to be an England player. Graveney had told me I would be touring as Alec Stewart's number two, with the promise of playing in some of the games between Tests. That would do very nicely, thank-you.

Most of the squad had been in Kenya for One-Day Internationals and were travelling to Pakistan from there, so when I headed to Heathrow in October I only had four others –Mike Atherton, Ian Salisbury, Dominic Cork and Michael Vaughan – for company, and after meeting at our hotel we were asked to carry out a few pre-tour formalities. One of these was the regulation signing session, which saw us ushered into a room by ECB staff and invited to autograph various items of memorabilia.

I have to confess that I enjoyed this immensely. Like many boys, I had often practiced my signature in preparation for the time when I would be famous. Now I was to be an England player, I took pride in adding my scrawl to every item, but others were less enthusiastic. Atherton, for one, had an approach all of his own to this task, seemingly aiming for a world record time as he seized a photo, dragged his pen across it in a straight line, and then moved onto the next. I watched him and wondered if he realised that somebody out there might be awaiting his autograph like an item of treasure. 'Not very impressive', I couldn't help thinking.

I thought my trips to India and Bangladesh had equipped me with all the knowledge I needed about the subcontinent, but I was wrong. India was a warm and colourful place, but Pakistan immediately seemed harder, colder. In India, when we travelled around in the team coach and waved to people in the streets, they waved back. In Pakistan, they just stared back. If that was the first surprise, the next was the introduction to Pakistani crowds. The last of the One-Day Internationals in Rawalpindi was interrupted by a riot outside the ground, when a mass of people turned up without tickets. Firecrackers went off and tear-gas floated across the ground as the police tried to regain control.

Things were calmer a couple of days later when I made my first England appearance at the same ground. The records show that I first pulled on my gloves for my country against a Patron's XI, that my first of six dismissals came in the sixteenth over, that the opener Naved Ashraf was my opening victim, that the bowler was the unlikely figure of Marcus Trescothick, and that I contributed 31 runs in a stand with Craig White. But the detail was overshadowed by the sweet feeling that I was – at last! – playing for England, and loving it.

As the tour unfolded, though, things were not quite so smooth. The first thing I noticed about touring with England was that the squad was organised into distinct groups, a bit like Leicestershire in the old days. Newcomers like me were expected to know our place, while the established men like Atherton, Graham Thorpe and Nasser Hussain, the captain, had their own little clique. Those of us on the outside of this bubble barely got any time in the nets, or any attention from Duncan Fletcher, the coach. More often than not we had to practice among ourselves. It was clear from the outset that we were just seen as the backroom boys, there to help the main guys.

That frustrated me. I wanted to learn from the best, but it seemed that some of the senior players were only concerned with covering their own backs. None of them made the slightest effort to talk to me. I didn't like that, so I tried to do something about it.

After one practice session, I approached the group of giants.

'Right, I'm coming out with you boys for dinner tonight,' I announced.

You could have heard a pin drop. The looks on the faces of Atherton and Hussain were those of cool sixth-formers who had just been asked by a geeky third-year if he could join them on their big night out. I practically forced them to allow me to tag along to their meal. They were sociable enough at the table, but only just. They put up with me, but didn't embrace me as a team-mate. They basically gave me nothing.

It was because of this division that I first got to know Matthew Hoggard properly. He was another player on the outside of the clique, another in England's equivalent of the Shit Pit, and it was the start of a relationship that would get stronger as the years passed. Hoggy has always been a cricketer with a massive heart and a lovely guy 99 per cent of the time. Back then, though, he spent the remaining one per cent being a serious pain in the arse.

He had a repertoire of annoying habits which didn't endear him to the po-faced senior clique (or anyone else for that matter), ranging from sticking a finger in your ear when you weren't looking, to a crafty nip, to trying to wrestle you without warning. Nobody was spared, from the established players to the hopefuls. After so long on tour, living with the same blokes morning, noon and night, a man's tolerance can wear thin. It was a matter of time before Hoggy provoked somebody. That somebody was me.

One morning, on a long coach trip, I was nursing a sore neck from keeping wicket in practice, and Hoggy was up to his usual tricks, nudging and annoying people for no obvious reason. My tolerance threshold was particularly low that day, and as he walked past my seat after one of his latest wind-ups I turned around and gave him a meaty left hook, catching him flush on the arm. He reeled back a little, the look in his eye suggested that he knew I wasn't in the mood for a play fight, and my unplanned piece of corporal punishment on Hoggy became the talk of the tour for a few days . . .

'Did you see what Nico did?'

'Yeah, gave Hoggy a proper whack.'

'Fair play to him.'

Everyone – and the clique in particular – seemed to appreciate what I had done. Acceptance at last!

A less surprising predicament than finding the England squad operating on the 'know your place' principle was my place in the wicketkeeping hierarchy on tour. When it came to the more serious business of chasing a Test place, my chances of dislodging Alec Stewart felt a shade less than zero. Alec was, to his credit, one of the few members of the senior set who made time for me. I developed an immense respect for the way he went about his work: training hard, being professional in everything he did, but always retaining his sense of humour. He never forgot about the wicketkeepers' union and I did my best to support him. But he was, by some distance, the man in possession, and that picture was unlikely to change.

Then, out of nowhere, the picture began to change. As I walked off the pitch at the end of the first day against the Patron's XI, I found myself under siege from camera crews. Very quickly someone shoved a microphone under my nose and the questions began, each one a different version of the last.

'What is your response to the allegations?'

'How do you reply to what has been said about you?'

'Do you have any reaction to the news?'

What news? What allegations? I had no idea.

'Mister Stewart, Mister Stewart, how do you respond.'

It was an easy mistake to make, really: how were they to know what one of England's most capped cricketers looked like?

'Sorry fellas, you've got the wrong man,' I explained. 'I'm Paul Nixon.'

There was confusion all round, and a rapid end to my impromptu press conference. The camera crews scurried away, and I walked off the field chuckling to myself and shaking my head.

But what were the 'allegations'?

I found out when I got back to the dressing room. That day, 1 November, was the day Alec's name was linked in reports to an Indian match-rigging enquiry. It was alleged that he had been paid £5,000 for information on pitches, weather conditions and team morale back in 1993. The story dominated the cricket agenda for weeks and we talked about it non-stop in the dressing room and hotel, mainly to dismiss the idea that Alec, of all people, had been drawn into the shady world of match-fixing. This was the Gaffer, after all; Mr Integrity. It was almost laughable.

His hotel room was next door to mine, and I would often pop into his domain for a chat. One time after the storm erupted, I walked in as usual to find Alec and Darren Gough delving into a big cricket coffin full of English food, which had been sent over by Colin Graves, the Yorkshire chairman and founder of the Costcutter supermarkets. As Alec looked up and hurled a Pot Noodle in my direction, followed by a tin of baked beans, I instantly noticed a change in his appearance. He seemed to have lost weight and his face was gaunter than I remembered. From then on, he tended only to emerge from his room to board the team bus in the morning, and whenever he was asked about the allegations, he just shook his head. 'There's a lot of crap going on which I don't need, but we'll deal with it,' he said. And that was it.

Even with the Cronje case in the air, it seemed too far-fetched to assume that Alec had been drawn in. He had had an impeccable cricket upbringing, was the world's most driven man, was filled with pride whenever he pulled on his England kit, and always played the game the right way. If anyone was whiter than white, surely it was Alec Stewart?

As it turned out, there wasn't a scrap of proof that he had done anything wrong. At the time, though, I had to be conscious of the fact that the furore might work in my favour. There was always the possibility that Alec might need some time off, to take himself out of the firing line. I had to be ready for the door being flung open at any moment. I made a concerted effort to step up my wicketkeeping practice, and tried harder to get a net, just in case.

But the man was not for moving. Alec got his head down and played through the storm, and the tour continued as it was always supposed to: with the Gaffer firmly in position, and me back in the ranks.

In my second and final tour appearance, against a Pakistan Cricket Board XI in Lahore, Nasser Hussain declared our innings when I was one boundary away from my first fifty in England whites. There was no warning, no 'hurry up and get there, Nixon.' We were just whipped off, with me stuck on 47.

At the end of that game I couldn't help thinking that the timing of Nasser's declaration had been just another reminder of who was in charge, and who was making up the numbers. Whether deliberate or not, it rankled. But I don't want to give the impression that I spent all my time in Pakistan under a cloud, because that was far from the case. I was being paid good money to be on a cricket tour with England, after all, so it was hardly the time to get the violins out. There was plenty of satisfaction to be gained from working your nuts off and being an upbeat tourist. There was much to enjoy.

During that series, for instance, I saw Fletcher and Hussain start the long process of driving a winning mentality into a disjointed and unsuccessful team, with Duncan the master technician and Nasser the hard-nosed disciplinarian, who absolutely ripped into Thorpe on one occasion in the dressing room. 'You can fuck off back home if you want to keep giving it the big one,' the skipper bellowed at his close friend.

I don't recall what Thorpe had done, but Nasser's tirade must have had the desired effect, judging by their partnership which won the deciding Third Test in Karachi. As I ferried pairs of gloves out to Thorpe in the middle, as England got closer and closer to the victory target in failing light, Yousuf Youhana (now Mohammad Yousuf) came over for a word.

'What you think, Nixy?'

'Mate, we'll win this with an over to spare.'

My comment was made half in jest – I was just trying to imagine the perfect outcome, and wind Yousuf up in the process – but how prophetic it proved! Pakistan tried all the delaying tactics in the book, but Steve Bucknor, the umpire, infuriated them by insisting that play should go on, even as darkness descended. And I mean darkness – it was the darkest I have ever known at a game of cricket, darker even than the Edenhall Medals I contested as a boy in the Cumbrian gloom.

I sat on the boundary edge as Thorpe swept and cut his way to the victory target, fending off Waqar Younis' 90mph in-swingers, and finally inside-edging Saqlain Mushtaq straight past Inzamam-ul-Haq's feet for the decisive runs. It was so dark that Inzy barely saw it.

It was a wonderful moment, and as I later got stuck into the celebrations, dancing around in the dressing room like a three-year-old, I had a glimpse of the physical and emotional relief that came when a marathon Test series was won. I hugged Alec and saw that everyone else was wide-eyed with delight. It felt like a massive release.

That night, we drank beers in Fletcher's hotel room, and then met up in our team room. Duncan and Nasser stood up and said a few words about the massive effort that had gone into beating Pakistan in their own back yard. Both men made a point of thanking the lads who hadn't played in the Tests. 'You have been there for us in practice and helped keep our spirits up,' Nasser said. 'We really appreciate the part you have played.'

That was nice to hear. Then another voice chipped in.

'That's right, boys, you've got the David May Award.'

A few titters quickly died away.

It was Atherton.

I could have knocked him out.

Let me explain. David May was a Manchester United footballer who became notorious for his antics after the Red Devils won the Champions

League final in 1999. Following their victory against Bayern Munich at Barcelona's Nou Camp Stadium, May – an unused substitute and bit-part player – deliberately put himself at the forefront of the team photos. He was duly mocked and pilloried for grabbing an excessive share of the limelight.

This is how Atherton chose to describe those of us who hadn't played a Test in Pakistan. The implication was that we were hitching a ride on the success of the senior players. Players like him, in other words.

It was as patronising as hell. When he came out with that smarmy line I felt a strong urge to walk across the room and swing for him. We were professional cricketers, passionate about being where we were, trying to contribute as best we could. We were certainly not gatecrashers, trying to steal the glory. If Athers had got an injury on that tour, he might have ended up carrying drinks and spare kit for one of us instead. He could quite easily have been 'David May' himself.

To me, that comment summed up the attitude that prevailed in that England squad. It probably explained why the team had not been as successful as they should have been, until Hussain and Fletcher came in with their new broom. They had serious talent as individuals, but if you are not a united group you will never thrive, especially when you are on a long tour.

Athers was a good player and a very bright bloke with a lot going on in his life. But life isn't just about being clever and successful, it's about people and relationships, about seeing people as equals, not looking down your nose at your fellow man and dismissing a group of blokes which included England's future seventh-highest Test wicket-taker of all time (Hoggard), and others who were desperate to achieve good things.

I often thought back to that needless little jibe when watching the modern England of Andy Flower and Andrew Strauss sweep the board. They are a proper unit, the players clearly work in harmony and relish each other's company, and their results say it all. Back then, there was too much division, suspicion and negativity. Such a shame.

Before we left Pakistan to embark on the Sri Lanka leg, Duncan Fletcher was observing me in the nets, his eyes hidden behind his trademark shades, his face expressionless. After I had completed my batting, he walked over to me.

'Nico, I've been watching you, and I am going to tell you something,' he said.

What had he spotted? What flaw in my technique had he sniffed out? What door was the great coach about to unlock?

I stood and awaited the precious nugget of Fletcher wisdom.

'I can't tell you now, but I will tell you later, at the end of the tour. I promise.'

twelve

LIMBO

Lessons from Sri Lanka, March 2001:

1. You have never known heat until you have been to Sri Lanka
I mean proper, heavy heat. Humid heat. Heat that drenches your shirt with sweat. Heat that makes you look like you've been for a swim in the ocean, fully clothed.

When we arrived in Colombo, we did an early fitness session and then a 'bleep test' on a tennis court. It was so ridiculously hot that it actually burned my feet through the soles of my trainers. Not fun.

2. Jet lag is unsuitable preparation for facing Sri Lankan spin bowlers
The first tour game was against a Sri Lanka Colts XI in Moratuwa, a city on the island's south-west coast. It would have been a perfect chance to impress, had I not felt like a zombie.

As Atherton and Trescothick walked out to open our innings, our dressing room resembled an emergency dormitory. There were knackered bodies everywhere, and Graham Thorpe, due in at number four, was actually asleep. When I eventually made it out into the middle I was still in a daze, with no idea whether my foe was a leg-spinner or an off-spinner. He required two balls to claim the easiest wicket of his life.

3. Graeme Hick was on his last legs
As England's fifth wicket went down in the First Test at Galle, Hick rose from his seat and picked up his bat.

'Well,' he said. 'The journalists will be sharpening their pencils now.'

I couldn't believe that! Surely the last thing that should be on your mind as you walk out to bat for England is what the hacks are thinking?

Any time I threw to Hick in practice, it was a joy. His bat seemed wider than Sri Lanka when it came down. But he had been in and out of the team so many times by then that he was mentally gone. Atherton declaring with him on 98 not out in Sydney, back in 1995, cannot have helped.

4. Alec Stewart is made of granite

On the morning of the Second Test at Kandy, the Gaffer stubbed his toe on a wooden bench in the dressing room. There were fears he had broken it. His toe, that is.

The first I knew of this was when Duncan Fletcher came running over.

I had been enjoying a daft net with Hoggy, batting right-handed while he bowled spin, to relieve the tedium of having thrown to Atherton and Thorpe for the previous twenty minutes. In the blink of an eye, I was being briefed about my possible England Test debut. 'Get your mind on it,' Fletch said. 'You might be keeping wicket here.'

I didn't play, of course. Stewie got his painkilling injection in time, but knowing the Gaffer he would probably have played for England with his leg hanging off. The man was a machine.

5. Andrew Caddick can fix anything

Thorpe brought back a set of miniature speakers from a trip to the market one afternoon, only for them to break within the first two minutes of use. Enter Caddick. On a coach journey back from Galle, the big seamer offered to help. Thorpe handed over the dud speakers and Caddick duly disappeared into his own little world. After a lengthy period of fiddling and poking, he got the goods to work again. Thorpey couldn't believe it.

Moral of the story: give Andrew Caddick a matchbox and a Swiss Army knife and he will probably build you a Ferrari.

6. Any tour needs girls

Ignore anyone who says that wives and girlfriends have no part to play on a long cricket tour. By the time the womenfolk arrived in Sri Lanka, it's fair to say the players were ready for them. I won't spell out why. We were like coiled springs.

When Jen and the other girls came over, I was given a bit of time off to show them around. We went on a glass-bottomed boat cruise, looked around an elephant sanctuary and a turtle farm, and had a great laugh in the hotel bar as I got them all nicely lashed in time to greet the boys after a hard day's practice.

Their presence lifted the mood enormously. When they eventually left, and it was just the boys again, there was a noticeable slump around the camp.

7. International umpiring can be erratic

In the First Test, our lads were nailed with some terrible decisions as Sri Lanka won by an innings. In the Second Test at Colombo, the roles were reversed.

The umpiring in that game was the most bizarre I have seen. Nasser had about five lives; nicking off and being plumb lbw, but somehow not being given out. He proceeded to a hundred that helped level the series which England would go on to win.

In the same game, there was the infamous moment when Sanath Jayasuriya hit a wide ball from Caddick into the ground, before it flew off to third slip where Thorpe clung on superbly. To widespread amazement, Jayasuriya was given out by umpire BC Cooray.

As he walked off, the Sri Lankan batsman threw his helmet in fury. Cooray, meanwhile, was given police protection as he left the arena at the end of the session. It was a total joke. Later, he received death threats, which wasn't so funny.

8. Darren Gough is brilliant

I was the last one to do the bleep test on that stupidly hot concrete tennis court in Colombo. As the rest of the squad wiped their brows and sheltered from the 100 degree heat, I was hammering through my sprints and feeling every stride. To my surprise, Goughie then pulled his trainers back on and joined me, cajoling me along to a decent score, even though he must have been knackered and ready to step under a shower.

Goughie was a top man on tour. On the coach, he was always the one keeping spirits up with his funny stories. But he was deadly serious about his game, and inside his coffin he kept a list of the top England wicket-takers' stats. When his list was spotted, he took a bit of stick, but I admired him for it. It showed how driven he was.

9. Running still helped

When you are practicing from one day to the next, in the knowledge that you are extremely unlikely to be playing, you start to feel a bit remote. After a while you have to fight the urge to mope around. My way of fighting the urge was to run.

In Sri Lanka I got on very well with Tim Abraham, the Sky TV reporter. Tim was a fitness freak who would run for miles every night and then go for an hour's swim. When he told me about one route he had taken – through town and up the side of the mountain on the way back to the hotel in Kandy – I made a mental note. Then, after our next boiling hot net session, I loaded my gear into one of the minibuses and then started running.

I could see the lads watching me and thinking, 'What the fuck is he doing?' It was tough going, but the freedom of running was priceless to me. As usual, it helped clear the clutter. It was also my way of saying: 'I'm pushing here, boys. Look how much I want it. If I'm tough enough to run up that hill, in this heat, I'm tough enough to play.'

They probably just thought I was nuts.

10. The final step is the hardest

When I boarded the plane for home, I couldn't honestly say I felt much closer to a Test cap. It was gratifying to know that I was back in my country's thoughts, that I had been part of a successful tour and that I now understood the England environment. But the dream still felt distant. After weeks of hotel rooms, nets and running, I was ready to get some English air back in my lungs. And I was absolutely desperate to play some cricket.

Changes were afoot when I returned to Kent for the start of the 2001 season. John Wright had left to work with India and had been replaced by the Australian, John Inverarity. My living arrangements had also altered. That summer we decided to buy a house but, as the deal took forever to go through, I began the season as a lodger with Mark Ealham, the former England all-rounder, and his wife Kirsty.

I'm not sure whether Ealy had deliberately chosen to live in a place – Elham – that bore almost exactly the same name as him, but what I do know is that as people we were like chalk and cheese.

Ealy was a food lover and took his devotion seriously, spending hours strolling around the supermarket, scrutinising every shelf and methodically filling his trolley with pork pies, cheeses, sauces and anything else he could get his hands on. I was a creature of simpler habits, who believed food shopping required little more than five minutes of grabbing the meat, fruit and vegetables you needed and then getting the hell out of there.

My time living *chez* Ealham coincided with the period when I was at my most obsessive when it came to refuelling. I was now in my thirties and aware that I had to start working a little harder in order to keep myself in top condition. This meant signing up to a new religion. Protein was my answer to everything and dominated my feeding habits. I had made a Eureka discovery of 'meal replacement' protein tablets and powders in silver packets which, when dissolved into water, produced a gloopy substance which had the consistency of white emulsion. The sight of this would repulse Ealy but I couldn't get enough of the stuff.

Our dietary differences led to some interesting moments at the breakfast table. I was an eight-Weetabix-a-morning man, and when Ealy produced the goods from the back of a cupboard, I merrily tipped a load into my bowl and got down to it, only to gag at the taste of soggy cardboard.

'What the fuck's this?' I shouted, eyeing my bowl.

'What do you mean?' he replied. 'It's Weetabix, isn't it?'

I grabbed the box and found the sell-by date: NOV 1994.

I had been feasting on six-and-a-half-year-old Weetabix, which had been steadily fossilising with every morning Ealy had weighed up his options and then delved into his fridge for a packet of bacon and some sausages.

We were the classic odd couple, Ealy and me. I was Mr Positive all the time and he was a much more laid-back type, who lived for his days off. One of his more unusual theories was that if we passed a farmer's field on the way to the ground, and the cows in the field were lying down, it was going to rain. And to Ealy, rain was the stuff of dreams. I can hear him now, striding into the dressing room, clapping his hands and declaring: 'The cows are lying down in Elham, boys! It's gonna be a great day for the Spitfires! We'll have a big lunch and they'll call the game off before tea!'

I, on the other hand, hated days off and would have happily played in a swamp.

Ealy and Kirsty looked after me no end, if I'm honest, and sometimes our differences actually helped. Ealy despised the gym but some of my healthier ways did rub off on him (we found some common ground with a weekly game of squash, once playing for so long that it gave me tennis elbow), and equally, his more relaxed approach to life occasionally helped calm me down.

Within the club, John Inverarity's arrival brought a further change of philosophy. He was a quieter operator than Wright, more professor than tough-guy motivator. Nothing escaped his eye, or his memory. 'Nico – in the sixty-sixth over you slightly fumbled the third ball,' he once said, at the end of a session. 'Were you mentally in the zone at that point? Were you in the room?' He made extensive notes and his technical knowledge was unparalleled.

I found this new approach stimulating and I soon settled into a better summer with the bat and the gloves. After the England tour, it felt like a release to be playing again – and in a team that was confident and full of fun.

I don't think I have ever known a greater collection of jokers than at Kent. One incident still brings a smile. On a day off, a group of us piled down to the Getty Estate, with a warning from captain Fleming to make sure Symo didn't get injured or come to any mischief. A few hours later, the skipper took a grave phone call and learned that his warning had not been heeded.

'You won't believe what's happened.'

'What?'

'Symo and Nico?'

'Why, what's happened?'

'Well, Symo went off somewhere fishing and took Nico with him. Seems like he was teaching him how to fly-fish. Problem is, Nico's accidentally cast the hook right into Symo's eye.'

'Oh, Jesus.'

'Yeah, he's in a bad way. He's had to go off for surgery.'

Fleming slammed the phone down, proceeded to dial the number of every eye surgeon from Harley Street downwards and had worked himself into a real lather by the time the wind-up was explained to him.

Dave Fulton was another who bought into the upbeat spirit, but in a more serious way – and the results were profound. Kent had been close to releasing Fults at the end of the previous summer, but Ealy and me had spoken up for him when the decision was being discussed. Eventually he was given another chance, John Inverarity introduced him to some new drills, he sorted a few things out in his personal life and in no time he was on fire, churning out 1,892 First Class runs as we came in third to Yorkshire in the new two-tier Championship.

We made up for that near miss by winning the 45-over National League. The climax came at Edgbaston, where Warwickshire fell to pieces in the face of Symo's heavy seamers. The hosts cracked under pressure and played a bunch of stupid shots; our Aussie talisman ended with 5-18; and we celebrated our title by hitting Birmingham hard.

The chosen venue was a Walkabout bar and we all got well and truly smashed, nobody more so than McCague, who was in the thick of the party despite not having figured in much cricket that summer. At one stage the big man staggered back from the bar with a tray of forty sambucas in one hand and the trophy in another. In what seemed like slow-motion, he then proceeded to fall flat on his arse, snapping a big metal ring off the silverware in the process, but heroically saving the sambucas. For this selfless act he was rewarded, a few hours later, by Fleming, Matt Walker and me taking a razor to his pubes and his eyebrows (I'm still waiting for the thank-you card).

All this foolishness masked a more important truth: Kent was feeling like home.

The following summer, Symo departed and was replaced, late in the season, by his fellow countryman, Steve Waugh. The day after the legend landed, I found myself in the middle with him, trying to chase down a target of 169 against Leicestershire in a National League game at Canterbury.

When I walked out to the wicket, we were, to use the technical term, in the shit. But Steve was completely unflustered from ball one, even as

I struggled to get going at the other end. I was picking out fielder after fielder and failing to get the scoreboard ticking. It was winding me up and between overs, I tried to reassure Steve that I was able to contribute to the chase. 'Keep playing, I'm coming with you,' I insisted. Then, a word of advice: 'Don't go too high-risk just yet.'

I'm not sure whether he was listening, because in the very next over he went down on one knee and subjected Darren Stevens, the Leicestershire bowler, to the biggest slog-sweep of all-time. The connection made a noise like nothing I had ever heard and the ball sailed over the lime tree and into the middle of next month. It was a phenomenal sight.

'Right, mate,' said Steve, catching my eye. 'We're away.'

And we were. That example of his signature shot was our trigger, and batting got steadily easier. In front of a big, expectant crowd, my confidence grew (I don't think Steve's ever faded) and our partnership flourished. By the time we had put on 72 in the space of twelve overs we had finished the job nicely.

Knocking off the runs with Steve Waugh – how did that feel? Bloody awesome.

It might sound unlikely, but the nerves were shared equally when Steve joined us that summer. Despite his status as one of the most hard-nosed winners in international cricket, he was still anxious about coming to a new club and being expected to produce the goods. On the team's part, there was an obvious nervousness; the first time he walked into our normally boisterous dressing room, a sudden silence fell. The lads were in awe of him, and it took a while for him to be regarded as just another team-mate rather than the great Steve Waugh.

I was in the lucky position of being able to get to know him better than most. Steve was housed in a rented apartment in Canterbury's city centre, near the railway station. By this point I had moved with Jen to a place in a little village just around the corner, and since most of the other players lived further afield, I started inviting Steve for meals and nights out, to help him settle in. We talked about cricket and life until the sun came up and quickly developed a great friendship. He spoke about his charity work in India, and about how much he missed his family, something that was obvious whenever he got his kids' schoolwork e-mailed to him and he responded with a phone call home to praise them.

It was impossible for someone like Steve Waugh to walk around a cricket city like Canterbury without being spotted, but he handled the attention effortlessly. One night we found ourselves in a rough-looking bar where everyone looked up from their pints and started eyeing up the Aussie legend. A less certain customer might have thought better of the venue but within minutes he had them eating out of his hand, buying them drinks and having a laugh.

I began to look upon him as a bloke rather than a sporting icon, and I think he appreciated that. At the club, he needed to have the piss taken out of him, rather than spend all his time being revered. Once, when he took a catch at gully, he broke a nail and I instantly piled into him, followed by the rest of the lads, branding him an Aussie soft-cock. We gave him grief about his surprisingly girly choice of drink (Southern Comfort and lemonade) and later laughed about the chirp he had given me back in 1989 – 'Fuck me, mate, what time does the cricket start?' – but this was only a small example of the Aussie mentality which nobody represented better than Steve.

Once, when commenting on my approach to wicketkeeping, he paid me the greatest compliment a bloke from New South Wales could possibly give: 'He's like a mosquito buzzing around in the night that needs to be swatted but always escapes . . . Nico should have been born an Australian.' It wasn't a comparison every Englishman would enjoy but I was humbled. From the time I played club cricket Down Under I have always found much to admire in Australians. They play tough, they are scrappers and they are always up for a battle, but they never fail to have a beer with you at the end of the day. The ethic seems to be: you give shit and you take it, and you play to win at all levels from club cricket upwards, but you never lose sight of the fact you are playing a game.

Nobody won more than Steve Waugh, but he never let his head drift into the clouds. We have remained mates ever since that summer of 2002, probably because I recognised something in him that I have always aspired to myself; a belief that life is about being a good bloke first, and a cricketer second.

One other thing I admired about Steve? His walk.

It was the same walk that Australia's Test opponents had seen for years – that brisk stride from the boundary rope to the middle – and it never failed to impress me. It was the walk of a man who meant business; a batsman who was keyed up and ready for battle, not someone who was uncertain about the challenge.

Sometimes I found myself watching him walk out to bat for Kent and imagining myself in the shoes of the other team. How must that have felt, seeing Steve Waugh pace out to the crease so purposefully after the fall of a wicket? That feeling, that knowledge, that the game was not about to get easier, but a hundred times harder?

I never asked him how he learned to do such a simple thing in a way that somehow set him apart. Maybe I should have done, because I always thought it said something important about the man. 'A walk?' you might be thinking. 'How bloody trivial!'

Not me. I believed, and still believe, that you can tell a lot about a cricketer from the way he walks.

The night before the last game of the season at Headingley, Dave Fulton – standing in as captain for Matthew Fleming – walked up to me and, without warning, kicked me flush in the bollocks. Not literally, I should say, but it hurt just as much.

'Nico, you're not going to like this,' he said. 'The club is going to release you.'

'Release me? What do you mean?'

'Look, mate, I don't agree with it. But as a friend and a bloke, I've got to tell you. It's up to you whether you want to play in this game or not.'

I was frozen to the spot. I couldn't believe it. I thought I was going to end my career at Kent. And why, now you mention it, was this coming from Fulton, and not the club captain?

Matthew Fleming had made me feel welcome at Kent from day one. He embraced me and Jen as he embraced everyone at the club, and invited us for meals at his parents' huge manor house in Tunbridge Wells – a quintessential English home, with an orangery the size of Kew Gardens, a doll's house big enough to live in and one of those olde-world portraits whose eyes follow you around the room and which once led a frightened Rob Key to sleep with the lights on. We had great laughs and great times, so it was disappointing that Fleming, a former Army officer and leader of men, didn't then have the balls to tell me that Kent were letting me go.

It fell to Fults to explain the rationale behind the decision, which was this: in Geraint Jones, Kent had a talented young wicketkeeper-batsman who was scoring double hundreds for the seconds. This was true enough – Geraint was a genuine talent and someone I'd spent a lot of time mentoring. He was a great lad, and promoting him in my place would save the club a lot of money; unless, that is, I took a ridiculous pay cut – too ridiculous even to consider. So that was that. There was nothing I could do.

But did I want to play against Yorkshire? You bet I did. I wanted to score a hundred and remind Kent that they were letting a good man go. But my mind, not for the first time, wasn't where it should have been, and after 21 gruelling balls I was run out for five when Ryan Sidebottom sidefooted the ball against my stumps. I walked back to the pavilion feeling even more pissed off and confused, and it fell to Waugh to light up what was now going to be my last game in Kent whites – playing Steve Kirby, a bowler I had seen battle back from a back injury at Leicestershire and someone I really admired, with a stick of rhubarb ('Mate, you can try moving the stumps a bit closer if you like,' Waugh told the famously fiery Kirby. 'Because you are shit').

His magnificent 146 would have been more fun to watch had I not been staring into such an uncertain future.

Less than two years earlier, I had been Alec Stewart's understudy, next in line for my country. I had given up the prospect of a benefit at Leicestershire in order to move to Canterbury and had not missed a match for Kent in three years. My form had been OK, in the main – not sensational, but not bad by any means – and I had helped the club win a trophy. Now I was being cast adrift!

I was absolutely gutted and the news hit me hard. I rang Dad and poured my heart out. To make things worse, I discovered that all the other counties seemed to have their wicketkeeping positions sewn up for the 2003 season. Where was I going to go? Where was I going to make a living?

My options seemed stark. If there wasn't a first-team space anywhere, I would have to give up First Class cricket and join a club on a young player's wage, and try to unseat their first-choice wicketkeeper. Back to the beginning, basically. Otherwise, it was back into the outside world. But what else did I know? I spent the next few weeks stalking around with a cloud over my head. I couldn't believe it had come to this.

Eventually, after a few weeks in limbo, my agent struck gold. He discovered that Leicestershire, of all clubs, were releasing Neil Burns and there was an opening at my old haunt. There was a new regime at Grace Road, Jimmy Whitaker was now the general manager, and the club was keen to have me on board.

Talk about timing. There was no point in staying bitter about how it had ended there three years earlier. In any case, it was my only offer, so I gratefully accepted.

Not that going 'home' was as smooth as it should have been. No sooner was I back at Grace Road, I was putting on a suit and heading to the Employment Tribunal Office at New Walk in Leicester to defend my reputation. Burns was, along with the off-spinner Carl Crowe, suing the club for unfair dismissal, claiming the club had gone back on a promise of a new contract. My day in court was to establish whether I had been approached by Leicestershire before they had given Burns his cards – had I been sneaked in by the back door in other words?

I had not, whatever the other rights and wrongs of the matter, and however oddly Burns had behaved before Steve Waugh's debut at Canterbury, when I had walked into the Leicestershire dressing room to see some old friends, passed Burns' kit and picked up his gloves.

I was just taking an interested look at his kit – as wicketkeepers do – but Neil reacted strangely when he spotted me:

'Er . . . Can you put those down please?'

I'm not sure why he was having none of the wicketkeepers' union that day – he was a talented player, but a bit different as a bloke – but the most important thing here was that I had emphatically not set out to nab his place. I said as much in the tribunal, explaining when I was approached, what had happened, who had spoken to me and what meetings had taken place. I knew I had nothing to hide, so I was quite relaxed when I gave my evidence. Jimmy, among others, wasn't so relaxed. It was a rotten time for the club. The case had wide-ranging implications for cricket and for Leicestershire in particular. The players won their case, forcing the club to introduce a performance review system which meant that any player about to be released now had to be given due notice.

Personally, though, it was a relief to be back in familiar surroundings with my future safe. Did I play like the returning hero in my first season back? Not exactly – my knees were feeling the strain and crying out for an operation. I wasn't at my best.

Had I rejoined the title-winning Leicestershire of old? Not really – it was a squad in flux and bound for relegation in both the Championship and the one-day National League.

But was I happy with how it had turned out for me? I can't say I wasn't, when I considered how it had ended with Kent. And had my second Championship debut for Leicestershire – by coincidence, at Canterbury, the following April – not been one of the most satisfying occasions of my career?

Was it not hugely gratifying to go back to the St Lawrence Ground, receive a lovely, warm ovation and score 113 unbeaten runs, on the wicket I knew like an old friend, against the county who had let me go? Yes, it was. And did it matter that Jones then stole a little of my thunder with a hundred of his own, after receiving the life of all lives on 99 when he was dropped at fine leg?

No, it didn't, not really – I was privately pleased for Geraint. Anyway, I had plenty more to look forward to myself. I just didn't realise how much.

thirteen

BATTERY

September 2003.

I am sitting in a darkened room, without my shoes, and with electrodes fastened to my head and my underarms. There is a strip of red light on the wall directly in front of me and I am thinking of where I have seen this sort of light before. Then it hits me! Knight Rider, *the 1980s TV series, starring David Hasselhoff as Michael Knight. It is exactly like the red lamp that flashed at the front of his KITT car! How weird is that?*

My task is to watch a row of small dots as they light up along the red strip and start moving from side to side, at a gentle pace.

Left.
Right.
Left.
Right.

Easy enough.
After a few seconds, the dots start moving faster.

Left, right.
Left, right.
Left, right.

Then they get even quicker.

Left, right, left, right, left, right, left, right.

Within a couple of minutes, my eyes are shooting backwards and forwards so quickly it feels like I'm watching a tennis rally in fast-forward . . .

Leftrightleftrightleftrightleftrightleftrightleftright.

Beyond the room I can hear the faint bleeps of computers and other machines. As I say, very odd. And you should have seen the things they had me doing earlier! What was the purpose, for example, of strapping me into a harness, instructing me to balance on a wobble board (the kind used by NASA to train astronauts, they said) and challenging me to focus on a little moving picture as it darted around on the wall? Where were they going with all the spinning around, and the hopping, and the reciting of times tables?

Search me. I'm sure I'll find out soon.

Now the dots are racing:

Leftrightleftrightleftrightleftrightleftrightleftrightlefrighlefrighlefr . . .

I strain hard to keep up, but I can't. Too fast. And I'm absolutely knackered! Who knew that following a load of tiny lights was so exhausting?

Eventually the lights go off and the door opens.

Jen was very happy to have settled back in Leicester, and so was I. We hoped that it marked an end to the upheaval for the foreseeable. But, as content as we felt to be back, there were times when I continued to drive my poor wife round the bend.

The following scenario is a routine example of what I'm talking about:

Jen is cooking dinner and asks if I can nip out to the shop and buy a pint of milk. 'No problem,' I say, grabbing my wallet from the table and walking briskly down the road.

When I get to the shop, I make for the refrigerator, where my eye is immediately caught by a can of Coca-Cola. *I am thirsty. I could really go for a Coke.* Into the basket it goes.

I then wander vacantly down the aisle. I see a colourful box of Cadbury's Creme Eggs on the shelf. *I love Creme Eggs!* I stop and throw a couple in.

Then my gaze falls on the newspapers. There aren't many left, so I grab one, and by the time I get to the counter, my basket is full. I pay, say a cheery farewell, and leave the shop. I walk back, drinking the Coke. When I get home I open the door and enter the kitchen, where I empty the plastic carrier bags and display my haul to my wife, who is arranging various items of food.

'That's lovely,' says Jen, scrutinising the items. 'But where's the milk?'

The milk!

The milk, of course, is still in the shop. The sole reason for my little outing has completely upped sticks and vanished from my mind. So I roll my eyes, reach for my wallet again and curse myself as I fling open the door and repeat the trip.

When things like this happened, Jen thought I was just being forgetful. Bills would go unpaid, letters would be left unsent, and other little jobs she asked me to do would travel from one ear through to the other without touching the sides. The assumption was that I was a bit of a scatterbrain, and I wasn't in much of a position to argue. I mainly had to hold my hands up and resolve to remember the next household task I was assigned.

By 2003, Jen had left British Airways and was working as a PA for a property company in Leicester. During the summer she became involved in organising a golf day, which required contact with various property owners and businessmen. At the golf day, she had a conversation with one of the businessmen, a man called Barry Fitzpatrick.

Barry described himself as a forgetful type, and explained that he had constantly been battling to get his handicap down, but without much success, and he put this down to his 'cluttered' mind. He explained how his head was always buzzing, how he would flit from one thing to the next, and then the next, and then the next, the result being a state of mental congestion and an inability to think and focus clearly.

Jen's ears instantly pricked up: 'That sounds just like my husband.'

Barry then spoke about a man who had helped him, a man called Wynford Dore, who apparently ran a pioneering dyslexia foundation and had worked with the rugby player Kenny Logan and the Olympic rowing legend Steve Redgrave, with startling results. It transpired that this Wynford Dore was now looking to expand his portfolio by studying a cricketer.

When Jen came home and passed this information on, I was all ears.

Since day one I have always been open-minded towards anything unusual if I thought it would give me an edge. The fitness and the protein and the Bikram Yoga you know about. I can't think of any innovation I haven't enjoyed testing out, other than one acupuncture session in my early years at Grace Road. Why didn't I enjoy it? Because a few team-mates very kindly sneaked in while I had been left on my own, flat out on the bench, and started meddling with the needles. They left me in a cold sweat and in the grip of panic. The memory still makes me shiver.

Those saboteurs weren't invited on the latest venture, however: to a big house in Kenilworth, Warwickshire, towards the end of the 2003 season. I walked through the door and was ushered to a waiting room, where a group of children were playing on the floor with small, coloured bricks. After a short while, a big bloke with dark hair and a Welsh accent greeted me with a handshake and showed me to a consulting room.

Wynford became animated as he explained his story. He spoke about his daughter, who had been diagnosed as severely dyslexic and had sunk into depression as a result, eventually trying to commit suicide. He explained that he had sold his successful paint company and ploughed his money into setting up a research institute, staffed by doctors and neurological scientists, whose aim was to disprove the theory that there was no known cure for dyslexia. He described the work he had done with all kinds of people – from children with learning disabilities to international sportsmen – and then he focused his attention on me.

'Tell me if this sounds like you,' he began.

'OK,' I replied.

'Sometimes you are forgetful. Sometimes you go into a shop and you don't buy what you went in for. Sometimes you feel dizzy and light-headed. Sometimes you feel in a rush to get your words out. Sometimes you stutter, because you want to get them out before they have gone. Does that sound familiar?'

He sat back in his chair. I looked at him agog. It was as if he had secretly been living inside my head for years.

'Thought so,' he smiled.

Then we left the room and the tests began. When the strange sequence of exercises was over, Wynford explained the results that had shown up on the computers, through the sensors.

'Basically,' he said, 'your eye-tracking is very good from far to close, but poor from side to side. It very much looks like you have a mild form of dyslexia.'

'So you can tell all that from these tests?'

'Absolutely. You see, it's all to do with the cerebellum?'

'The what?'

'The cerebellum – it's a little walnut-shaped thing at the bottom of the brain, near the top of the spine. That is your little nerve centre, your processor. Think of it as a car battery: if it's not stimulated, it coughs and splutters and barely works. But when it *is* stimulated, it's up and running. And so are you.'

I had to take his word on the last bit, but what he said about eye-tracking really made me think. What if he was right? What if this explained everything?

When I looked back, and applied this new theory to some of the strange difficulties I had encountered over the years, it seemed a perfect fit.

As a young footballer, for instance, I often played in central midfield, because I had energy to burn. But whenever I received the ball in the middle of the pitch and had to look for a pass, I rarely sent it wide to the wingers. I was seldom very good at spotting their runs. As a result, I would mainly aim the ball down the middle, towards the strikers, which wasn't always the right choice.

1. (Above) Langwathby Hall Farm, the playground of my youth. When I wasn't snagging turnips, sometimes I drove the tractor.
2. (Left) Mum and Dad.
3. (Below) The grip is familiar, but I'm not sure about the shoes.
4. (Below, right) Kitted out for Langwathby May Day.
   (© Harringtons of Penrith)

5. My first team, Edenhall. That's me on the right of the bottom row, next to Dad.

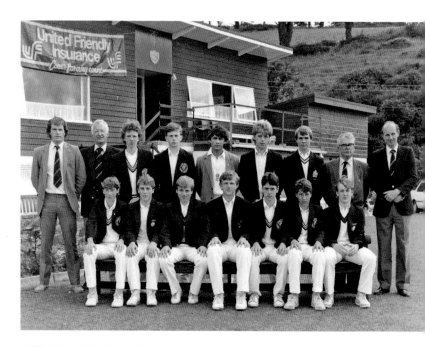

6. The England Under-15s line-up at Truro. I'm on the back row, third right, next to Chri Adams (fourth right). But it was Mark Ramprakash (back row, middle) who ruled the roost. (© R.E. Hughes, Truro)

7. Fresh-faced and yet to graduate from the Shit Pit in my first season at Leicestershire. (© Leicester Mercury)

8. Gordon Parsons congratulates me on my first hundred, after I had survived a barrage from the great Malcolm Marshall. (© Leicester Mercury)

9. When Winston Benjamin stared at you, it was rarely a good thing.
(© Leicester Mercury)

10. Hansie Cronje was an inspirational team-mate and fellow fitness nut before he fell into scandal and then tragedy.
(© Leicester Mercury)

11. A champagne moment, as Leicestershire clinch the 1996 County Championship. (© Leicester Mercury)

12. Jimmy Whitaker and Jack Birkenshaw transformed Leicestershire – and my mindset – in the mid-1990s. (© Leicester Mercury)

13. Adam Hollioake was a true competitor and sportsman, and we had more to discuss further down the line. (© Leicester Mercury)

14. The talented but flawed Chris Lewis earned a hero's reception after his innings against Northants in 1998 – the most insane game of cricket I have known. (© Leicester Mercury)

15. Lewis 'Brandy Time' Springett was one of Leicestershire's most devoted fans. When he died, he was cremated wearing one of my old shirts.
(© Leicester Mercury)

16. Jen and me tie the knot in Penrith, supported by (from left): Paul 'Macca' McKeown, Tim Holliday, John Holliday, David Young, Jimmy Whitaker, Dad and Mark Holliday.

17. Unlike some, Alec Stewart was a great team-mate on the England tours of Pakistan and Sri Lanka – but he wasn't giving his place up lightly. (© PA Photos)

18. My first game in England whites, against a Patron's XI in Pakistan. Graeme Hick, fielding at slip, was about as certain of his place as me. (© PA Photos)

19. Swapping some expertise in exchange for some green tea at a market in Pakistan. The England clique would probably have considered it a fair deal. (© PA Photos)

20. Andrew Symonds, whose head I'm obscuring here, was a fearsome customer, whether with bat, ball, gun or rod. Here he bowled Kent to glory in the National League at Edgbaston in 2001. (© Kent Messenger Group)

21. On Steve Waugh's Kent debut, everyone else faded into the background. (© PA Photos)

22. Darren Maddy has always been a great friend, and together we teamed up for Twenty20 Cup glory at Trent Bridge in 2006. (© Leicester Mercury)

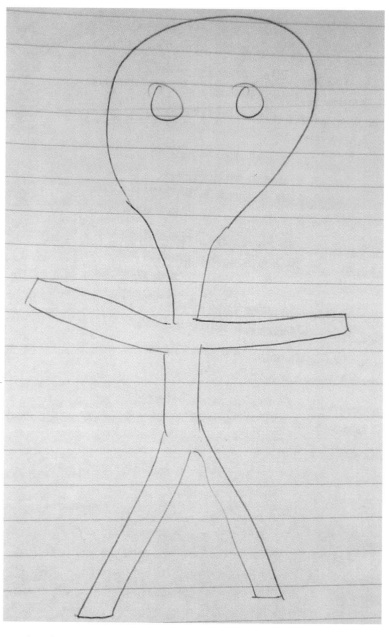

23. There he is – my most faithful companion. My little negative man.

24. Leicester is a great sporting city. Football fans at the Walkers Stadium were always keen to share our Twenty20 joy. (© Leicester Mercury)

25. Jeremy Snape (left) had a huge influence on my mental approach. It's a shame Mohammad Asif (right) wasn't able to think quite so straight a few years on. (© Leicester Mercury)

26. Mike 'Mr Cricket' Hussey was my first England victim Down Under – but that wasn't the end of our battles. (© PA Photos)

27. While some England players were weary of the media circus, I couldn't get enough of it. Posing for pictures in Sydney meant I wasn't cooped up on my own. (© PA Photos)

28. Kevin Pietersen in the nets, and in the middle, was an awesome sight. (© PA Photos)

9. Get in there! The northerners' union account for the old enemy at Melbourne. (© PA Photos)

30. The Barmy Army snaffled my sunglasses at the SCG – but they weren't getting my cap. (© PA Photos)

31. It took a while, but I won Freddie over as an England player – not that it helped us much in the turbulent 2007 World Cup. (© PA Photos)

32. The signature shot, this time in the thrilling run-chase against the West Indies in the World Cup. (© PA Photos)

33. This fresh-faced young man has become a half-decent international player.
(© Leicester Mercury)

34. Stardom, at last, on the hallowed turf at Carlisle United's Brunton Park – the half-time draw. (© Cumbrian Newspapers)

35. The good people of Birstall Cricket Club in Leicester produced this superb work of art to mark my benefit year. Note how the graffiti vandals have targeted W.G. and not yours truly.

36. Batting with Johnno during my benefit year event at Keswick. I wasn't about to deny him the strike. (© Cumbrian Newspapers)

37. Isabella Rose, age two days, is treated to one of her first Nixon protein drinks. (© Leicester Mercury)

38. Neil Davidson (left) and Tim Boon (right). Things weren't always so cheerful in their later years at Leicestershire. (© Leicester Mercury)

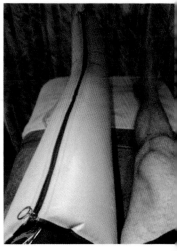

39. (Left) I was up for any challenge – like this Outward Bound course – but the challenge of captaining Leicestershire was more than I had bargained for. (© Leicester Mercury)

40. (Above) This compression sock was my best friend during my final, painful months.

41. After our incredible Twenty20 quarter-final victory against Kent in 2011, Grace Road went crackers – and so did I. (© Leicester Mercury)

42. Fairly soon, the contents of that pint glass were sliding down my throat.
(© Leicester Mercury)

43. The Catch, Part One – Wayne White bowls . . . (© Ed Melia)

44. The Catch, Part Two – Kieron Pollard swings . . . (© Ed Melia)

45. The Catch, Part Three – I'm already feeling the goosepimples . . . (© Sky Sports)

46. The Catch, Part Four – Titch Taylor leads the charge, and soon I'm engulfed.
(© Ed Melia)

47. Jacques Du Toit introduces me to a new kind of pain – champagne in the eyeballs. (© Ed Melia)

48. Hoggy used his Finals Day interview to take the doubters to task – and could have picked a worse target. (© Ed Melia)

49. In Cumbria, there is a fine tradition in the art of gurning. (© Leicester Mercury)

50. A more civilised celebration, with Dad. (© Ed Melia)

51. My last dismissal on English soil happened during a two-day hangover. (© Leicester Mercury)

52. I don't know where I'd be without Jen and Izzy. (© Leicester Mercury)

53. The future – coaching the cream of Cumbrian talent back in Penrith. (© Cumbrian Newspapers)

And reading – it always sapped my energy the moment I started moving my eyes across a page. I would start to read something and then give up, because my head would be hurting. This applied from the classroom to adulthood, and the frustration often built to the point where I would have to put down the book or the magazine, get the trainers on, head outside and run.

This eye-tracking problem had not, I reasoned, posed me many problems in wicketkeeping, because the ball was always coming directly towards me, rather than from the sides. But there were other things. At Leicestershire we used to do an exercise which required the players to spin around three times and then take a catch. Most of the lads managed this easily, but I always found it impossible. When I spun around it felt like the world was toppling off its axis and my head became so clouded that I would routinely put the catch down. Strange.

On other days I would get out of bed with what felt like a hangover, even though I had not touched a drop of alcohol the night before. Sometimes, in the field, I would feel so drained that I just wanted to be back at home, in bed. Not physically tired, but mentally shattered. As a result, it prevented me from focusing and led me to flit from one random distraction to the next, creating an environment where my little negative man could thrive. Hence my very inconsistent form, which had sometimes threatened to go into orbit but never quite managed it. And all because of an unstimulated walnut-shaped thing I didn't know existed!

Wynford then told me there were exercises that could help, and ended the day by sending me home with a workbook and an important word of advice: 'Wait until your cricket season is finished,' he said. 'Sometimes they can make you a little dizzy and affect your balance.'

Summer rolled into autumn and, as directed, I began trying the exercises. Some were similar to those I had done at Wynford's place in Kenilworth: the balancing on one leg, the reciting of times tables while hopping. Another involved lying in bed, focusing for ten seconds on one corner of the room, then slowly switching focus to the opposite corner, and repeating the process five times. I was to do this first thing in the morning and last thing at night.

I religiously followed Wynford's exercises for two weeks and had started to feel a change by the time I headed off to Spain with Jen. At the airport before our flight I bought a pair of books written by Lance Armstrong, the inspirational cyclist, and threw them in my bag.

Once I started reading them, I couldn't put them down. In the space of two days I had finished both.

This was a revelation: I had never completed a book before in my adult life.

I was an instant convert to these new theories and continued the exercises through the winter and beyond. When I did them, life somehow got easier. It was as if a slow-down button had been pressed; my thoughts started becoming calmer and clearer and I found myself – to Jen's delight – becoming less susceptible to distractions and forgetfulness.

The other major development of 2003 was Jeremy Snape's arrival at Leicestershire from Gloucestershire. Snapper, one of the wiliest all-rounders in the game, was also studying for a psychology degree, and wasted no time in using me as his guinea pig. Snapper had worked with Ted Garratt – a psychologist who had spent time with us at Grace Road in the 1990s – and was a very bright guy with his own ideas on the inner workings of the sportsman's brain. We hit it off straight away as I showed him around Leicester, and it was Snapper who first introduced me to the ideas of physical and mental routines which could keep the internal negativity at bay.

'What you need to do,' he said, when I explained some of the things that were going on in my head, 'is override that doubting voice of yours with some clear and positive words of your own.'

He described how I could regain control of my focus by chanting positive things to myself at the crease. So, instead of the little man intruding . . .

What's the bowler going to do here? Is he going to bounce you? Can you get one past mid-off? What about your other areas? Where are you going here?

. . . I should get in first with my own self-talk:

Watch the ball, watch the ball. Play straight, play straight. Watch the ball.

It was all about having something in the mind to keep the demons at the gate – to stop all the shit flying around when a bowler was running in.

When keeping wicket, Snapper suggested other routines.

For example: the second the bowler starts his run-up, I should 'switch on' and think only about the batsman nicking it to me. Instead of half-concentrating, instead of muttering something to first slip about something that happened last night, my whole world must now be about the nick. If it doesn't come, I quickly analyse my foot movements, check I had been in the right place for the catch, then wrap the entire experience up and hurl it into an imaginary black bin bag. Then my mind is free to wander off, and I can talk a minute's worth of rubbish to the bloke next to me, until the bowler turns and starts running in again. Then the switch should be flicked back on.

'You know me,' I said to Snapper, after absorbing all this. 'I'll try anything.'

When England introduced Twenty20 cricket to the world in 2003, my thoughts immediately shot back to a conversation I had a couple of years earlier with Richard Bevan, the chief executive of the Professional Cricketers' Association. At a function in London we were discussing the problem of dwindling crowds in county cricket. During our chat I shared an idea with him.

'If you want to make county cricket more accessible, we need to go back to the grass roots,' I argued. 'People need to play cricket like they did when they were younger.'

I explained how, as a kid, I had played 17-over games in the evening leagues in Cumbria. I argued that the only time cricket could be regularly accessible to people is after 6.00 p.m.

County cricket was, to me, crying out for something like that; something which club and league players could identify with. Something short and snappy that would get the families in the grounds.

'What we need,' I said to Bevan, 'is a bit of a thrash.'

It was a wide-ranging chat during which I threw a few more commercial concepts at Bevan. One was bat stickers. 'A cricket bat should be an advertising board,' I said, and a few weeks later I spoke to a lawyer about patenting the idea. The reply was that it couldn't be done, because there was no way it could be policed if it caught on globally.

I didn't bother trying to patent the idea for a reduced overs thrash in county cricket. Such is life . . .

A couple of months before starting life as a Leicestershire player for the second time, I had headed off to Australia with Jen for a holiday of pure excess. We teamed up with the Maddys and the Mullallys in Perth and properly let our hair down (relatively speaking). The highlights included an episode of late afternoon skinny dipping which horrified the picnicking families nearby (we were so drunk we thought it was midnight); Justine Maddy sliding comically down a bank and emerging smothered in duck poo (a substance which, I can report, does not give off a very pleasant aroma); an experiment on the effects of washing-up liquid in a jacuzzi (the result was so much overflowing foam it nearly flooded the place); the learning of a new life skill (puppetry of the penis was now a viable career move if cricket didn't work out); 24 empty wine bottles (ouch), and a bonce like a Belisha beacon, thanks to an aimless five-hour drive in Mullally's open-top sports car (so much for his local knowledge).

If that helped clear the head (again, relatively speaking), life back at Grace Road was not so carefree. The club had been through massive upheaval after the Burns-Crowe court case, the squad had gone through wholesale changes, and the long slog of a four-day campaign had proved too hard to sustain. In limited overs competitions things were not a great deal better.

As captain, Phil DeFreitas was the ultimate professional, but leading us at that time cannot have been an enviable job. Daffy had settled down from some of his wilder early days and tried to lead by example, but deep down I don't think he enjoyed captaincy. It didn't help that he more or less had to carry our attack, once Devon Malcolm had broken down injured and then announced his retirement, and nor did the presence of two richly talented overseas players help us avoid our fate, despite providing some great entertainment along the way.

One of them, Brad Hodge, was a run-machine when in form, a pocket Aussie dynamo who turned up at Trent Bridge in August, scanned the wicket and declared: 'If I don't get a double hundred on this today, I'm fucking going home' (he failed, spectacularly, scoring 302 not out – a club record in the Championship). The other, Virender Sehwag, was the most relaxed man I have ever known, all natural talent and calm belief. He wasn't around for long, but in his short spell he managed to score three hundreds, all of them before lunch.

During one virtuoso display against Middlesex at Southgate he gave Jamie Dalrymple the charge and hit the poor bloke onto the side of the church, which was just ridiculous. And after any rare failure at the crease he would never smash up the changing room, or shout and swear, or tear off for a run around the park, like me. He would simply pull off his pads, have a little sigh, and say: 'The sun always shines for the next innings.'

I only saw him get angry once – when Daffy wanted him to play against the touring India A team. The calmest man in cricket suddenly transformed into the most furious. 'Daffy, I don't fucking play against India A,' he shouted at the skipper. 'I tell you. No fucking way.'

It was all to do with the big hierarchy system over in India, in life and cricket. A herd of galloping horses could not have pulled Viru onto the field for that India A game. Sadly, that tarnished his relationship with Daffy. He eventually left, mid-season, citing a back problem, but the truth is he seemed to lose interest after his dispute with the captain.

This was a snapshot of the stresses which clung to the club as we floundered in the Championship. As a result, the freshly-minted Twenty20 Cup came as something of a release. Some counties regarded it as a bit of a hit and giggle competition, with dancing girls, paddling pools by the boundaries, and a beery, early-evening atmosphere, but at Leicestershire we set about it more methodically. We saw an opportunity to master a new form of cricket, and with Phil Whitticase driving us as our new coach we spent time analysing it, practicing and working out intricate plans. Even Daffy, as experienced and as proud as they came, spent hours in the nets on his own, working on new slower balls in readiness for the challenge. We took it down to the finest detail, encouraging bowlers to think on their feet and vary their deliveries on a ball-by-ball basis, and fine-tuning our batting order.

The idea was that Hodge and Maddy would be tasked with getting us off to a flier. Then the likes of me and Snapper would work it around in the middle of the innings. With the ball, our high-class spinners like Snapper and Claude Henderson – who would have played a hundred Tests for South Africa, rather than seven, had it not been for apartheid – would, in theory, tie teams in knots.

It is often assumed that this was the time I started to play the reverse-sweep, which many people regard as my signature shot. That's not necessarily true. I certainly worked on it more when Twenty20 came in, because it was an unorthodox stroke that could beat many conventional fields and I found it a useful, low-risk shot against the spinners. But it's something I had employed long before the media started highlighting it. Two years before Twenty20, in fact, I had dispatched Muralitharan for a reverse-swept six in a Championship game for Kent against Lancashire. The difference was that the cameras weren't there, so not many people noticed.

We were so far ahead of the game that we reached Finals Day in the first two years of Twenty20. The atmosphere at these occasions was more reminiscent of a big football match than a genteel game of cricket. There was razzmatazz, excitement, glamour and Atomic Kitten singing on stage. It was brand new and I loved it. In 2003 we lost to Warwickshire in the semi-final, but the following year we came storming back.

I had a patchy season in 2004 after a knee operation but was in decent nick by the time the Twenty20 games came around. Maddy batted magnificently all through the competition and then it was Surrey, in the final, at Edgbaston.

I always enjoyed playing at Warwickshire's great old ground, and on Finals Day it was packed to the rafters. And to make things even better, most of the people seemed to be supporting us in the final. Not many Surrey fans had travelled up, and the few supporters they did bring were drowned out not just by our followers, but by those of the losing semi-finalists, Lancashire and Glamorgan, who latched onto the underdogs as they took on the aristocrats from the Oval (where have we heard that before?).

It was, briefly, just like the good old days, when no challenge seemed too great. Surrey's 168-6 was a decent effort but Hodge, our new captain, took them to the cleaners and then Snapper hit the winning runs with five balls left (I was due in next).

That day is up there with the best. It all comes flooding back: the tingle of excitement as the ground reverberated to the strains of 'Leicestershire, la la la'; the unmistakable buzz of knowing that I was a winner again; the hugs with Snapper and the jumping around on the podium as the champagne sprayed; the singing and the dancing in our dressing room as plans were formulated for the evening's carnage. I remember also, a few minutes later, slipping quietly into the mainly deserted Surrey dressing room and offering a consoling beer to the few people who were still there. I remember talking to Jimmy Ormond and Ally Brown, saying hard luck, it wasn't to be, next year it might be you, the usual things you come out with to try to appear humble in victory. I then remember seeing Adam Hollioake sitting in the corner of the sweaty dressing room, alone with his thoughts, and quite suddenly realising that there was one more conversation I needed to have.

fourteen

MARGARET

Some years ago, I went to see a psychic medium. For as long as I can remember I have been intrigued by that sort of stuff. Don't ask me to explain why; it just absolutely fascinates me. When one of the Leicester Tigers rugby players' wives told me in the late 1990s that she had been to see a clairvoyant in Countesthorpe, I couldn't help myself; I had to give it a try.

So I visited the same woman. I was immediately impressed when she identified me as a sportsman – a goalkeeper, she insisted, which wasn't a bad guess – and further encouraged when she then informed me that I would be successful in life, get married and have kids. But I wasn't sure what to make of her next claim.

'You have a guardian angel with you,' she said. 'I feel this very strongly. Someone who is looking after you.'

That was a strange thing to say, but she was completely adamant. And the more I thought about it, over the years, the more I conceded that she might be right. Why? Well, consider the evidence.

The car crash with Mullally, for instance, when I pleaded with God for mercy? Not a scratch. The occasions when I drove under the influence of alcohol in South Africa? Nothing. The stupid time I did it in England, on the night of Jimmy Whitaker's benefit dinner in 1993? I got home safely. That terrifying moment on the long trip back from Truro, when I was absolutely convinced we were going to plough into the oncoming car? There was no collision. The time in Cape Town, when I was motoring along the notorious Hospital Bend with John Holliday and witnessed a ten-car pile-up, with cars flying everywhere and a look of absolute horror on one poor woman's face? The metal sea parted and we managed to drive through the gaps, miraculously untouched.

Then there was my accident in the dressing room in the early days at Grace Road, when I was using a scalpel to adjust my bat handle, only to become distracted and put the knife down on the bench. A few seconds later, Cliff, the physio, pointed with alarm to the growing pool of blood by my hand. I had leaned right back onto the scalpel and was later told that, had it penetrated by just one more millimetre, it would have sliced through a tendon and I would have lost a finger. But I didn't.

A more distant incident, from my youth: it is a beautiful summer's day and I am on the farm with Dad, helping him load a trailer with hay bales. This involves a lot of tight packing and squashing, so I decide to climb to the top of the bales, in readiness to help Dad rope them together. Then I slip and fall between some of the bales. Soon, I feel the force of the tractor as the bales start to squeeze around me. The straw is pushing into my face and my body like the points of a million pencils.

I'm being crushed!

Panicking and struggling to breathe, I wave my hand in the air. I am fearing for my life when Dad, who has come around the side of the tractor, spots my fingers waggling above the hay. He pulls me out. I wheeze my relief.

'I don't know why I came round that side,' he tells me later. 'Normally I would just have gone back and carried on ramming into the bales. You'd have been squashed. And I mean squashed.'

One more: aged 4, helping Dad bring in the milking cows. As he heads into the parlour, I stand in the gateway and find myself suddenly stuck into the mud. I sink until my Wellingtons and half my legs are deep into the shit and, as I do so, a hundred cows come lumbering towards the gate.

Do any of them trample me, as I wail and scream? No – the beasts somehow manage to give me a wide berth. 'What the heck happened to you?' Dad enquires, once I have dug myself out with my hands and run into the parlour. He then hoses me down and I eventually stop crying.

I have had so much luck over the years that I am now certain someone is looking out for me. Maybe it's Uncle David, or one of my grandparents, or somebody else. I just feel like I'm being protected, somehow.

It would be very easy for you to dismiss this belief as crazy. Each to their own, and all that. But I am convinced that I have somebody with me, and that there is something out there that we cannot control or fully comprehend.

More evidence? How about this. (I swear on my wife and my daughter's lives that the following is a completely accurate account of events).

The month is July 2004 and the scene is our team hotel in Durham, where we are contesting a Championship match. Outside it is raining with Biblical force and our base is a big, old building out in the sticks, supposedly haunted. One of those places that, for reasons you can't quite put your finger on, just feels a bit funny. Well, the act of kicking around a hotel for hours on end can leave a bunch of blokes in sore need of some mental stimulation. And so it comes to pass that, as a group of us sit in

Brad Hodge's room talking nonsense to each other about what might be floating around this haunted hotel, Darren Maddy speaks up.

'Come on boys,' he says, excitedly. 'Let's have a séance.'

It would be a first for me. I remember Dad once telling me not to get involved in 'that sort of thing', and while Jen had done one in her younger days after coming home drunk with her mates, here we are stone-cold sober.

Another voice. 'If we're going to do this, we're doing it properly.'

That's Darren Stevens, who has taken part in a séance before and insists he knows what to do. He sets about rearranging the room and assembling the necessary equipment – a circular, wooden table, around which we all sit; several pieces of paper, on which Darren writes the letters of the alphabet before arranging them around the edge of the table's glass top; two more pieces of paper, placed at opposite ends, on which the words 'YES' and 'NO' are written; and a small drinking glass, which is turned upside-down and rested on the middle of the table. With the lights turned down, and a lit candle on the table, we all reach out and place a little finger on the upturned glass. Then Stevens speaks again.

'Spirit world . . . is there anybody there . . . we are here . . . will you please come and join us?'

Silence. And more silence. A minute passes. Nothing.

What a load of bollocks, a few of the lads are clearly thinking. But the two Darrens remain keenly serious. So does Hodge. So do I.

'We're not pissing around here,' interrupts Hodge, sternly. 'I don't want anybody pushing the fucking glass. We're doing this thing right.'

Another ten minutes go by. A few arms are starting to ache. Five more minutes and some are losing interest, joking around and singing, 'Is there anybody theeeeeere,' in a pub-singer voice. Some take their fingers off the glass. Stevens explains that, as long as two of us keep touching it, we are OK. Then, the glass moves, a couple of inches to the right.

We all look at each other.

'Right, who pushed it?' Hodge asks.

Nobody confesses. Everybody is suddenly deadly serious.

The truth is, so lightly are we touching the glass, with the tips of our little fingers, that it would be impossible for one person to force the glass in a short sliding motion without it being blatantly obvious. Those of us who have been watching the glass closely have seen no such interference.

'Is there anybody there?' a few of us ask.

The glass slides to the left, in the direction of the piece of paper marked 'YES'.

Fucking hell! We're away!

'What's your name?' Stevens asks.

Slowly, the glass starts sliding around the table, making short, scraping motions from letter to letter.

M-A-R-G-A-R-E-T, it spells out.

'Margaret!'

'Margaret? Who is Margaret?'

'Our spirit guide,' confirms Stevens.

One by one, we all take turns to ask Margaret questions. When one player speaks, the rest sit motionless. At the start, we resolve to test 'Margaret', to see if it isn't one of the boys who has somehow found a way of manipulating the glass.

When it comes to me, I ask her to tell me the name of my late granddad's favourite dog. Nobody in the room knows this, I am certain.

The glass dutifully slides in the direction of J. Then I. Then P.

J-I-P. 'Jip! Granddad's dog Jip!' This is unreal!

Hodgey's turn. He asks Margaret to name the pub where his old Victoria coach and fellow Aussie David Hookes had died after an assault a few months ago.

The glass duly slides again.

NO

'No?'

It then starts moving again.

H-O-T-E-L

Hotel.

Yes! It was a hotel where he had died, not a pub. Then the glass moves again.

B-E-A-C-O-N-S-F-I-E-L-D

This is getting seriously scary.

Everyone takes his turn, firing questions at Margaret. Some of the lads ask her about family members who have passed away. Each enquiry is answered with terrifying accuracy.

My go again.

'Margaret, do we all have to be touching the glass?'

A slide to the right: NO

'Do three of us have to be on it?'

NO

'What about two of us?'

YES

'What about just one of us?'

NO

'Can you touch me, Margaret?'

YES

I close my eyes, and feel a faint brush on my right arm, as though someone is very gently tickling my arm hairs. I shoot my eyes open. Nobody is laughing, or guiltily withdrawing an arm.

Suddenly, the silence is shattered by a loud knock on the door. To a man, we shit ourselves. Into the room bursts another figure from the next world – a big, hairy figure wearing only a pair of white Y-fronts.

'What the bloody hell's going on here, lads?' Phil Whitticase enquires, rubbing his eyes.

'Phil,' someone whispers. 'Margaret's here. Put your hand on this and ask her a question. Something none of us knows.'

Phil steps forward, gingerly kneels down, puts his finger on the glass and poses a question. On cue, the glass does its thing, and Phil's eyebrows go north.

'Fuck me lads, I'm out of here,' he splutters. 'This isn't for me.' Back into his room he scampers.

More questions.

'Is this your first time as a spirit link?'

YES

'Can we talk to other people?'

YES

'Is my granddad there?'

YES

And so the evening proceeded. I asked Granddad questions; he answered without fail. I then contacted Dickie Davis, a good mate who had played for Leicestershire and Kent, and who had died from a brain tumour the previous year. I asked about his funeral and back came the details, down to the letter.

All this happened a couple of weeks before our Twenty20 Cup Finals Day appearance. Surrey were one of the four teams who had qualified. Surrey . . . Surrey . . .

I took a deep breath and asked to contact Ben Hollioake, who had been tragically killed in a crash in Australia two years earlier. Ben was a beautifully gifted cricketer and a fantastic bloke with a lovely sense of humour whose loss stunned the game. I had so much time for his brother, Adam, who remained Surrey's captain.

'Ben . . . are you there?'

YES

Fuck me.

'Are you OK, up there?'

YES

'Ben, is Daffy a good captain?'

NO

'Are Leicestershire a good team?'

NO

'Who is the best team?'

S-U-R-R-E-Y

Well, he would say that.

This surreal business went on for hours.

'Ben, have you got any messages for anyone?'

P-L-E-A-S-E M-A-K-E O-T-H-E-R-S A-W-A-R-E

Please make others aware.

'So . . . you want me to tell people we have done this?'

YES

'OK.'

But who was I supposed to tell? And how?

When it was time to stop and go to bed, Stevens said the correct way to end a séance was to turn the glass back up and rinse it out with water.

'If we leave it like this, on the table, will you be angry, Margaret?'

YES

At breakfast, the lads who had not been involved in the séance listened to our stories and, predictably, concluded we were bullshitting. And you might read all this and agree: surely the man is nuts. Communicating with the late Ben Hollioake? He's lost his mind. Or having a big, sick joke.

Again, each to their own. But I know what I saw that night, and so did the others who were there. It was like being on a magic carpet ride. I was in awe of the whole thing and I didn't want it to end. Hodgey, on the other hand, was so spooked by the experience that he was unable to sleep in his room once it was over (I think he ended up spending the night in John Sadler's bed). And quite what Durham's batsmen were thinking the next morning, when we made joking references to the night's events as we chased their wickets, is another matter altogether.

'Come on lads, let's get one for Margaret!'

'Margaret says we're gonna get a catch at first slip!'

'Margaret says a wicket's coming in two overs and one ball!'

Another thing Margaret had 'mentioned' was about goosepimples, the heebie-jeebies. These, she said, with a few scrapes of the glass, were a sign from the next world, one we would only understand once we had passed over ourselves.

I now think of this every time I drive past a certain place on the road to Langwathby. On Boxing Day 2004, while driving to Mum's, I witnessed a crash. Two cars skidded on the icy tarmac and met in a head-on collision. I stopped and rushed straight to the vehicles. The driver of one, a man, was conscious and groaning about his legs. The other car, containing two women in their sixties, was silent. 'Always go to the person who is quietest', they taught us at school, so I reassured the man that help was on its way, called the emergency services, and then tried to speak to the women. One was barely conscious, but the other was not. I tried to keep them alert, talking all the time, until the police and ambulance arrived. After explaining to them what had happened, I was eventually left to complete my journey.

Weeks later, I learned that the women had both died. And now, whenever I go past that precise point on the road, I shiver. Every year it happens, without fail. These days I drive along telling myself not to break out in goosebumps, trying to steel myself against it. But out they come, regardless.

A couple of weeks after that strange night in Durham, I walked into Surrey's dressing room at the end of our Twenty20 Cup victory and saw Adam Hollioake sat in the corner. It didn't feel like the time or the place, but I had to say something.

We shook hands, embraced, sat down and exchanged some small-talk about the game.

'Listen Smokey, mate,' I then said. 'You know I've always been straight with you. Well, there's something I've got to tell you. Something I've been asked to tell you. Right, well, no bullshit, this is what happened . . .'

But before I could go on, he looked me in the eye and asked: 'Is it Ben?'

'Yeah,' I replied, taken aback. 'The thing is, we did a séance . . . and he was telling us things . . .'

Adam broke into a little smile.

'I know, mate, I know,' he said. 'I know he's been trying to contact me.'

'Really?'

'Yeah. Little things keep happening at home. I've turned the TV on and the name 'Ben' has been spoken. Books have appeared in places they shouldn't have. And I keep seeing the number eleven. Any time I look at a clock, it seems to be eleven minutes past eleven.'

Ben's birthday was 11 November. The eleventh of the eleventh.

'So I know, mate,' Adam added. 'And I appreciate you telling me this. Thanks.'

It was quite a surreal conversation, coming so soon after our victory celebration. I went on to explain the details of the séance, and Adam listened intently. We eventually parted with a handshake and a hug, and I left with a funny feeling inside, a feeling I found hard to explain.

I can explain it now.

It's not a feeling of uneasiness or worry. Quite the opposite, in fact. It's a feeling of certainty. A feeling of comfort.

A feeling that I will go to my grave without any fears or worries.

Don't get me wrong, I don't exactly look forward to dying. But when my time comes, I know I will be relaxed about the prospect. I am now convinced there is something else.

This isn't a religious belief, even though I do say the odd prayer for people. I don't believe there is a God, as such. But I do believe there is an energy out there, a leader of some kind. And I believe, from what happened with Margaret that night, that there is a place where our spirits go. I have not one ounce of doubt about it.

I've often felt like doing another séance since David Young died.

I'm not really the nervous type, but my first encounter with my future father-in-law was filled with apprehension. David had a reputation for being quite a tough bloke and the suspicion was confirmed the first time I went back to Jen's house. He extended a handshake, I responded, and he proceeded to squeeze my hand so tightly I thought it was going to fall off. When his face then creased into a mischievous smile, and he let go, I finally relaxed. My laughter was perhaps more nervous than his that time but over the days, months and years, that brutally strong handshake became a part of our rapport, our mutual calling-card.

We hit it off almost immediately. For one thing, he introduced me to the magic of the Whisky Mac (a golden cocktail of whisky and ginger wine), and for another, we shared a lively sense of humour. I will forever remember the night I returned drunk as a skunk from a night out with Jen and gave him the shock of his life. On our winding route home, I appropriated a huge yellow cone from the local police station, and when we got back to Jen's I sneaked upstairs with the cone on my head. In one swift movement, I leapt on David's bed, yanked the lightswitch pulley above my head, and made a stupid noise at top volume. The look on David's face when he woke up and saw me was priceless. In my defence, I should say that he got me more times than I got him.

David was a larger-than-life bloke who didn't know the meaning of taking it easy. He would drink until all hours on a Friday night and then get up at the crack of dawn to do a 15-mile walk in the Lakes with his mates. When they set off together, with their spicy tuna sandwiches and a few crafty Whisky Macs tucked into their rucksacks, it was like a scene from *Last of the Summer Wine*. When he came to visit in South Africa, we went for a hike up Lion's Head, which I tried to use as a leg-strengthening exercise, putting a little boulder in my backpack to create resistance. One stage of the climb required us to lever ourselves up, using a chain, but by the time I got to that point I just couldn't get any higher. I battled, strained and sweated but eventually had to lose the boulder, otherwise I would still have been there now.

David loved that. For years he ripped the piss out of me for not being able to get up. He thought it was hilarious. And when David started laughing, he used to cry. It was the same when he accompanied me to the Getty Estate, the first time I got picked for England. 'What do they need an old bastard like you for?' he boomed, as the tears streamed down his face.

On 29 July 2006, David died. He went down with a heart attack during a fell walk with his mates and couldn't be revived. Somewhere in the hills around Ullswater there is now a little plaque, with David's name on it. Only his closest family and friends know the place. We scattered his ashes on one of his favourite fells, too. It's where he loved to be.

Even now it's hard to believe he's not around. Sometimes, when lights go off in the house at random and things seem to fall over of their own accord it feels like he's having a joke with us, the way he always used to. He was such a massive part of our lives and one of my most treasured memories is of that emotional car journey in 2000, when he was there to share in my dream as it started to come true.

He would have loved what happened in the winter of 2006. He would have laughed and cried and punched the air all over again.

England had not come back for me after Pakistan and Sri Lanka. Alec Stewart remained in command of the gloves until his retirement in 2003, James Foster and Chris Read had been given opportunities before and since, and then another younger player had risen to prominence.

The 2005 Ashes series was compulsive viewing, and at the heart of it was the man who had taken my place at Kent. I bore Geraint not the slightest grudge, because he was a good bloke who worked hard and had serious talent, but when he took that defining catch off Kasprowicz to seal England's famous two-run victory in the Second Test at Edgbaston, I have to confess to mixed emotions. I was delighted for Geraint, delighted for England and delighted for English cricket, but I was also gutted, because it wasn't me.

I wanted to be there, taking the catch. I wanted Geraint's job.

I knew England had always thought fairly highly of me, but by the 2006 season I was 35. I still felt fitter than players ten years younger than me on the county circuit, but some talented young men were now shooting through the ranks. For example, at Leicestershire the place was full of talk about the young fast bowler who had been pulling up trees in the seconds. I remember the way an 18-year-old Stuart Broad performed on his Championship debut at Oakham School, against Somerset, swinging the ball beautifully at a decent pace, taking wickets and scoring runs.

He was part of the new generation. I was twice his age.

But I couldn't deny that I was feeling uncommonly good about life. For one thing, my mindset had improved no end and my form with the bat and the gloves had gone skyward in a way that felt a shade more than just a late-career purple patch.

Since taking on board Snapper's advice and Wynford's work, I had started to make more of the right decisions, and the little man's impact had been reduced. In my head, I had learned to heed his negativity as a warning, rather than lose myself to his distracting jabbering. Since 2003 I had stopped more than one bowler during his run-up and lied that I had something in my eye. This was one of my new tricks, a way of buying myself a couple of extra seconds to deal with my little friend.

I had also, thanks to Snapper, started to appreciate the value of positivity, and had been spreading this precious commodity around more liberally than before. Snapper had certain phrases that would stick in your mind and make you think. One was: 'We are all managing directors of our own company.' What did he mean by this? We are all responsible for our own actions, every second of every day, and that it is ultimately down to us to do everything in our power to be positive and successful. In his terms, my company had steadily become one that people wanted to invest in and associate with. I spoke more clearly and brightly to my fellow players and was now a better team-mate as a result.

Since coming into the professional game, I had been known as Paul Nixon the joker, the party boy, the enthusiast, the fitness nut, the bloke who is tough and gutsy and determined. But all that stuff was quite raw and natural. After three years of Wynford's weird exercises, I began to understand what I was thinking and doing and was able to execute my thoughts and plans much more clearly. At the crease I gradually started to feel that I had more time to think of my scoring options. My mind felt stiller and more peaceful.

It was an absolute cracker, that summer of 2006. I scored nearly 500 one-day runs and helped Leicestershire to another Twenty20 Cup triumph. In the semi-final, against Essex at Trent Bridge, I walked across my stumps to Darren Gough and lifted him into the stand over deep square leg, on my way to a decisive 57 not out. I was named man of the match in one of the biggest games of our season, and then Maddy won the final for us against Notts with more brilliance.

I was buzzing. I felt in a blissful place. But was I expecting the call from Michael Vaughan that came in September? Hardly.

'Between you and me, Nico, keep hitting cricket balls,' he said. 'I don't pick the team, but you never know what can happen.'

I'm not daft enough to ignore the signs when the England captain rings you and tells you to keep in shape – Vaughan wasn't just trying to look after my well-being.

I spent the autumn flitting back and forward to Grace Road, netting with Tim Boon, who had replaced Phil as our head coach. I hit ball after ball as the seed sprouted in my head.

Could this really be it?

During that autumn, some words of wisdom from Alan Knott came back to mind. 'They always have to talk about somebody,' the legend had advised me, all those years ago. 'You're doing alright. Keep going.' I kept going, but heard nothing more as autumn shifted into winter. Then, in December, as I packed up some belongings in readiness to drive back to Cumbria for Christmas, my mobile went. David Graveney's name appeared on the screen.

'Hello Nico.'

'Hi Grav.'

'Nico, I've got some good news and I've got some bad news.'

Just give me the good news. I want the good news now.

'The good news,' he went on, 'is that there's a good chance you are going to come to Australia for the one-day series. The bad news is that I can't tell you for certain, right now. But I've got to warn you, because we are going to send you some things with a courier, to beat the Christmas post. There's a selection meeting in a few days' time and a few things to sort out. I'll keep you posted. In the meantime, look out for the gear in the post.'

I felt my heart quicken as the call ended.

England!

No, stop . . .

I knew I couldn't allow myself to get over-excited. What if the kit arrived and then Graveney told me I wasn't going?

When the big bag of England gear duly came, I couldn't bring myself to open it. It would have felt like tempting fate. My blazer from the Pakistan and Sri Lanka tours was in my wardrobe, unworn, because I had only played in warm-up matches. It didn't feel right to put it on. So I wasn't about to jump the gun this time.

It was on Christmas Eve when Graveney called again.

This time, he was only bearing good news. It was confirmed: I was going to Australia. More than that: I would be going as England's main one-day wicketkeeper. In the front-line. To play.

I sat down in silence.

This is it, I thought.

I've done it.

This is what it has all been for.

I'm going to be an England player! At last, I'm going to be an England player!

It was like the curtains had been thrown open and the sun was shining brighter than ever before.

I rang Mum to share the news. Then Dad, who was already in Australia on holiday, watching the Ashes series. As I spoke to the old man, Jen phoned her mum. In no time, my phone started blaring again. The press had got wind of my call-up and the Leicester media wanted interviews and photos of me in my England gear.

With pleasure, chaps.

As in 2000, life sped up when England called for the second time.

One day I was packing my bags for Christmas, wondering if I had made it, the next I was back in the homeland, trying to make the best of our first winter without David, and the next – Boxing Day – I was on a Virgin Atlantic flight from Heathrow, reclining in seat 1A in First Class, thinking: 'Yeah, this will do nicely'.

It was hard leaving the family behind at a time like that. Christmas was tough and David's absence naturally hit Jen hard. But all I got was encouragement and support, from her and from everyone else. They were with me, in spirit, on that plane, and so was David. I felt sure of that.

When I arrived in Sydney with some of the other one-day players, bleary-eyed but excited, I was whisked through the airport and driven to the Star City apartment complex. I stepped into my allocated digs and scanned the scene. It was a nice two-bedroomed number, with a kitchen, living room and reasonable view of Darling Harbour, in all its shimmering glory. 'I could get used to this', I thought, as I heaved my bags onto a chair and then paused at the sight of a piece of paper on the floor, by the door.

I bent down to pick it up, and studied the handwritten words.

Congratulations and welcome to the England squad, Paul.

It was a note from Duncan Fletcher. Inside I was dancing with delight. Among the words was an instruction . . .

We have had some disappointments out here over the last few weeks, and we would like you to keep your distance from the Test players for the time being. Please don't mix with any of them until the Test series has finished. Their wives and girlfriends are here and we would like you to stick to your own group of one-day players for the moment. Thank-you and good luck.

Welcome to Australia, England style.

fifteen

BOUNCE

The Ashes were, of course, a disaster. England had received three beatings in the first three Tests by the time I boarded the plane. As I arrived, they were on the brink of another, in Melbourne. A fifth and final trouncing then took place in Sydney while I adjusted to my new surroundings. When the humiliation was over, and it was time to start preparing for the Twenty20 international, I saw exactly why Duncan Fletcher had been so keen to keep the one-day specialists apart.

For my first few days in Sydney, my closest interaction with the Test squad had been to bump into Andrew Flintoff's wife, Rachael, in the taxi queue and share a cab with her into the city. But when I pulled my kit bag down from the apartment to load onto the coach, and finally greeted my new team-mates before our first morning of practice together, the Test boys looked – to a man – like absolute zombies. Since November they had been knocked from pillar to post and every single day was written into their faces.

Here we were, then: Ground Zero. It was clearly going to take some rebuilding.

The bus to practice was quiet, with no buzz and no Goughie to lighten the mood, but during the short coach ride Fletcher sat with me and asked if I would be willing to say a few words to the rest of the group when we got to the dressing room. He wanted me to share my experience of winning Twenty20 Cups with Leicestershire. I happily agreed and he returned to his seat, as I realised that, in one brief chat, Fletch had given me more attention than he had on an entire tour six years earlier.

We arrived, unloaded, got changed and then the coach piped up.

'Guys, can we have a minute please?' he called out. 'Nico's here, he has played in lots of Twenty20 games in England and been very successful. We've got an important game coming up and we need to have our preparations right. Nico, can you talk a bit about Leicestershire's plans, about how you went about it and why you were successful?'

I cleared my throat and spoke. As I started to describe how the Foxes had become a Twenty20 force, my eyes scanned the room. All the players were watching me intently. This was a new experience – an entire England dressing room hanging on my every word! Well, almost an entire dressing room. The exception was Flintoff, who looked bored and distracted throughout. At one point I thought I saw him roll his eyes. If there was a thought bubble above his head, it might have said: 'Here we go again, Nixon with his theories. What the fuck's he talking about?'

Fair enough. He was an international player and I was not. Not yet.

Duncan thanked me and scribbled down some notes. Then we went out and trained like demons. The following day, Fletcher and Vaughan sat me down at a table and discussed my role. In summary, it was to be a number six or seven batsman capable of finishing games, and an upbeat wicketkeeper who could get into the Aussies' minds. 'Our body language hasn't been as strong as it could have been out here,' Fletcher explained. 'We think you can make a difference for us.'

I knew exactly what he meant. In the Sydney Test it had been well-documented that Chris Read had declined to join in when Paul Collingwood and Shane Warne had been trading angry verbals. To me, silence from a wicketkeeper in those circumstances is a criminal offence. Fletcher agreed.

The Sydney Cricket Ground. The famous old SCG. My first game as a fully-fledged England player. The detail will stay with me forever: the physio's room, the rehab room, the battered lockers covered in graffiti, a big table bearing trays of food, a TV in the corner, and a little viewing gallery outside next to the members' pavilion.

I stood in the dressing room filling up with emotion, and then when we all jogged out to warm up we found that the ground was rammed to the rafters with English supporters. That was a good start. Then, when we went through our drills, I felt like I was floating across the outfield. It was akin to an out-of-body experience. I was so devoid of negative thoughts it was scary.

We were like coiled springs by the time play started, but straight away we noticed something unusual about our opponents. Australia were all relaxed, cracking jokes and smiling. They even had nicknames on the back of their shirts. Were they treating this as an exhibition game? Were they taking the piss?

Not quite. We soon saw the result of Australia in relaxed mode. From the start, Hayden and Gilchrist started pinning us against the ropes with a barrage of boundaries, with Gilchrist, who was miked up to the Channel 9 TV commentary crew, offering a running commentary on his plans:

'Next one's going over midwicket.'

. . . and then Gilchrist delivered his promise by launching Jon Lewis for a six. He picked another target for Lewis' next ball and was as good as his word again. It was a bit like Lara against Warne at the Getty Estate, only with a massive wall of sound for accompaniment.

Australia bashed their way to 221-5 from their twenty overs, but during their assault I claimed my first international victim: Mike Hussey, stumped, after galloping down the wicket to Monty Panesar. The first one is always special, and I was pleased Monty was involved. When he wasn't sleeping in his room with his eyes open and with his long hair out of his patka – a scary sight, the first time you witness it – Monty was the most enthusiastic man in the world, a puppy eager to learn new tricks. I knew I would be keeping to him a lot during the series so I made sure to spend time with him in the nets, in order to feel his drift and turn with the Kookaburra balls.

Monty's control was world-class, but he wasn't the greatest thinking bowler. So I encouraged him to develop some signals that we could take into a game. For a normal delivery, for instance, I would put my hands on my knees, and for a fuller ball I would drop my hands a bit lower. Sometimes, too, I would mouth the word 'slower' just before he bowled. That's what happened when we got rid of Hussey: Monty held one back, Hussey went through it too quickly, and I knocked off the bails.

If it was nice to see that little plan come together, the same couldn't be said for our reply. We fell massively behind the run-rate early on, and though I made 31 not out, aided by a woeful dropped catch by Shane Harwood and the bonus of a nice six in the last over on a pitch like a brick road, we were never really in the game. The enemy reined us in to 144-9, and my international debut ended to the familiar sound of Sydney sitting back, cracking open a beer and enjoying yet another triumph over the beleaguered Poms.

My sudden arrival as an international cricketer did not go unnoticed by the press. A 36-year-old coming from nowhere to take on the best team in the world? That was certainly a good story. And, unlike some of the established players, I quite enjoyed the attention. Most of the lads were quite world-weary when the reporters and photographers were around, but I couldn't get enough of it. A chat by the pool? No problem. A photo in front of Sydney Opera House? By all means. Any reason to be out of the hotel room; any reason not to be cooped up on my own, with just my mind for company.

A tour, though, can never be perfect unless you are winning, and England were certainly not doing that. With the Commonwealth Bank Series coming up – a three-team contest involving Australia and New Zealand – a disquieting thought was going around the media. If the Aussies could do so much damage to us in twenty overs, how were we going to get close to them in fifty? We were in the losing habit, after all – that much I knew after one game.

It had to change.

1. Melbourne, 12 January 2007

My One-Day International debut, against Australia, at the cavernous Melbourne Cricket Ground. With 70,000 people watching, we batted first and Kevin Pietersen whipped his way to 82, before breaking a rib to a Glenn McGrath delivery and suffering a premature end to his series. That was a massive early blow to us, but in the short-term Paul Collingwood and Freddie tried to repair some of the damage with a useful stand.

Me? A fucking duck.

Unlike most grounds, the MCG requires you to walk onto the field from one place, and then leave it in another direction. In the moments after my fourth-ball lbw dismissal to Mitchell Johnson, this information vanished from my head. As I departed, I was greeted by Jamie Dalrymple, our next batsman, who had a puzzled look on his face.

'Where the fucking hell are you going, Nico?' he enquired, in his posh voice.

I suddenly realised I was marching off the wrong way. *Shit! The Aussies are going to love this.*

'Tell you what,' I whispered to Jamie. 'I'll start waving my fingers around to make it look like I've come to tell you what the ball is doing. Then I'll turn around and go back the right way.'

'Er . . . OK.'

I carried out a few elaborate hand-signals, as Jamie looked on patiently. Then I turned around and trudged off towards the correct gate. As I crossed the boundary rope, with thousands of Australian spectators passing comment on my performance, one voice rose above the cacophony.

'Nixon, you fucking Pommy bastard,' a supporter screeched. 'We know you were walking off the wrong way. Look at me and tell me I'm wrong, Nixon! Look at me mate!'

Don't look at him, I ordered myself, as I made my way past. *Don't feed the beast.* For some reason, I changed my mind at the last moment and indulged him with a glance.

'Aaaaaarrgggh!' he exclaimed. 'I knew you were wrong!' It looked like I had made his day.

We set Australia 243 to win, and our defence got off to a strange start. I got nowhere near Flintoff's opening delivery to Gilchrist, which flew down leg side and kept swinging. Then, in the second over, Jon Lewis' first ball snaked and dipped, and banged against my elbow. His next ball caused yet more mischief, hitting me flush on the knee.

If that had happened ten years ago it would have opened the gate to the little negative man. Not here. Those little mishaps went into the black bag and I faced the next deliveries with a fresh mind. I didn't drop anything else and claimed a nice pair of catches to account for Hayden and Gilchrist, but Australia still won at a canter.

During their chase, Michael Clarke had struggled to get going and I had regularly been reminding him of this fact. 'There's only one successful Clark in Australia at the moment, Mike,' I taunted, referring to bowler Stuart who had enjoyed a stunning Ashes series.

'Nixon, you're just a fucking clubby,' Clarke shot back, clearly unhappy. 'Nobody's even heard of you.'

Poor effort.

'Well,' I replied, 'how is it going to feel to be caught by a club cricketer, eh? How. Is. That. Going. To. Feel? You're going to make a club cricketer's day, Mike.'

He was really uncomfortable, squeezing his bat handle tightly, and I thought it was a matter of time before we would have him. But the club cricketer's catch never came, because at the other end Ricky Ponting played a blinder to see his mate through the storm. He stole a single at the right time to keep the strike, gave Clarke one ball to see out an over until he got his bearings, and chatted intently to him all the way through.

Trying on the verbals with Ponting was a futile act. 'I don't know how your legs aren't tired from carrying this useless fucker,' I said to the Australian captain at one point.

'Just concentrate on your own fucking job and catch the fucking ball, mate,' he answered, and then got back to work, making 82 unflustered runs. He was as tough as old boots and remained in total control throughout. A class act.

2. Hobart, 16 January 2007

On the night before our first meeting with New Zealand, I met Dad and Irene for dinner. We went to a nice restaurant on the harbour and I opted for oysters. A couple of hours later, I began to regret my choice. Back at the hotel, I started throwing up and continued vomiting into the night, and when I headed down for breakfast the next morning I still felt like death, not sure if I was capable of playing.

But I *had* to play! My appearance record in county cricket was up there with the best. To miss one here would have been a disaster.

I played. I was dehydrated and my head was in a thousand pieces, but after being given a few tablets by our physio, Dean Conway, my stomach settled and I managed to keep wicket without any traumas, and surprised myself by connecting bat with ball, despite feeling dizzy at the crease. I made fifteen in a partnership with Freddie before I was run out by a whisker. No matter – we knocked off our target with a ball to spare.

Our first victory! For some of the players, it was their first victory in 72 days of thankless slog! What a bloody relief!

In the dressing room afterwards, Matthew Maynard, the assistant coach, dished out pieces of card, which displayed the lyrics to the England team song. As I squinted at the words, Matthew stood on a table.

'Lads, that was a great victory and we're back in business,' he roared. 'We've nailed New Zealand, so it's onwards and upwards and now it's time to shove it up the Aussies.'

We all bellowed our approval and belted out the song in a huddle. As we sang, it felt like a massive, oppressive weight was lifting from us. When we stopped, I started to feel like crap again, and it was such a relief when I could finally get back to my room, cast off my clothes and collapse into bed.

3. Brisbane, 19 January 2007

Before we went out to warm up at the Gabba, Vaughany called everyone into a circle and summoned me forward.

'Congratulations, mate,' he said, holding out a blue cap with the number 199 stitched into the fabric. 'It's an honour for me to give this to you.'

I felt my lower lip quiver as I looked at the little white numbers. One-hundred and ninety-nine: my official place in the order of England one-day players. Ok, I confess – I then tried to swap with Monty, because his 200 was a nice, round number, but he was having none of it, so I had to make do with 199. That was a hardship I could live with.

Vaughany missed the Ashes, but returned from injury for the ODIs, before his old knee injury came back to haunt him again. So Freddie, who led the Test team, took the reins again. The big all-rounder and me later found ourselves together at the crease as we tried to salvage a competitive score after a wobbly start.

For some reason I felt absolutely fantastic from ball one. Beyond fantastic. At one early stage in my knock, I timed a hook off Glenn McGrath so sweetly that I barely felt any impact.

'Fucking hell, you nailed that one,' Freddie observed.

He was right: I felt as though I could have batted forever. Then I hit Johnson for an effortless, back-of-a-length four . . .

Nico, you're in here. This is your day.

With my confidence brimming, I then attempted to run Brett Lee down to third man. I got a bit less on the shot than I wanted, and the result was a simple slip-catch for Hayden. I got back to the dressing room and hurled my bat. I was furious with myself. I wasn't supposed to be out for nine, not here, not feeling as good as I had felt. I had given it away, big style.

We were rolled over for 155, but then made some good early inroads with the ball. When Mike Hussey, one of the remaining big beasts, then nicked off during Jimmy Anderson's first over after a rain break, I took the catch and tossed the ball in the air. We had nailed Hussey! Surely this game was ours now.

'Not out.'

Daryl Harper, the umpire, disagreed.

Not out?! Unbelievable! It was a proper edge and Hussey knew it. Did he walk? Not a chance.

For the rest of the innings I gave 'Mr Cricket' heaps, but he didn't flicker. He kept his head down and guided the Aussies home.

We were getting closer, much closer, but still no cigar. After the game, we went to the hotel bar to unwind. A few of the Sky commentators were milling around, along with the Kiwi and Aussie players. It was a pretty relaxed affair, and in the case of Freddie and Ian Botham, who were sat together at a table, extremely relaxed. They were in their own little world, and going hammer and tongs at the drinks. When Beefy bought one, Freddie bought two. When Beefy bought two, Freddie bought two, plus a shooter. It was quite a sight. When I went down for breakfast at 7.00 a.m. the next day, they were still there, fully clothed and asleep, with empty bottles and glasses strewn across their table.

'Fletcher must have seen that', I thought, as I tiptoed past the slumbering giants.

4. Adelaide, 23 January 2007

After the Brisbane game, my ding-dong with Hussey was picked up by the TV and newspapers and I had a mini media frenzy. Even more people wanted a piece of the old bloke who had a lot to say for himself in the heat of battle. The feeling was that England were rediscovering some fight and some spunk, and my verbals were supposedly a major reason for that.

Against New Zealand at the Adelaide Oval, we then had an absolute shocker. I was caught behind for six off Jacob Oram, who had earlier batted beautifully, and they buried us by 90 runs. After the game we were all really down. Coming so soon after the near-miss at the Gabba, it felt like a big step back.

Later, the Aussie coach John Buchanan appeared in the press to claim that his team had been beating us so easily that they weren't getting enough quality practice ahead of the World Cup. He said:

'In essence, the batting efforts of our opposition are not assisting the development of our bowlers' one-day skills and the decision-making that accompanies being placed under the microscope of competition.'

Charming.

5. Adelaide, 26 January 2007

I woke on Australia Day to a call from Steve Waugh.

'I just wanted to wish you well today, mate,' he said. 'You guys have been getting some bad press lately and I think Australia are getting a bit ahead of themselves. Maybe this could be your day.'

I thanked him and told the lads as we got changed. A few words of encouragement from one of the greatest living Aussies could do us no harm, surely? A few minutes later, as we lined up for the national anthems, I found myself crying again. I was so proud and so up for it I could hardly contain myself.

We got stuffed, of course.

It was a day/night match but, to our acute embarrassment, it was all over before the floodlights came on. I played a diabolical shot to Brad Hogg's spin – caught and bowled for four – and we were knocked over for 110.

When the Aussies replied, I began by laying into Hayden, who was not in great touch and at the centre of speculation about his place in the team. 'This could be your last knock for your country, mate,' I said, with Strauss egging me on in the slips.

The big Queenslander looked a worried man. But Ponting, again, flew to his mate's rescue, just as he had with Clarke at Melbourne. They finished us off without many dramas.

This wasn't just a defeat. It was an absolute, royal hiding and we knew it. The dressing room afterwards was like a morgue – a scowl on every face, with kit being thrown and equipment being kicked to the sound of catcalls from angry spectators outside. Not a pleasant place.

I was livid with myself. After that phone call from Steve Waugh, and after walking out with a perfect opportunity to get my team out of the mud, I played that shot, that pathetic leading edge to Hogg.

We went out that night for a few drinks, then a few more, then a few more, and tried to forget about it.

6. Perth, 30 January 2007

It had been pouring down just before we got to the nets, and there was talk of further storms before our game against New Zealand at the WACA. To make things worse, the surface in the nets was terrible. It reminded me of Edenhall on a wet Saturday afternoon.

As we milled around after practice, a few people mentioned that Freddie was a bit the worse for wear and actually smelling of booze. I didn't see much of him, because I was doing a lot of my own wicketkeeping work that morning, but the whispers were certainly going around.

Whatever the truth of them, I never felt that Freddie was the ideal captain. I'm a big believer that, if you have a genius in the team – and Freddie was a genius with the ball – you should let them be free to perform without any extra burdens. Captaincy is hard work, a fifteen-hour-a-day job, but Freddie liked his life away from cricket and hated the idea of being consumed by the role. His session with Botham should have been a giveaway. A cry for help? I don't know, but I do know that when Reggie Dickason, our security guy and motorbike nut, sorted Freddie out with a Harley Davidson for a couple of days, he went away and had a whale of a time, and came back buzzing. He needed more time like that.

The game confounded the forecasts and went ahead. Jen had flown out by now, Al Mullally was there and a load of my old friends from my younger days in Australia had also turned up to watch. It always fired me up to think that there were a few extra people in the crowd who had come along to see me and gee me along, but I had to wait a while to impress them, because New Zealand first piled up 318-7, taking Chris Tremlett and Freddie for plenty. Ed Joyce then played a decent hand at the top of our order but we duly fell miles behind the rate. As it became apparent we were getting nowhere near our target, Fletcher came to me and the other guys who were still to bat and explained that our aim was now simply to deny the Kiwis a bonus point, so that we still had a realistic chance of reaching the final.

At last, I went in and clicked. I shared a 76-run partnership with Liam Plunkett, hitting Daniel Vettori for a couple of sixes, reverse-sweeping for fun, nailing Shane Bond out of the screws for four and annoying the hell out of the Kiwis. Fantastic fun and games, and it ensured that the bonus point was saved. Job done.

Nearly. There was one ball to go, and I was on 49.

We still weren't guaranteed to be in the final. There were only four men in the circle. There was an easy single on offer for my 50.

Smack it, smack it! This could be your last ball in international cricket! England are losing games and you could be dropped at any time. Go out with a bang, Nico! Go out in style!

For once, I was in perfect harmony with the little man. Fuck it, I thought. My chips are in.

Bond sent it down and I swung hard. I got plenty on it, but not enough. Oram took a brilliant diving catch and the Kiwis celebrated with abandon. Afterwards, I had twenty messages on my phone asking why I didn't get a half-century. But I was seriously not bothered, and I swear on my life that I would do the same thing again. I was playing for England, and I wanted to hit what I thought was my last ball for my country into another universe. Simple as that.

7. Sydney, 2 February 2007

It wasn't my last ball, as it happened. I was still in the team. Back at the SCG, Ed Joyce got a brilliant hundred, but I perished for four after hitting a Shaun Tait delivery off the splice, giving Brad Hodge an easy catch.

It was one of the fastest balls I had ever faced and its predecessor, which I managed to top-edge into the sightscreen for four, wasn't much slower. Tait was really fired up, but soon after my dismissal I saw Ravi Bopara deftly running him down to third man for four. 'Hold on,' I thought. 'I've tried to hook a ball I knew was coming and only managed to splice it, but Ravi has gone in and played Tait with his bell-end?' It told me Bopara was a special player in the making.

We assembled 292-7, and then Plunkett bowled Gilchrist first ball. We got right on top of the Aussies, for whom Andrew Symonds was batting at five. Once, when playing for Kent against Gloucestershire, I had seen Symo give Jack Russell heaps of stick when the great man walked out to bat. As Symo approached the wicket here, I resolved to give a bit back on Jack's behalf.

I met him twenty yards before he got to the middle . . .

'Hey Symo, dog-breath, it's all down to you now, son. And I'll tell you something – when you nick it to me I'm going to send you the scorecard every day for a year.'

Symo was always a worrier at the start of his innings and tended to play with his heart rather than his head. I also remembered Steve Kirby winding him up something rotten in a county game, to the point where Symo came charging down the wicket and got bowled.

I kept chipping at him, not giving him a moment's peace.

'Come on, you dingbat, you're not bright enough to get these Aussies out of trouble.'

He got more and more charged up. He made a quick 39, and then hurtled up the pitch for a massive whoosh. He missed the ball and then pulled up, clutching his arm. A torn bicep. Retired hurt. Without the big man, we made short work of the rest of the Aussies. I took a nice, diving catch to get rid of Clarke and we won by 92 runs. The whole game, in fact, went like a dream. We had beaten them at last. Were things finally starting to turn?

Emboldened by the experience of caning Australia, I caught Fletch at a quiet moment during our next net session and scratched the six-year itch.

'Fletch, do you remember when we were in Pakistan and you said you'd seen something in my game, but you couldn't tell me until the end of the tour. You didn't get round to telling me. Can you remember what it was?'

'Really? Oh, no, I haven't got a clue.'

8. Brisbane, 6 February 2007

Vaughany was now back, but this game was all about Paul Collingwood. Colly hadn't enjoyed a prolific series but here he made a high-class hundred and then bowled ten tight overs as we squeezed the Kiwis. Only Fleming, their captain, hung around for long enough, but his century was unsupported and they fell fourteen runs short.

Fourteen sweet runs.

It meant – as unlikely as it had seemed a few games ago – that we were in the final.

A two-legged final, against the Australians.

Game on.

9. Melbourne, 9 February 2007

In the first final, Australia scored 252, which we felt was just below par. At the start of our reply we lost three wickets cheaply, but then McGrath dropped Ian Bell and we steadily picked up the pace. Freddie had a lusty cameo before falling to Shane Watson for 35. Then Dalrymple was run out for three.

I inhaled deeply and walked out briskly to join Colly, who had compiled another magnificent hundred. We required 25 from three overs, and I required some runs to avoid an MCG 'pair', following my duck on 12 January.

Colly greeted me and was clearly in the zone. 'Right mate, it's the northerners' union here, a Geordie and a Cumbrian,' he said firmly. 'Let's do it. Let's beat these fuckers. Just give me the strike.'

He was fired up and playing beautifully. He kept walking up to Nathan Bracken's left-arm swing and playing fine sweeps over square leg. I was facing McGrath and was just determined to get bat on ball. I got a couple of quick twos through square, settled down and steadily nudged my way to eleven. I felt fine. Relaxed. Sort of.

At the other end, meanwhile, Shotley Bridge's finest was playing the ODI innings of his life, and eventually hit the winning runs through midwicket – a golden moment which was followed by another meeting of the northerners' union in the middle.

'Get in there!' Colly roared. 'We've beaten these Aussie fuckers!'

I hollered some other expletives into his ear as we embraced. It was dream stuff – knocking off the runs to beat the old enemy.

The next morning's papers captured that moment for all eternity, with a big picture of me and Colly walking towards each other, bats aloft, with Ponting scowling in the background. That night a few of us celebrated by hitting the Crown Casino in Melbourne, where Vaughany had a ridiculous run on the roulette and paid for all our dinners. Talk about a change of luck.

10. Sydney, 11 February 2007

Colly again. The bloke was on fire. In the second final he kept cramping up but that didn't stop him making a gutsy and crucial 70. I had a short stint at the crease and was in at the end, for McGrath's final over. The last ball of the innings was a lowish full-toss which I tried to deposit over cow corner. I couldn't get enough on it, and Brad Hodge took the catch. Minutes later, I put my bat down in the dressing room and gave it a kick. It thumped against the lockers. Another minute passed before a figure appeared at my shoulder.

'Here you go mate,' said Rocky the dressing room attendant, offering a pen. 'Write your story down. Should be a good one – McGrath's last wicket in Australia.'

I suppose it was my little place in SCG history. I scrawled a few words on the lockers, next to my dent, and then we set about winning the game.

After a rain delay, Plunkett bowled Gilchrist with a brilliant in-swinger. Then they fell in a heap. I held a nice, low two-hander to remove Clarke for a duck, Dalrymple took an unbelievable diving catch at backward point to get rid of Watson, and then the rain came again. We were miles ahead on the Duckworth-Lewis formula and our victory was confirmed while we were in the dressing room, eyeing the heavy skies. We had done it again.

England 2 Australia 0. How sweet.

After the first final, our third consecutive win, Maynard insisted that we mark the occasion by sitting on the floor, one behind the other, as if in a rowing boat. We all gleefully obliged, rocking back and forth and chanting: 'Three in a row, three in a row,' at the top of our voices. This time, the coach leapt onto a table, urged us to follow suit, and then ordered us to jump up and down repeatedly. We all gleefully obliged again. The chant? 'Four on the bounce, four on the bounce.' It was gloriously giddy, but as we jumped and hollered and sprayed beer around the place, and celebrated the moment like it was the best thing in the world ever, another strong feeling prevailed.

It was that we had well and truly shoved it up John Buchanan's arse.

After victory had been confirmed, Freddie beckoned us back outside to greet our jubilant followers. The Barmy Army were there in force, as they had been all winter. I walked across the boundary rope towards a group of English fans.

'Nico, throw us your shoes,' someone shouted.

I pulled off my stinking boots and hurled them in.

'Let's have a picture, Nico,' bellowed another.

I crouched down by a bunch of blokes and suddenly felt myself being dragged back. As the flashlights went off, and I pulled the biggest smile of all time, my sunglasses disappeared into someone's hands. Then, amid the chaos, someone made a grab for my precious cap. I held on for dear life.

Casual theft aside, we were so pleased for the Barmy Army. They have no idea how much they mean to the England players. When you are out there, toiling to make something happen, their songs give everyone a lift. They had been with us through thick and thin on that trip, and that night they were swarming around Sydney to share in our elation.

We had a big night out, which started in the hotel and continued in a bar called the Establishment until the small hours and beyond. It was about 7.00 a.m. when I staggered back to the hotel, blind drunk. The bus was due to leave for the airport in an hour's time.

I approached the hotel foyer to the sight of police, everywhere. It was explained that Dean Conway had returned a few hours earlier and had been robbed at knifepoint by a gang of four. A couple of phones and a wallet had been taken. Fortunately Dean was OK, but it was a sombre way for the trip to close.

I felt thoroughly wretched on the flight home. I was sick and struggled to get much sleep. I walked off the plane in chilly England with a thick skull, red eyes and a few nagging doubts about whether I had done enough to prolong this amazing journey.

Yes, doubts. Well, you know me. I had kept fine, but my batting hadn't been great. I knew I had tried to score too quickly before getting myself in. As a result, my stats with the willow were not brilliant, and it was in the back of my mind that England might end the experiment the moment my feet hit the Tarmac at Heathrow, and turn elsewhere for the World Cup.

As we said our goodbyes, Freddie lingered for a moment.

'Nico, you've been brilliant for us,' he said, pumping my hand. 'You were just what we needed.'

After the way he had rolled his eyes at my Twenty20 speech, that felt good. It suggested I had won him over.

Fletcher was next to come my way.

'Well done, Nico,' the coach said, with a smile. Then he winked.

sixteen

REVERSE

Want to know about the trappings of international cricket? Try this. One morning shortly after returning from Australia, I woke up to find a beautiful, gleaming Volkswagen 4x4 on the street outside my front door. Well, that was very nice, but what was it doing there?

The vehicle, I discovered, was a perk of the sponsorship arrangement with the England team. After a few thousand miles, it could then be exchanged for another. *Don't mind if I do.*

Then there were the cheques; the steady, satisfying stream of cheques. After a couple of days back in the cold and grey of a Leicester February, £10,000 floated onto the mat from another sponsor. A few days on, another cheque for £15,000 arrived. Those sweet little slips of paper continued coming from different sources until I ended up with around £60,000 in bonus money for my first tour as a front-line England player.

I can't deny it was a pleasant way to be welcomed home – I was used to receiving no more than a couple of grand for wearing a certain brand of kit at county level – but the perks aren't everything. The cash doesn't take away the doubt. The cheques didn't stop me wondering if my lack of runs in Australia, which had been glossed over in the media due to our incredible series victory, were going to come back to nail me when the World Cup squad was put together.

The fear that it was all over lingered right up to the moment the squad was announced on 14 February, as I directed builders around my dust-covered dining room which was being readied for an extension. When the news came, I knew immediately that the wink from Fletcher had been the hint. It was pinch-myself time again. At the age of 36 and a bit, I was off to the World Cup!

Things were going better than I had dared hope and there was no way I could stop myself from looking forward to the Caribbean with big ambitions for English glory. After Australia, anything now seemed possible – and we did have at least one world-class matchwinner in the ranks. Watching Kevin Pietersen in the nets was to observe genius at work, a maestro who got into rhythm by batting a yard out of his crease and smashing our quickest bowlers on the up. There was an ego with Kevin, certainly, and at times you could sense some tension between him and Freddie as the team's two big guns. But he was meticulous in his preparation and the recipient of a lot of misguided crap in the media about his supposedly disruptive personality. Kevin wasn't a 'team man', according to some sages, but that piece of received wisdom just made me think back to New Year's Eve in Sydney Harbour, when most of the squad, Kevin included, had toasted the arrival of 2007 in the Flying Fish restaurant, while Freddie had hired a boat for himself and a few friends and separated himself from the group.

Differences aside, they were both indispensable players, of course. And if they clicked . . . Well, we could only hope.

The mood was upbeat as we landed in paradise. After the warm-up games, there was the opening ceremony and photocall in Jamaica, and an impromptu reunion with Brian Lara. Most of the teams were based in the same hotel, and as I strolled down the corridor before the event and passed an open door, Brian (with whom I shared an agent) caught my eye and called out: 'Nico, come on in . . .'

I entered his domain, chatted for a minute, and then turned to see a bronzed beauty stepping out of the shower, wearing a towel on her head and not much else. Lara flashed a big smile; I made my excuses and (very slowly) left.

The practice facilities at our St Lucia base were not so glamorous. Some of the outfields were strewn with potholes, and on one occasion we turned up to find the dressing rooms locked. But we were in good spirits and made the best of it.

We were stationed in a little boutique hotel on the beach, next door to the Australians' base. A few of the press were also there, which was a bit of a downer for Fletcher, as he was never completely relaxed when he knew that journalists were in the vicinity. But there were certain benefits, such as the early morning stretches on the shimmering sand as the Caribbean sun did its thing, and the sight of Michael Clarke's model girlfriend, Lara Bingle, oiling up in her bikini and then swimming out to a private island eighty metres away.

Our first match of the tournament, against New Zealand, did not begin well. We lost early wickets and found it difficult to raise the tempo. We were tottering on 138-7 when I was joined in the middle by Liam Plunkett. Seventy-one unbroken runs later and we had repaired some of the early damage wrought by Shane Bond and Scott Styris.

I loved batting with Liam. We had good, open communication and he was always positive with his talk. I had learned my lesson from Australia not to get anxious for runs too quickly, and the result was a nice, unbeaten knock of 42 from 41 balls. Our total of 209-7 was never going to be enough, though, and the Kiwis – Styris and Oram, mainly – knocked them off.

It wasn't the perfect start, but we knew an opening defeat was far from the end of the world and nobody was too down afterwards. The tournament was always more marathon than sprint, and even in that loss to the Kiwis there had been some decent personal performances which could be built on.

It was certainly going to take more than one measly defeat to knock me down from cloud nine. I had just posted my second-highest international score, I was a member of a happy and buzzing team environment on a heavenly island, I was part of a World Cup in my mid-thirties, and I'm sorry, I'll have to stop now, because there goes Lara Bingle again, gliding serenely through the ocean, and I have some urgent warm-downs to take care of.

Very nice indeed.

The calm before the storm.

After returning to our hotel following the New Zealand game, Vaughany mentioned going across the road for a Chinese. I agreed, and Colly was also keen, but by the time I joined them in the restaurant they were halfway through their meals. I had been waylaid in the hotel, talking to supporters, posing for photos, greeting somebody who claimed to know Dad, and making a quick call home to Jen. When I eventually pulled up a chair next to them in the restaurant and ordered a drink, their conversation had reached the subject of the press. Neither man seemed to have a good word to say about the English media.

'Lads,' I said, chipping in. 'I don't give a flying fuck what the press think or say.'

Colly raised an eyebrow. 'That is absolute bollocks, mate,' he snapped.

'I swear to you, I don't care,' I retorted. 'When I'm cleaning my teeth at night and looking in the mirror, I'll know if I've dropped a catch or played a shit shot. They'll write whatever they have to write, because that's their industry.'

'Yeah, but they could write it in a different way,' argued Colly.

'I think you're talking crap, Nico,' offered Vaughany.

The debate went on for a while, then we rose and left. As I went back into the hotel, a few of the other players were heading out: Jon Lewis, Jimmy Anderson, Ian Bell and Liam Plunkett. And Snapper, too, who had been invited to join the squad to pass on some of his psychological expertise – a great idea, I thought. Vaughany and Colly went off to their rooms and, still hungry, I returned to mine and ordered some room service. After eating, it was about 10.30 p.m. and I was still wide awake and buzzing. Bed was the last place I wanted to be. I didn't fancy the hotel bar, which was full of disappointed supporters, so I decided to hop back outside and set off in the direction where the other boys had been headed. I saw them in the first bar on the left, a place called Rumours.

Together, in jovial spirits, were Plunkett, Bell, Anderson, Lewis, and a few cricket journalists from the national papers. Our next game against Canada was a couple of days away and the atmosphere was merry. At the bar, oblivious to the main gathering, were Snapper and Freddie, locked in what appeared to be a deep and meaningful conversation. Snapper saw me and winked. 'Maybe he's getting through to him,' I pondered.

The other lads were in more boisterous mood. Jimmy kept reaching over and trying to kiss me, which was one of his daft habits after a couple of drinks. When a girl then appeared from behind the bar with a camera, requesting a group picture with the players, I volunteered to take it, mainly so I could wriggle free of Jimmy and his lecherous antics. As I pressed the button, the barmaid accidentally knocked Jon Lewis' drink down his shirt. The bowler pulled a silly face by way of response.

I had a couple of drinks there and a couple more in another lively bar down the road. A while later, I decided it was time to knock the evening on the head, so I walked back to the hotel, on my own, pausing to have a bit of banter with a few of the New Zealand players who were around the hotel swimming pool. We said our goodnights and I climbed into bed to the sound of the sea outside the window. It was not long after midnight and I still couldn't sleep, so I flicked on the TV. An hour later I switched it back off and drifted away. The next thing I heard was a thundering knock on my door.

As I bolted upright, I saw a note come flying into the room, under the door. I clambered out of bed and picked it up.

Duncan Fletcher requests that you come to the team room immediately.

I glanced at the clock. 8.00 a.m. I hurriedly climbed into my tracksuit, not bothering to find any undies or socks, and sped downstairs, wondering what was up. Had I got back too late? Were those four – I think it was four – Bacardi and Cokes a couple too many?

I opened the door to our team room; an expanse roughly twenty metres square and filled with gym equipment, medicine balls, protein powders and other paraphernalia. As I walked in, I noticed a bunch of chairs arranged in a horseshoe shape, with a flipchart set up at the head of the room. The other lads came in dribs and drabs and sat down. In the corner, splayed out on his back on a physio's bench, was Freddie. The big man looked barely conscious. He was wearing a singlet vest, a pair of long boarder shorts, and his lower legs were covered in sand. There was a pervading smell of Jack Daniels and Coke in the air. A few of the lads glanced at Freddie and winced as they took their chairs.

On the flipchart was a series of initials – the initials of every player. Next to the flipchart was a stern-faced Duncan Fletcher. Silence fell as he began to speak.

'There was an incident last night which we are not very proud of,' the coach announced. 'The first thing I'd like you to do is come forward, one by one, and tell the room what you did last night. And if you could also write down what time you got back to the hotel on the chart. Nico, can you go first please?'

I got to my feet, stepped forward and briefly recounted my evening's activities: the restaurant with Vaughany and Colly, the four Bacardi and Cokes in the bars, the encounter with the Kiwis in the hotel foyer. I apologised for having been out drinking at such a stage during a World Cup. Deep down, I knew it had probably been a bit too much. I said it wouldn't happen again, and then wrote my time on the chart.

'Thanks Nico, you can sit down,' said Fletch.

One by one, the players and staff walked to the front of the room, explained themselves, and added their times. When the ritual was complete, Fletcher spoke again. This time he looked furious.

'Right,' he exploded. 'The jokers here who think they can pull the wool over our eyes can think again. I asked security to write down all of your times when you got back to this hotel. So I know some of you haven't told the truth this morning.'

Several pairs of eyes stared straight ahead. It was a proper, headmasterly telling-off. Fletch then went on to explain that Freddie had commandeered a pedalo in the early hours of the morning, fallen off it and could quite easily have drowned in the sea. He had been stripped of the vice-captaincy, Fletch said.

Snapper, my new Leicestershire captain, was among the motionless group. He looked mortified. Freddie, meanwhile, remained flat out during the whole dressing-down, occasionally lifting his head with one eye half-open.

The meeting ended with a strict warning not to discuss it with the press, and to refer any questions to Andrew Walpole, our media officer. We spent the rest of the day walking around on eggshells. Later there was another meeting with the management, in which Freddie, now upright, apologised for his behaviour. Five of us – me, Anderson, Plunkett, Bell and Lewis

– were then told we were being fined, because a stance had to be taken. There had been no curfew, but a notional line was drawn at midnight and those of us who had returned after that time were punished. I was relieved of £1,500 from my pool money, and one or two of the other lads were docked a bit more.

Then the fun really began. The photo I had taken in the bar had somehow found its way onto a tabloid front page:

'BOOZE SHAME OF WORLD CUP STARS'

And then, to make things worse, the 'Fredalo' story broke in the *News of the World* and all hell broke loose.

We were shocked by what had gone on with Freddie. We knew that he was the sort of bloke who could wake up one morning with a brutal hangover and bowl at 90mph in the nets – that was why he was a national treasure and a player all our opponents feared. But we also sensed he had lost control this time, and hoped the controversy had brought him to his senses. We now know he was suffering with depression, but at the time we just felt he had gone too far off the rails.

As a team, it certainly focused minds. Going out for a beer can sometimes relieve the tension of being cooped up in your room on a long trip, but we were probably a bit over-giddy at the thought of being in a World Cup and had pushed things too far. Fletch had rightly aimed a rocket up our backsides. Freddie was dropped for the Canada game but the rest of us were challenged to prove our minds were back on the job by giving one of the minnow teams a hiding.

Before that game, our fielding drills were exceptional. Every player was as sharp as a tack, throwing down the single stump again and again without fail. Even the backroom staff had a fresh determination in their eyes. We were desperate for it and it was a proper relief when play began and we could start focusing on cricket again.

After Joyce and Vaughany had played nicely, I made 23 not out in a quick partnership with Colly and while Canada put up a reasonable fight, our total of 279 was never under threat. We achieved the comfortable win which we needed more than ever, and tried, against the prevailing media climate, to move on.

Bob Woolmer's sudden death made moving on impossible. When it was announced that the Pakistan coach had died in his hotel room in Jamaica, after Pakistan's incredible loss to Ireland, it cast a shadow over the rest of the tournament.

Bob was a big, engaging professor of cricket. I first encountered him during my early winters in Cape Town, enjoying regular barbecues at his beautiful house with some of the Warwickshire lads. I got to know him more intimately than I had hoped when he twisted his ankle on a long walk up the Stellenbosch mountains, obliging me to help carry him back down the hills, but he rewarded me and the other boys with a few big glasses of red wine when we got back to the house.

A lot of the lads knew Bob closely and were knocked for six by the news. Ian Bell, who described him as one of the biggest influences on his career, was in a terrible state.

No disrespect to Ireland, who had obviously played a blinder, but they should not have been able to beat Pakistan that day. And yet, as history has shown, it does not always pay to rely on Pakistan. There was some talk of match-fixing surrounding the game, with the suggestion that Bob's death was in some way connected to that. Unproven, of course, but I remember a few of the England lads sitting down to watch that game and saying to each other, 'This one could be interesting.' We had our suspicions. Lo and behold, the Irish came up trumps.

The investigation also seemed to raise more questions than answers. Why, for instance, were the Irish players on the same hotel floor as Bob not even spoken to by police officers afterwards, to find out what they might have seen or heard? At best, it was haphazard. At worst . . . well, we won't go there. It's impossible to know the truth of it but it leaves a very uncomfortable feeling, even now. At the time the tragedy left us sad and angry in equal measure.

Getting our minds back onto the World Cup wasn't easy. We wore black armbands in memory of Bob during our last group game against Kenya, which we won comfortably in front of a crowd full of Brits to secure our place in the Super 8s stage. Freddie was back in the team, and the tournament carried on, under a cloud.

In our first Super 8s game, we overcame the spirited Irish. It was in this match that I suffered my first dismissal in World Cup cricket: caught in the deep for a quick 19. I suppose the run had to end sooner or later. That result in the bag, we next faced the considerable challenge of Sri Lanka, at the Sir Viv Richards Stadium in Antigua. Before confronting Muralitharan and friends, though, we first had to confront an even bigger test. Our hotel on the island was an absolute dive, like a shabby B&B in Blackpool which hadn't been upgraded since the 1960s. Paint was peeling off the walls, and I even saw a rat in one of the rooms. So much for the trappings of international cricket.

Because we had finished second to the Kiwis in our group, we started the Super 8s halfway down the table. This meant we had to get some early victories on the board to give ourselves a chance of making the semi-finals. The Sri Lanka game was massive and our preparation was thorough. Fletch had identified the experienced opener, Sanath Jayasuriya, as our main target, assuming that if we got him early, it was game on.

When the match began, we gave him both barrels. Jayasuriya was the most fidgety player I have ever come up against, making even Graham Gooch resemble a picture of serenity between deliveries, and I quickly started chuntering in his ear about his little foibles. With the rest of the team also giving him plenty, he stuck around for 25 but then lost his castle to Saj Mahmood.

That pumped us up anew. We kept up a strong war of words with their remaining batsmen, with me as the ringleader, and restricted them to 235 – a decent score on a tricky pitch, but one that didn't scare us. We were happy enough and felt we could chase it down.

The reply stuttered when Vaughan and Joyce fell cheaply, but Bell and Pietersen repaired the damage and got us moving along nicely. But when those two tumbled in quick succession, Colly and then Freddie were on their way to the middle, and I was hurriedly padding up in the dressing room with Ravi Bopara, getting our minds on the challenge.

'How do you think you'll play Murali?'

'I don't know . . . sweeping might be a good option.'

'Yeah, I think you're right.'

On the floor I then spied a couple of black, rubber mats and recalled a tip from Alan Knott. 'Always look for things that can help you in your preparation,' he had once advised. Well, a ball will jump off one of those mats, I reckoned – perfect for creating some exaggerated spin. So we set up a small area of the dressing room as an impromptu net and I gave Ravi some throws with a tennis ball, which dutifully spat off the rubber at a sharp angle.

'I'm going to look for one into midwicket against Murali,' I said, mid-throw. 'But if it's turning too much, I'm going to reverse him.'

Ten minutes later, Ravi was on his way out. Freddie had fallen. In a matter of moments, Colly went too. I gathered my bat and set off for the middle. Things were happening quickly. But before the rubber mat duo could come together again, I had to pass through an unusual guard of honour.

'Your mother's a fucking whore!'

'You're a fucking old cunt, Nixon!'

'We'll break your fucking fingers, you fucking arsehole!'

'You're going to throw it away for your fucking country and you're going to look a fucking idiot!'

I had never known a barrage like it. The Sri Lankan fielders were piling into me like a pack of wild animals! When the verbal assault subsided, it was down to Ravi and me to rebuild our crumbling innings. We were 133-6.

Early on, Ravi tried to play a few awkward offside shots. 'Come on,' I admonished him. 'We've talked about our gameplan – don't change it now.' He nodded, went back to Plan A, and creamed the next few balls. He soon looked at ease against Lasith Malinga's slingy action. I wasn't so comfortable with Malinga, but felt confident against the spinners. When Murali started bowling to me, I noticed straight away that the boundary to my offside was quite short. I gathered my thoughts and my options, activated my mental routines, and . . .

Come on, take Murali down, hit him out of the ground, look at that short boundary, you really fancy this, go for your shots, remember the reverse-sweep, what about a reverse-sweep in the air for six, come on, look at that boundary, it's obvious . . .

What was this? Positivity? Well, that was a new one, but no. I couldn't. I thanked the little man for his input, focused my mind afresh and opted to milk the bowling for a while.

Dealing with Murali's incredible turn was always a challenge, but more so, I believed, for right-handed batsmen. We left-handers are used to the ball turning sharply away from us, because of the rough that commonly appears outside our off stump. It's a different kettle of fish for right-handers, who aren't so often tested by off-spin spitting in to them at a right-angle.

Yes, Murali could rip it further than most, but I found that I could cope. I picked off a few comfortable singles and a nice couple of fours and we steadily ate away at our target. After bringing up our fifty partnership, we got it down to a gettable 29 from fifteen deliveries. By then, I knew it was time to go big, but I was at the wrong end to reverse it over the short boundary. This one was much longer. Having said that, the wind was with me, and we would have to get cracking sooner or later.

I decided that there was no time like the present. Murali jogged in and bowled. I shifted into position for the reverse-sweep, got my weight into it and connected like a dream. It sailed over the rope for six. The English fans went crackers. I could see people leaping up and down and a few sunburnt figures splashing around in a pool.

Ravi walked towards me with a slightly bemused look on his face. 'Fucking hell, where did that come from?!'

I went back to the crease and thought about doing the very same to the next ball. But Murali, who despised being hit for six, brought a fielder in at short third-man. That made the big reverse a bit too risky. So instead, when he fired the next one in a bit quicker, I used the pace of the ball to flick it more delicately over the fielder for four.

Ten runs off two balls brought the target right down. We were getting there. But then, in Malinga's next over, disaster. I went through a shot too early and toe-ended his slower ball to Mahela Jayawardene at mid-on. Out for 42 with victory in sight. Nightmare. 'You can win this, Ravi,' I said, walking off – and he got so close, taking it to the last ball, from which three runs were needed.

Dilhara Fernando ran in and feigned his delivery, failing to let go of the ball. Back in the pavilion, with my pads still on, I was willing Ravi to pull out of the next one himself, to give a bit back to the bowler. But he was too sporting for that. When Fernando finally bowled, Ravi swung and missed and his bails went airborne.

We were as devastated as our opponents were jubilant. Afterwards, everyone was in a state of disbelief that the game had come back within our grasp and then slipped away again. The chances were that our World Cup hopes had gone with it.

My signature shot against Murali sparked a new surge of media interest, and a couple of days later I was invited to Sky Sports' house on the beach. I was greeted by Bob Willis and David Gower and then asked to offer a masterclass in the art of the reverse-sweep. It was a good laugh, if a bit surreal, but I couldn't stop thinking about that Sri Lanka game. It felt like the stuffing had been knocked out of us and I struggled to sleep for the next couple of nights.

Next, as luck would have it, was Australia. This obliged us to stay in the same Barbados hotel as our old foes, and one morning before battle I stepped into the lift with Jen (our wives and girlfriends had flown out to join us in Antigua) to find Andrew Symonds already there, accompanied by his girlfriend.

'Symo, how you doing, bud?' I said.

No response.

'Symo, you good, mate?'

No response.

Symonds continued staring at the floor, declining to return my gaze and barely registering my presence. Mind games? Or had I really pissed him off with that stuff about the scorecard in Sydney? Surely not. As we stepped out of the lift in silence, I was none the wiser.

The game failed to go to plan, as Ponting and Clarke put us to the sword in front of Prince Harry and his girlfriend Chelsy. This again left us scrambling to stay alive. We scrapped our way to a victory against Bangladesh, which I sealed with another big six, but we were surviving by the skin of our teeth. Then South Africa put us out of our misery.

The kill was short and painful. Andrew Hall took 5-18 and Graeme Smith blasted us out of the World Cup in less than 20 overs. The dressing room afterwards was mostly silent as we packed up our gear. We felt numb.

The South Africa loss triggered Duncan Fletcher's resignation. During practice at the Police Ground in Barbados a couple of days before our final, dead-rubber game against the West Indies, the coach called us into a huddle and broke the news with tears in his eyes. It was almost as though he didn't want to go, but he had to. There was a feeling that the press had pushed him, which was ridiculous, but his mind was made up. When he stopped speaking, he properly broke down and we gathered to console him.

When Vaughany later nominated me to give the team-talk in the huddle before the game started, I spoke from the heart. I talked about how we had underachieved and how it was one final chance to perform for everyone who had backed and believed in us. That included our leader. 'There's a great bloke in there who is sadly not going to be in his job much longer and he has given everything for English cricket,' I said. 'Let's win it for Fletch.'

The West Indies match happened to be the farewell game of another giant, with the Kensington Oval packed to the rafters for the Brian Lara tribute show. When he walked out to bat, we formed a guard of honour, and the party was proceeding very nicely for the host nation as Lara made his way to 18 without any trouble. Then the script was torn up, as Marlon Samuels ran him out.

As the legend walked off for the last time, and a stunned stadium took stock of the situation, I wasted no time in reminding Samuels of what he had just done. He looked aghast at having played a role in Lara's premature end, and responded in the only way that would have spared him a public lynching – by playing as though his life depended on it. He belted his way to 50 from 37 balls on a dream of a pitch and looked like he might bat us into smithereens. He was going along like a man possessed, and it quickly became obvious that we needed to remove him as soon as possible.

Then I remembered something.

In between the Commonwealth Bank Series and the World Cup, I had been invited onto the Sky Sports show *Soccer AM* to talk about, among other things, my love of Carlisle United, and sledging. While debating the latter topic, somebody mentioned a brilliant comment a darts player had once made in order to psyche out an opponent. Before throwing, Player One asked Player Two whether he breathed in or out at the moment he released the dart.

It was a work of genius. You actually can't avoid thinking about it.

Always look for things that can help you . . .

For some reason, this clever little technique popped into my head when I was thinking of ways to disrupt Samuels' flow.

'Hey Marlon,' I said. 'Do you breathe in or breathe out when you hit the ball?'

The very next ball, he played a complete mess of a shot, lobbing one of Vaughany's looping off-breaks straight to Colly. Good darts!

The West Indies eventually bowed out on 300 with a ball to spare. Then, in a grandstand finish, we knocked them off. During an anxious stage of our chase, KP smashed Jerome Taylor for an enormous six to bring up a magnificent hundred. 'OK, Kev, that's six,' I said, after he had milked the crowd. 'Just follow that with a few singles and it's been an amazing over.' He took one look at me and then tried to hit the next ball even further. His stumps were separated.

At the business end, it came down to me and Broad, Leicestershire old and Leicestershire young. I pinged Corey Collymore for three boundaries in four deliveries, before Dwayne Bravo bamboozled me with a slower ball that I'm still searching for now. I walked off in a daze, but then Broady nervelessly clobbered the winning runs and I galloped back on to embrace him.

I was sweating like nobody's business, but I couldn't help noticing that the young pretender was as cool as a cucumber. It was impossible not to be impressed by the man.

Very quickly the Broady and Nico show again became the Brian Lara show. After a lap of honour, the icon briefly appeared in our dressing room, shook a few hands and signed some shirts before being whisked away. When I sat down, and the commotion started to fade, it began to dawn on me . . .

This could be the end for you, too.

I desperately hoped it wasn't, but there was no point in deluding myself. *It might be over, here and now. Don't let it pass you by.*

So I reached for my bag, fished out my handheld video camera, flicked off the lens cap and pressed record.

seventeen

NEW BEGINNINGS

The ball is short and juicy outside off stump. The wicketkeeper-batsman cuts it merrily for four to bring up his hundred. He removes his helmet, kisses the face of his bat and accepts the ovation from all corners of Lord's. A century on Test debut at the home of cricket. The stuff of dreams!

The stuff of my dreams!

Except someone else was living them.

Ever since I had sat with Tony by the scoreboard during my groundstaff days, my fantasy had been crystal-clear. I would get a hundred for England at Lord's and it would be bloody brilliant. That summer of 2007, the dream came true down to every last detail but one. The bloke enjoying the moment of his life was Matt Prior, not Paul Nixon.

Deep down, I suspected my short England career might be over the second they chose Sussex's Peter Moores to replace Fletch as coach. Even though I was receiving plenty of positive press after the World Cup, a new regime probably meant one thing. But it didn't stop me dreaming, or hoping. Possession is nine-tenths of the law, after all; I felt an integral part of the unit, the selectors had shown faith in me through Australia and the Caribbean, and was that not the very same Peter Moores who had given me a breezy 'well done' after a game early in the '07 season?

Maybe, maybe . . .

No such luck. I was named in a 25-man squad for the summer series against the West Indies and India, but the word was that Moores wanted a fresh approach, and that fresh approach was likely to mean the player he knew well from Hove. I learned the news that they had gone for Prior for the 17 May First Test while I was at Keswick Cricket Club in Cumbria, hosting a black-tie dinner for my benefit year. There was no phone call from England, no hard luck message and no offer of an explanation. It just came out in the media and that was that. It didn't feel like the right way to find out, but I certainly wasn't the first player to be left a little deflated by the ECB's communications. Once you are out, you are out.

Fair enough – I had enjoyed my taste. I went into the ODI side on a high and in good form, and came out on a high and in good form. At 36, the fact they had decided to move on without me wasn't going to tear me to pieces. I had my memories, on my camcorder and in my head. And if England were going to proceed without a backward glance, I had no choice but to do the same.

Other things cushioned the blow as I came back down to earth. The benefit was certainly an enjoyable diversion after the end of my international career. It was launched at the Walkers Stadium in Leicester, hosted by Willie Thorne before an audience of nearly 500 and was followed by a whirlwind of appearances and functions, notably the cricket and football event at Keswick, which featured the unlikely sight of Martin Johnson, the giant of Leicester and England rugby, going into soccer battle with Carlisle United players and the stars of *Emmerdale* (not many were keen to tackle him, oddly enough) and then a golf day at Woburn, a cricket match against the Lashings team, a celebrity poker competition, a dinner at the posh Hurlingham Club in London, a Christmas lunch in the Long Room at Lord's and plenty more besides (I was also allowed to have an ECB logo on my brochure, a little badge of prestige available only to those who have played for England).

It was chaos, but brilliantly organised chaos, thanks to a first-rate committee headed by Brian Groves, the former Leicestershire chairman. We raised about £250,000 and gave more than £30,000 to our charities: the Great North Air Ambulance, who had flown to my father-in-law's aid during his fateful fell walk; and Movers & Shakers, a Parkinson's charity (Jen's mum, Christine, was suffering from the disease).

The response from the public and from cricket was fantastic, and not just towards the benefit. I had returned from the World Cup with a buzz around me and more people than ever seemed to want to associate with me. I was asked to do the half-time draw at Brunton Park (allowing me to boast that I had at last been cheered by the Carlisle United faithful), people at Grace Road were quick to slap my back (including one or two who had been less inclined to do so before) and when the season started, opponents were full of warmth. It was as though I had been a flag-carrier for all those journeymen who wonder if their country will ever take notice of them. It felt like I had given them a bit of hope. I liked that.

I also liked what international cricket had done for my mind. The moment I had reclaimed my things from the baggage carousel at Heathrow I had just wanted to carry on playing. Facing world-class bowlers had sharpened me up no end and in the first few weeks back it felt like the average county trundler was easier to face. I felt as good as I had ever felt, my head was clear, my thoughts were diamond-sharp – *Come on, bowl at me, bowl at me* – and the runs piled up accordingly.

Then life started to get even more interesting.

Halfway through the 2007 season, I was asked to take over from Darren Robinson as Leicestershire's four-day captain. This was the first unexpected development of a strange year. Captaincy had not come easily to Darren, a bright and talented guy but one who seemed to be taken aback by the heavy demands of the job. He was a naturally gifted player, but the weight of the world rested on his shoulders when the team's form – and his own – had failed to lift. Darren, who had joined us from Essex in 2004, could be a volatile man who was not oblivious to the red mist, and there were times when you feared he might punch somebody's lights out, or just give up cricket for good.

If captaincy wasn't for him, I wasn't sure whether it was for me, either, but when Tim Boon asked me if I fancied taking on the job for the remaining couple of months of the season, I could hardly say no. I was experienced and felt I had plenty to give, and if things didn't pick up much for the team from that point onwards, I turned out a couple of nice hundreds and was starting to thrive on the challenge of leadership. And when Tim and David Smith, the chief executive, sat me down at the end of the summer and laid the future on the line . . .

'Nico, I hope you realise this is going to be the most frustrating time of your life.'

. . . it still felt more like a challenge than a problem. I signed a three-year deal to be Leicestershire's captain in all competitions and went home feeling excited about where it might lead.

Never meet your heroes, they say. They'll only let you down, they say. Bollocks, I say. When I watched Carlisle United in my youth, one of my favourite players was Chris Balderstone, a princely midfielder who also happened to be a first-rate batsman for Leicestershire. Chris made history in 1975 by playing professional football and cricket on the same day; turning out for Leicestershire in the morning and afternoon, pulling on his boots for Doncaster Rovers in the evening, then coming back the next morning to complete a century. Later, he became an umpire, and often brought his old Carlisle scrapbooks to Grace Road to show me. I was like a pig in muck looking through his old reports and photos.

I was actually less in awe of Viv Richards when I threw to him on the groundstaff in the summer of '88. I was too young and just too up for it that I didn't fully take it all in. But I never forgot the experience. And nor, to my surprise, did Sir Viv.

In the autumn of 2007 I flew to Grenada for an over-35s tournament. Organised by Allan Lamb and Nigel Felton, it pitted an old England XI against a team of West Indies veterans: Haynes, Croft, Greenidge, Logie, Richards and Joel Garner, the Bajan giant who drank half a bottle of rum before loping in to bowl.

After the game, Felts suggested we go into the West Indies dressing room. As we did, that familiar, smiling figure sprang to his feet . . .

'Nico, come and grab a beer and sit down.'

He led, I followed.

We exchanged a high-five and clinked bottles. 'You know, man,' Viv said, 'I followed your career ever since you were a young kid at Lord's and I never forgot the passion and energy you had. You wanted to throw to me more than anyone else . . . I knew you would play for England and I was so pleased when you did. I should have got in touch with you sooner but I'm pleased we can have this conversation now.'

I was choking back tears as he spoke. That conversation with Viv, in that dressing room – it was a haven, a place I could have lingered for hours. It made me feel warm inside. Calm.

The storms would come later.

But first, another adventure. Dave, my agent, was enthusiastic when he called. 'There's this new Twenty20 tournament starting in India,' he explained. 'And there's a chance we can get you in there. Do you fancy it?'

He laid out the details. Its name was the Indian Cricket League, a tournament of just six teams, which entailed a handful of games in the space of a few weeks and offered serious money to anyone taking part. Every team required five experienced, overseas players to mentor the young locals, there was lucrative backing from Zee Entertainment Enterprises, a huge media company in India, and it was intended to be a very big deal.

The big deal for me was that I could earn the equivalent of my annual Leicestershire salary, plus bonuses, in a tiny fraction of the normal time. Did I fancy it? Bloody right I did! I threw my hat into the ring, resulting in a deal with the Delhi Jets, in a squad of twenty players including four other imports – Shane Bond, Niall O'Brien, Dale Benkenstein and Marvan Atapattu – and a cluster of Indian hopefuls.

I had been to India before, on the England A tour and on pre-season trips with Leicestershire, and I thought I knew what it was all about. Wrong. India in the grip of Twenty20 fever is a different place to normal India. When I arrived in Delhi it was as though the place was on steroids, morning, noon and night. Almost from the moment we landed we were hurled into a never-ending programme of PR commitments to push the Delhi brand. We visited shopping malls and schools and conducted TV interviews by the dozen. We travelled around in a Delhi Jets bus to the sight of kids pouring onto the streets to greet us. When the press conferences began, it felt like there were a hundred cameras present.

The opening ceremony took place in Mumbai and was conducted with full-on razzmatazz. As fireworks popped and dancers gyrated, Subhash

Chandra, the founder of Zee TV, told the excited thousands how big it was going to be. Tony Greig was involved as one of its founders and among the other players who had signed up were Brian Lara, Chris Cairns, Damien Martyn, Ian Harvey and Inzamam-ul-Haq – seriously big names. It was impossible not to get swept along by the glamour.

Home for me and my overseas colleagues was a four-star hotel in Delhi, and this allowed me to renew acquaintances with Dale Benkenstein. I had known Benky since meeting him on a pre-season trip to South Africa, and had since locked horns with him plenty of times in England. We tried to get him to Leicestershire many years back but he ended up at Durham and soon rose to legendary status. He was a serious professional and a man I respected immensely. Along with the rest of the imports, we bonded straight away.

The young Indian players, meanwhile, were full of enthusiasm, and none more animated than the keeper, Dishant Yagnik. He quickly became my little shadow, following me around and constantly asking for tips. It was like me with Alan Knott all those years back and I enjoyed the responsibility of being his mentor. And we were all mentors, we senior players. Our coach was the former India all-rounder Madan Lal, but I use the term loosely; Madan was as keen as mustard but a bit old-school in his methods. 'Try harder' seemed to be his main motivational message. He didn't really embrace modern thinking, but that was where we could come in. Team meetings started by Madan would invariably be taken over by Benky, Bond and me, and the Indian lads, who had great natural ability but didn't have much understanding of game plans and communication, all hoovered up our wisdom.

Essentially, it was a happy time and the schedule was not exactly gruelling. We would play a game and then, in the knowledge that our next match was five days away, set up camp in the hotel bar and live like kings. The next day we would sweat out the indulgence with a gym and pool session, before building up to the following game. Some days it felt like there wasn't much to do other than walk around the nearest shopping mall, but your spirits would lift every time you looked up and saw a massive Delhi Jets poster, with all the lads' faces smiling back. The posters were everywhere.

The tournament itself was how you imagined cricket in the future would be played. Think of a modern-day England tour, with all the luxuries money could buy, then enhance it some more, and that was the ICL. We had massage therapists, strength and conditioning coaches, video analysts, you name it. The broadcasters were all over it, too, with players miked up and overhead cameras sailing down a wire to follow a bowler as he ran in. It was basically a much more elaborate version of English Twenty20, with games subjected to massive build-up.

We threw ourselves into it and I made a couple of match-winning contributions with the bat and the gloves, helping us reach the semi-finals, a clash with the Chandigarh Lions under the floodlights at Panchkula. I sat that one out, and watched Chris Cairns and Andrew Hall see us off with two balls to spare – an agonising fall at the last hurdle. But for me the blow was softened by the fact we had such an enjoyable time getting there. The healthy pay packet for a few short weeks of fun was another welcome cushion which made the thought of going back even more appealing. I didn't give a moment's thought to the idea that it might just have been a little too good to be true.

For one reason or another, times had become hard at Grace Road and the club had tried to adjust accordingly. Young players had been given more opportunities, instead of big-name signings we could no longer afford. There had also been a deliberate move, under the control of the chairman, Neil Davidson (we'll be meeting him again, later) in the direction of hiring Kolpak players. These were foreigners, often South Africans, who carried EU passports, and as such were not included in a club's two-man quota of overseas signings. Leicestershire were one of the first counties to exploit the new ruling and came in for criticism as a result, much of it harsh.

In the short-term, we were flooding the squad with players who weren't English, but there was method in the madness. In place was a five-year plan, by which the club would reduce the number of experienced Kolpak players each year, as our young hopefuls became more battle-hardened. The theory was that a good blend would be created and new foundations laid, so the club could rise again. 'But in the short-term,' Davidson said, 'we want to compete.'

It was hard to disagree. Tim had a wide network of contacts and knew he could bring in people he trusted, and Gordon Parsons, now based in Potchefstroom, had been another great ally in identifying South African players who could help. Claude Henderson, our first Kolpak, had helped us win the Twenty20 Cup but had also begun sharing some of the secrets of spin bowling with the emerging Jigar Naik. HD Ackerman, from Cape Town, had scored runs aplenty but had also mentored the likes of James Taylor and Josh Cobb, helping the latter through the nervous nineties to his maiden century at Lord's.

In 2008, my first full summer as captain, I scored 954 Championship runs, the second-best return of my career. I was also incredibly proud to be captain and made sure I walked out for the toss at every ground in my Leicestershire blazer and cap. Leading the team out at Lord's, after shaking hands with a few old groundstaff faces, like the groundsman, Mike Hunt, was a moment to treasure like few others. And the thought of nurturing our exciting new wave of young players was increasingly stimulating. But for every benefit, there was a challenge.

When I think of HD Ackerman, two pictures form in my mind. The first is of the virtuoso player who should have played more than four Tests for South Africa; the bright and astute guy who had inherited his father's incredible cricket knowledge, helped my own game considerably over the years and has since become a great friend. The second is of a sometimes difficult customer.

HD, who had captained us in 2005, was the sort who needed to be kept in the loop about everything, all the time, because he could get pissed off very quickly. And when HD disagreed with you during a game, he had a way of organising his body language in a way that would inform not just you of his opinion, but the entire ground. When I needed him to come and have a quiet word, he would shout his views across the field. It took me a while to figure out that HD captained every game in his own mind.

His passion, too, was undeniable, but sometimes it overflowed. One of our typical pre-match warm-up routines was to play touch rugby on the outfield. This was a ritual HD loved, but one he took more seriously than most. Before a match in Cardiff, such a game was in full swing with the younger lads, as usual, throwing themselves around exuberantly and failing to observe certain rules. When HD saw someone failing to go back five yards in this particular game, he wasn't impressed. And when the placid and friendly Dillon Du Preez loitered deliberately offside for a couple of seconds too long, HD ran up and booted the ball at him from point-blank range.

He was absolutely livid and I thought things were going to come to blows. It didn't, thankfully, but I couldn't get that image out of my head as I drove home that night. *All that, over a game of touch rugby!* Towards the end of my captaincy, worrying about HD became a regular feature of my car journeys. I would drive to Grace Road thinking about him, and then drive away thinking about him. He was a magnificent player but managing his moods could be exhausting.

As captain, I was keen to bring back a few traditions that had served Leicestershire well during the good times, such as the prestige that came with having your club cap and blazer. Receiving your cap is supposed to be one of your proudest days as a cricketer; I had never forgotten the feeling when I accepted mine from Nigel Briers in 1992. I saw that little embroidered fox as a mark of what I had earned. People around the county circuit (umpires in particular) loved those great old customs and I wanted us to embrace them again, but this was easier said than done. Some of the lads were issued with caps that didn't fit, and when I took this up with the management I was informed that they were too expensive to replace. When I found myself lending mine to my wicketkeeping understudy Tom New, just so he could enjoy the kudos of having a club cap on his head, I felt uneasy. It would never have happened ten years earlier.

A bigger frustration unfolded one morning when I drove into Grace Road to see our chief executive David Smith out in the middle with Andy, our groundsman. 'What's going on there?' I wondered.

It later transpired that they were discussing which pitch we should use for the next game. I had made it clear that I wanted slow, turning pitches, because we had one experienced spinner (Claude) and another up-and-coming one (Jigar), both of whom were capable of doing more damage than our raw seam attack. I also thought our young batters would be able to find some form on a surface that didn't zip through quite so quickly.

When I found that my request had been overruled, and that Smith had apparently decided we were to play on a green 'result' pitch, alarm bells started ringing. Tim, as coach, was a man I always had time for, but he didn't side with me on this, and the upshot was a nagging feeling that we weren't operating as a unit, from captain to coach to chief exec. Results were bearing this out and it really pissed me off. I felt my authority as captain was being attacked, and it wasn't the end of the friction.

From an early stage in our marriage, Jen and I had often talked about having kids, but by 2006 nothing had happened. This led us to try IVF. When that didn't work, we tried a different kind of IVF. This time – success! Isabella Rose Nixon entered the world at 4.30 a.m. on 13 May 2008. The records say I scored 79 for Leicestershire against Northamptonshire in a Championship match the next day, but I could just as easily have created a new mode of dismissal: Asleep Before Wicket. When I made my way out into the middle I was walking on air but running on empty. I have never felt so happy and so knackered at the same time. At one point at the non-striker's end, I took my helmet off, put my hands on my head and felt that it would be very, very nice just to fall asleep on the spot. I was a proper nodding dog, constantly fighting the temptation to drift off, and more or less batting by instinct.

It was a very pleasant kind of tiredness after a long and hard journey.

The process of IVF sets all kinds of unexpected challenges. Biting your tongue when you are around young families is one. All of a sudden you regard other people as very blasé about their kids and have to fight the urge to be very bitter. Then there were the physical and emotional hardships for Jen. At the start, her hormones were shut down, before being brought back with double the force thanks to an absolute battery of drugs. This knocked her sideways and at times she didn't know whether she was Arthur or Martha. On other occasions she would wake up in the middle of the night, or drop fast asleep in the middle of the day. She would also get very emotional without warning; during one tea interval at Grace Road she called me in floods of tears, but when I tried to calm her down it just led to more confusion:

'Hey, come on, what's wrong?'

'I don't know!'

My own role in the procedure was comparatively simple. I had to produce a sperm sample and hand it over to the Assisted Conception Unit at Leicester Royal Infirmary. Piece of cake? You would have thought so. When the morning came around, I produced the goods and then set off for the hospital. First lesson – never underestimate the power of a hospital car park to drive you around the bend. It took me forever to locate a parking space, and by the time I found somewhere to pull in I was starting to run late. I grabbed my little pot of magic from the passenger seat and dashed around the building, eventually bolting through the doors and striding briskly to the desk.

'Hello, I'm Mr Nixon,' I announced with a smile as I proudly offered my afternoon's work to the girl behind the desk. 'I've brought this in for you.' The girl accepted my test tube and looked at it quizzically for a few seconds.

'Well, that's very generous of you, Mr Nixon,' she replied, battling the urge to smile. 'Unfortunately, there's not much we can do with it here. But if you'd like to walk fifty yards up to the left and drop it into the Assisted Conception Unit, I'm sure they will help you out.'

As she handed the tube back to me, I looked around. On the wall was a sign: PATHOLOGY. Lord knows what they would have done with it. Anyway, the confusion was cleared and we then had to sit tight for two weeks to learn if the treatment had worked.

Two weeks? Try two years! It felt like forever and I can only compare those fourteen endless days to the act of standing on a platform for a train, and waiting, and waiting and waiting.

Our train never came in. Two days before the results were due, Jen's dad, David, died. When we then found out that Jen wasn't pregnant, it really knocked us back and left us low for a while. Life could be seriously cruel, sometimes.

It took a while to pick ourselves up from two of the worst pieces of news you could ever receive, but time being a healer, we eventually rallied around and the following year we found out about a different treatment. We did our homework and resolved to give it another go.

This, again, required a sample. This, again, wasn't without its obstacles. The first was the doctor's order to stay off the booze for a couple of days so that my sperm count wouldn't be affected. Well, nice idea, Doc, but two days before I was due to give my sample I enjoyed my first win as Leicestershire captain. Naturally, this had to be celebrated, so I invited everyone back to the house and got the champagne out. As the drinks started flowing, Jen whispered in my ear:

'Just be careful what you're doing. Don't forget Monday.'

I nodded and pledged that I wouldn't do anything silly, but a couple of hours later her warning had fallen by the wayside as I participated in a drinking contest involving a Swiss Ball and a four-pint funnel. Jen watched this with increasing displeasure.

'I'm not doing this IVF just so you can piss everything up the wall.'

Eventually the party stopped and I stumbled up to bed.

Then there was the obstacle at the clinic – the grainy, black-and-white obstacle in the cubicle masquerading as 1960s pornography. I did my thing against all the odds (memo to the NHS: invest in some new gentlemen's magazines urgently) and it was while keeping wicket at Grace Road some weeks later that I looked to the boundary to see an animated Tim Boon gesturing something to me.

I looked closer. It was a thumbs-up sign. That was our signal. It meant Jen's blood test results had arrived. I felt my heart leap and start to rattle until the interval came around, at which point I dashed off the field and called Jen. The news was good. Our train had come in!

Jen's pregnancy was mainly an enriching experience, except for the antenatal classes, which were a bit too touchy-feely for this farmer's boy ('Ah, we'll get on with it, I'm sure we'll survive'), and she was amazing throughout her five-hour labour. When she was on the gas and air she gripped my hand so tightly I thought my wrist was going to snap. She was focused and determined beyond belief and I was so proud of her. And when I then held little Izzy for the first time my mind went into overdrive:

I would kill for this little thing.

I can't wait for our journey together.

I hope her childhood is as happy as mine.

Lucky girl – all that fun in front of you!

I thought of how nice it would have been if Granddad, who had died ten years earlier, had been alive to see her. I thought of how nice it would be when Mum and Dad came to see her; I thought it was a shame that they wouldn't be able to do this at the same time.

I also thought of the close bond Jen had enjoyed with David, and hoped I could have the same with Isabella when she grew up. I was feeling all sorts of things, really; nostalgic and emotional, happy and sad; and then, at random, a line from a favourite Beverley Craven song popped into my mind:

'Everything she's going through will be her memories.'

Why was that one a favourite? Because it's exactly what life should be about. Your memories are the things you treasure the most, the things that keep you going along your journey. The things I would now be able to share with the little bundle of joy I was cradling in my arms.

I still shudder to think about how close I came to ruining all this.

eighteen

STORMS

October 2008.

'OK, guys, who's winning this one?'
  No reply.
  'Come on, guys, who's getting the diamonds and the watches today?'
  No reply.
  'Who's going to be a millionaire, boys?'
  No reply.
  It's almost like they don't understand!

Not long after the ICL came into being, the Indian Premier League was also
born. One competition was officially recognised by the International Cricket
Council, and one wasn't. The ICL wasn't. Before the second tournament,
in 2008, attempts were made to marginalise it. The Board of Control for
Cricket in India (BCCI) refused to authorise it, while back home, the ECB
started issuing warnings to any English player who was considering signing
up to the 'rebel' league. The thrust was that we might no longer be allowed
to play for our counties and I might lose my registration as a result.

One problem, guys. I had signed a three-year deal to play in the
tournament and was also captain of Leicestershire. It started to get very
messy. The previous year five ICL players had won a court battle with the
ECB but the problems didn't go away, and with others in the same boat,
there was talk of further legal cases being mounted.

At Grace Road, though, David Smith and Tim Boon eventually gave
me the green light to go back to India. They were concerned about the
implications but, as things rumbled on without a clear solution, they
didn't feel there were any grounds for standing in my way as things stood.

So off I went again.

But the 2008 tournament was different. The Delhi Jets were now the
Delhi Giants, and one or two players had changed, but those were the
superficial differences. There was something else; a certain atmosphere
hanging over some of the games. A feeling that things maybe weren't

as wholesome as they had seemed in the beginning. Then there was the strange business of 26 October.

That was the date of our meeting with the Lahore Badshahs, a team flushed with Pakistan internationals, in the city of Gurgaon on Delhi's outskirts. Right from the outset it was a little, well, unusual.

Lahore won the toss and batted first. Bond sent down the first over, and Taduri Sudhindra the second, but it was what developed afterwards that alarmed. The batsmen's running between the wickets became increasingly haphazard. The openers, Imran Nazir and Imran Farhat, grew increasingly frantic and the others followed in similar fashion, giving run-out chances aplenty. I know Twenty20 is a more frantic game than the other formats but this seemed a bit more chaotic than normal. At one stage during the Keystone Kops performance I looked towards Atapattu at first slip: 'Marvan, this is absolute carnage.' He just smiled back at me.

The game continued in the same, weird manner. Our main spinner was a young Indian called Ali Murtaza, who was an accurate enough left-armer but not exactly Shane Warne. When he came on to bowl, most of our fielders duly filed back to the edge of the thirty-yard circle, offering the batsmen singles instead of inviting boundaries. But when Ali bowled, the Lahore batsmen routinely defended his deliveries and declined to run.

In no time, the spinner became lethal. With world-class batters seemingly unable to figure out his offerings, which were keeping a bit low but barely turning a millimetre, he ended with four wickets for seven runs from his four overs.

That's right: 4/0/7/4. Astonishing figures for a Twenty20 game. He had tied them in knots! Hadn't he? I started laying it on thick from behind the stumps as Lahore, aided by a classy 67 from Azhar Mahmood, set us 148 to win, but not before some other unusual things had occurred. In stark contrast to Ali Murtaza's success was JP Yadav, a skilful swing bowler who in our previous game had bowled yorkers to order at the death. This time, he served up a disappointing diet of waist-high full-tosses, long-hops and other very hittable balls. He saw his four overs taken for 45 runs, and when one of his deliveries was hit behind square and then aimed at the stumps by a fielder, he made no effort to back up at his end. The ball scooted past. I put my hands on my head and looked at him. He barely glanced back, and said nothing.

Lahore's defence then threw up yet more oddities. When their spinners came on, for example, there was no fielder positioned behind square on the leg-side – no protection, in other words, against the leg-side rubbish that was duly served up. We set about our chase without too many dramas, but not before Inzamam-ul-Haq, their captain, had brought himself on, sending down a couple of overs of filth and one wicket-taking delivery, when he had our match-winner, Syed Abbas Ali, stumped for 52.

We survived that surprise and I came out to help us win the game with an over and a half to spare, but I couldn't get all this strange stuff out of my head; the field placings, Murtaza's golden spell, Inzamam joining the attack. I had never seen Inzamam bowl before.

Afterwards, as we moved around our dressing room and started to get changed, the door crashed open and a huge, red-faced figure piled in. It was, unmistakably, Tony Greig. 'Right,' he barked, slamming the door behind him. 'You lot sit down.'

We all sat down.

'What I've just witnessed out there is absolutely disgraceful,' he roared. 'Now listen to me. There are some very good people in this dressing room, and they know who they are. And there is some scum in this dressing room, and they know who they are.'

He continued this *tour de force* for another couple of minutes.

'Let me tell you now – there are anti-corruption people here, and if I see, or hear, or find out anything that has gone on, and we have proof, then you are on the first plane out of here. Do you hear me?'

We remained silent.

'I am absolutely livid about what I've seen,' he concluded. 'And I'm going into their dressing room as well.'

He barged out, giving the door another slam. Nobody said anything for a few seconds. Then Madan Lal stood up and took his turn to go berserk, before pulling the Indian players in for a private meeting. The rest of us packed up quietly.

Now, I'm in no position to accuse any individual of anything, and maybe it was all perfectly innocent. Maybe certain players were just off their games, maybe some were having blinders, and maybe Greig's fears were unfounded. But by the normal standards of what you would expect from a Twenty20 game, the things going on that night in Gurgaon were ridiculous. I have never played in a game like it.

At the hotel, later, I sat down with Benky and Bond and chewed over the earlier events. All of us seemed to be asking the same question: 'Who can we trust here?' It wasn't an easy one to answer.

I can put my hand on my heart and say that I was never approached with anything dodgy, nor did I see any shady dealings taking place, but from that day on it felt like there was an undercurrent to the whole tournament. And when I thought back to other games, I reflected on the way certain batsmen came needlessly close to being run-out, about the crazy shots they played, the pointless blocking tactics they used, and the ridiculous leg-side wides that international bowlers sent down. I thought about other sloppy little pieces of cricket that came along a little bit too often.

As a team, 2008 wasn't a great tournament for Delhi. We didn't trouble the latter stages, and although we recorded the odd memorable victory – such as a thrilling bowl-out win against Chandigarh after I'd hit Andrew Hall's last ball for six to tie the match – it's safe to say we didn't light up the ICL. And that undercurrent: it was always there. Lots of rumours and lots of hearsay. It just wasn't the same as it had been in the beginning.

The mere idea that somebody out there might be using his skills in the wrong way worried and saddened me. The suspicions took the edge off everything and in the end I was quite happy when the tournament was over and I could go home.

The ICL folded in 2009. Was I glad to see it go? No, I wouldn't say that. Much of the experience was fantastic, the money was pretty useful, and the man-of-the-match awards were on a different level. After one game, for example, I received a state-of-the-art scooter, which I gave to a local orphanage to sell. If I was taken back in time, and asked to sign up for it all again, I wouldn't have said no. But a few warnings would have helped.

In November 2008, before the demise, I returned to India to play for an International XI in a round-robin style ICL Twenty20 tournament. We were based in Hyderabad, and while we were there a group of Islamist gunmen from Pakistan launched terror attacks on Mumbai, which was no more than an hour's flight away. We were scheduled to play against Pakistan's team, but news of the attacks instantly unsettled everyone. We watched the television footage in our team room and then received word that the Pakistanis intended to fly home immediately. There was some talk that we might stay and somehow carry on with the tournament, until the sensible decision was soon reached that we would also leave India. But our sudden departure, and then the collapse of the tournament, caused complications. I was fortunate that my ICL contract had entitled me to half my fee up front but, along with many players, I came home with about £50,000 still owed to me – and that's still the position today.

The global explosion of Twenty20 cricket continued unaffected by the ICL's collapse. The IPL went from strength to strength, the format's popularity in England seemed as high as ever, and then, in 2009, word spread that a new tournament was going to be launched in New York.

In no time at all, I received a call from an agent in the north of England, who filled me in on the proposals. Top players from around the world were going to be flown over for a six-week jamboree which was designed to take cricket into America in a big way. Cricket in America? I was sceptical, but then I read some stats which said there were roughly

35,000,000 cricket supporters living in the USA. Put that way it looked like a no-brainer. Soon, an offer came back, and I was tabled a three-year deal on very decent money. Did I fancy it? Bloody right I did. I felt it had the potential to be massive, but in order to commit to it I would have to pull out of the next two seasons of county cricket – possibly my last two.

I told the organisers I was keen and provisionally agreed the contracts, storing them away in a drawer until it was time to finalise things. I then started rehearsing the moment I would break the news to Leicestershire. That was a hard one to square. How do you tell your county, your home for most of your career, that you are upping sticks to play cricket in the good ol' US of A?

As it turned out, I didn't have to. A few months down the line, the idea died a quiet death. So the speech was left unsaid, the contracts gathered dust in the drawer and I was left to focus, as before, only on the job in hand.

But the job in hand was changing, too. Early in the summer of 2009, Tim Boon pulled me to one side and started talking to me about 'my role in the team'. It was the conversation you hope never comes, but here, at last, we were. At 38, I knew the time was eventually going to come when I would have to hand over wicketkeeping duties to a younger man, but nor was I yet willing to step aside for someone who wasn't better than me. Tom New was the main candidate to take the gloves, but I didn't think he was ready. I thought he was capped too soon and indulged when his performances didn't really merit it. I thought he, like other young players at Leicestershire, had too much smoke blown up his arse for the sake of a few happy headlines in troubled times. And times were certainly troubled, as I'll explain later.

On 6 May, we went to Bristol for a Championship game against Gloucestershire. My hands were really sore, and with Iain O'Brien bowling at a decent clip I wasn't entirely happy when the ball was coming through. As a wicketkeeper, the last things you should be feeling are relief when the batsman hits the ball and trepidation when he doesn't. And there were other problems: a ball down leg-side, which I had to take one-handed because I couldn't get two on it. A couple of fumbled chances. A heaviness in my legs. A bit of extra stiffness in my neck and back. Basically, I kept like a drain and I knew it.

After that match in Bristol, we went out for a team meal. Other than me and Claude it was like dining with a boy band. I felt myself ageing on the spot and it struck me there and then that I wasn't going to be around forever. When Boony then pulled me to one side again a couple of weeks later, and said he was going to give Tom a go, but I would be retained as a batter, I was inwardly gutted but I couldn't realistically object. Boony had always been fair with me and I knew some of the writing was on the wall.

Still, that first game without the gloves was as weird as hell. Moving a few steps out to the slips felt really strange. When we fielded, I had to fight the urge to go for the ball when it came through to Tom. When I opened the batting – my new role – I made 32 and 29 and began learning again.

But the transition could never be straightforward, because at Leicestershire in 2009 nothing much was straightforward.

Captaincy is a tough gig at the best of times, even harder when you aren't actually playing, and when I lost my place in the team for a few weeks in July it added to a list of deeper frustrations. After the minor problems with the caps, and the bigger issue of the pitches, there was the even more worrying case of the missing players. In the summer of '09 a lot of insecurity was spreading through the dressing room. Instead of backing our best talent with contracts of proper length, the club seemed to be sitting on the fence and leaving many players sweating about their futures. Things had grown unhappy behind the scenes and whatever decisions were being taken by Neil Davidson, David Smith and the rest of the hierarchy, it wasn't succeeding in keeping the camp happy and together.

The list of departures was long and illustrious. We lost Dave Masters, an absolute groove machine of a bowler, when he was desperate to stay and only wanted us to match the offer he had received from Essex. For one reason or another, we also surrendered the services of Darren Maddy, HD Ackerman, Garnett Kruger, Dillon Du Preez, Darren Robinson, Boeta Dippenaar, Jeremy Snape, Jimmy Ormond and Stuart Broad – serious players to a man. Well, supporters are no fools, and nor are players, and they could see we were not a stable ship. Results remained poor, the squad was growing steadily pissed off, I was starting to feel a bit disaffected with where it was going, and then there was the cherry on the cake.

Jimmy Allenby had a cracking summer in 2009, was a genuine match-winner with the bat, and had asked for a little more time before committing to a new deal. He wanted to know about the club's plans for the following year. Jimmy had become such a big player that it would have made basic sense to give him that extra time, but the club demanded a decision there and then and refused to budge. Jimmy, unable to commit to an uncertain cause, left for Glamorgan.

When Smith came into the dressing room and broke this news, my mouth fell open. I couldn't believe it. How on earth had we let yet another top player slip away? It was madness! I looked around and saw a bunch of players staring at the floor in disbelief.

My players, my colleagues.

Something snapped inside. Enough was enough. I couldn't stand it any more, so I stood up and spoke.

'Just to let you know, David, Tim,' I announced. 'I'm going to resign.'

Smith responded by telling me I was wrong to say what I did, when I did, and he was probably right. But I physically couldn't sit there and take it any more. I felt I had to show my team-mates that I was with them, that I didn't agree with the decisions that were being made over my head.

The job, in truth, had become one strain after another. Every week there seemed to be a new problem that was upsetting the applecart. I found myself wondering when it was all going to stop, and when we would be able to get back to playing cricket and enjoying each other's company? There was no fun in the camp, no harmony, no daft laughs, no silly japes like the stunt that was pulled on me in an end-of-season game at Sussex in 2003, when the boys secretly crushed up two Viagra tablets into my drinks and then flooded my area of the dressing room with porn, compelling me to spend the afternoon and evening sessions battling the forces of nature. That was bloody hilarious. It might also have been a different lifetime.

As captain I felt divorced from the big decisions and couldn't make the impact I wanted. I was captain in name only, my role confined to the call of heads or tails and the changing of field positions. It saddened me, because it could and should have been so much better. By the end it felt like I was running into a brick wall every day.

I was buggered if I was going to spend the final years of my career feeling so emotionally drained. I still felt I had lots to contribute, but I could do that as a player and a mentor, not as a figurehead. So I made things official, handed in my resignation letter, slipped back into the ranks and felt the weight lift from my shoulders, almost at a stroke.

From the moment Tom took over as wicketkeeper, I had moved into a utility role. Batting at the top of the order was a new challenge, but if I wasn't going to do my old job any more, at least I could have a bloody good shot at another. I had to train myself to survive as an opener, to knock the shine off the new ball, instead of coming in later and working the spinners. Fine. After all the bollocks with the captaincy, it was good to have something fresh to occupy the brain. Sure, sometimes it didn't work and I was back in the pavilion for not many. Sometimes it left me kicking my heels and dispatched to the seconds again. But on a few precious occasions it went like a dream.

There was always something about the St Lawrence Ground which brought the best out of me. What was it? I'm not sure. The pace and bounce in the wicket? Maybe. The crowd and staff who always had a kind word for me? Maybe. Whatever it was, the result was invariably the same when I walked out to bat at Canterbury – runs, and plenty of them.

Kent had wrapped up the Division Two title when we went there for the penultimate four-day game of 2009. I had played my way back into the team but Kent's players were in great nick and high spirits, and forced us to follow-on. When I walked out to open our second innings, with a day-and-a-half to save the game, Rob Key started chirping at me from minute one.

Rob's attempt at a Cumbrian accent is barely distinguishable from Swahili, but he had never been able to help himself in the years after I left Kent.

'Alright maaaaate . . .'

I chuckled and had a nibble back, and then we got on with the game.

Early in my knock, I flicked one off my legs and watched with a sense of foreboding as the ball flew straight towards Keysey at midwicket. The cherry plopped into his hands, and then, to my astonishment, popped straight out again and fell to the grass. A life! That would do for me.

My day. It's my day.

My mental and physical routines were operating like clockwork as I readied myself for the next delivery. By now they were almost second nature:

1. Two taps of the bat
2. Head pointing to mid-on
3. Watch the non-striker's end
4. Watch the ball, watch the ball, watch the ball
5. Backlift up
6. Back foot back and across
7. Front foot forward
8. Stay still, until just before the ball lands
9. Play the shot. Commit to the shot
10. Roll it all up and throw it in the little black bag. Now go back to Number 1, and start again

When you are so clear in your thoughts and so settled in your plans, the runs become a by-product. From that dropped catch onwards, I felt in perfect control of myself and the situation. I knew where I wanted to hit the ball and knew I could dominate the bowling.

I batted in a bubble of calm and control, and when I brought up my hundred I received a wonderful ovation. I then put my helmet back on and kept going, and going, beyond my previous highest score of 144.

I didn't want to stop. I felt like batting for weeks. Then, in the last hour of the fourth day, by which point my partnership with Matt Boyce had made the game safe, Keysey did the unthinkable and brought himself on to bowl.

'Come on maaaaate, play a reverse-sweep maaaate,' he kept saying, with a big, red-cheeked grin. 'Go for it maaate.'

I would never have heard the last of it if he had got me out. I couldn't let it happen. But nor could I give him the satisfaction of tying me down. *Decisions, decisions.* I played out a couple of careful overs of his ropey off-spin and then nailed him for a couple of big sixes, straight out of the screws. Then I took up his invitation and reverse-swept him over the ropes. I ended on 173 not out from 364 balls, having hit eighteen fours and five sixes. The product of a free and functioning mind.

Kent's celebrations afterwards were long and cheerful, and I joined in. Near the end of a difficult season, which we finished rock bottom of the Championship, it was nice to enjoy a couple of hours with some old friends to drink away the stresses of life. I clinked glasses with Keysey and Geraint and drained the ale. Later, on the way back to Leicester, I allowed myself to hope that next year might be better, happier, not quite so eventful in the wrong places. Maybe it was the beer flowing into my veins and the happy tiredness setting in, but was it really wrong to entertain the idea that there might be a slightly smoother ride in store?

What was that about calm and storms?

A sportsman's life is often a selfish one. Adulation is routinely thrown at you; it energises you and you come to crave it. No wonder some players get depressed when their careers finish. The adulation suddenly disappears and the world no longer revolves around me, myself and I.

The time Jen was going through IVF was another period when life could not conceivably be just about Paul Nixon. Something else was more important than me and my cricket. Something far more serious, challenging and deserving of my attention.

Around this time, my game wasn't perfect and my head wasn't exactly where it should have been. Where Jen was concerned, I had started acting like a dick and did some really stupid things that affected our relationship. At the time my wife needed my undivided support, at the time after her dad had died and following the trials of IVF which naturally knocked her for six, I wasn't there for her as much as I should have been and I gave in to selfishness too easily. Things came to a head a year after Izzy was born, and at that point she very nearly left me. She would have been well within her rights.

This might seem a vague account. I'm sorry about that. If you think it warrants more space here than I am giving it, I'm sorry about that, too. In the end I believe the fairest thing to do is record it only in terms of my own regret; my own wish that I could rewind to that time in 2008 and do things differently. I was out of order, basically, and nearly paid for that in a big way. Since then I have had to live with that knowledge. I always will, in some way, with one memory of that time sharper than all the others.

When Jen first put me in my place about how I had acted, when she spoke and when I listened, I heard the words in my head, as clear as anything, and I still hear them now:

I do not want anyone else to be with my wife, and I do not want another man to bring up my daughter.

Moving on wasn't easy, but clinging onto those words was, and when I think of all that happened afterwards I had to be deeply grateful that they were still going to be around.

nineteen

TURMOIL

The Gruffalo said that no gruffalo should
Ever set foot in the deep dark wood.
'Why not? Why not?' 'Because if you do
The Big Bad Mouse will be after you . . .'
(The Gruffalo's Child, Julia Donaldson, 2004)

At the end of the 2009 season, Tim Boon asked me if I thought we should sign Matthew Hoggard. My first response was to splutter.

'Fuck off,' I said. 'There's no way we could afford Hoggy.'

On 9 November, the club made an announcement on its website:

Leicestershire CCC can today confirm that former England seamer Matthew Hoggard has signed a three-year contract with the club and will also take over as Club Captain.

Davidson had made it happen. I was amazed.

The smell from the ICL's corpse continued to linger. Early in 2010, Leicestershire were informed that, because I still had an 'active' ICL contract, the club could be barred from qualifying for the new international Champions League if we got to the final of the English Twenty20 Cup with me in the team.

It was an old problem that refused to die. The club considered its options, and then decided to deal with the matter in the time-honoured way – by hitting me in the pocket. David Smith claimed that the ten or so Twenty20 games I would miss ought to wipe around £40,000 from my salary.

His thinking was that I shouldn't receive a penny during a 39-day period of the summer. In other words, I would be paid, as normal, until the Championship season broke off for the round of Twenty20 games. I would then have to wait until the four-day matches kicked in again for my wage to follow suit.

My thinking? 'David, it's your choice whether I'm picked or not – not mine. It's you saying I'm not eligible for the T20s – not me. I'm here and I want to play. I'm not pulling out; *you* are pulling me out.'

We were never going to get to the Champions League with such an inexperienced team – I knew that and the club knew that. My argument was that I could have played without any dramas, but Smith had decreed otherwise. There was no concession for training, or for days off. He had designated a theoretical 'Twenty20 period', seemingly for the purposes of cutting my wage, and it felt like they were trying to stuff me out of sight. When Smith put all this to me across the boardroom table at Grace Road I regarded it as so ridiculous that I actually started laughing. It was an absolute joke of a meeting and the discussion got a bit petty, as did our subsequent correspondence via e-mail.

Then the scene began to change. Some of the Pakistani and Kiwi ICL players had started reappearing for their international teams. The ban which had kept them out of international cricket therefore must have been lifted. Surely this meant my own shackles could now be removed? I made a few calls, and learned that the word from Dean Kino, who was in charge of the Twenty20 Champions League, was that because the ICL had folded, nobody was much bothered about any 'ban' any more, but in order to keep noses clean with clubs it was preferable to 'sign out' officially, and then the coast would, in theory, be clear.

In theory. David Smith did not view it so simply. I assured him that my agents had the relevant paperwork, but he was steadfast in docking me a shedload of my wage – which he duly did, without my knowledge – while being extremely difficult about the whole thing. It took forever to resolve, left me considering my options legally and with the Professional Cricketers' Association, and left a very bitter taste, but it fit neatly into a pattern at Leicestershire and was far from the end of the troubles.

My most vivid early memory of Neil Davidson is of a huge presentation he gave at Grace Road. It was a big Powerpoint job, full of charts, numbers and targets, the like of which Leicestershire had not seen before. After his election as chairman in 2003, he had set about implementing his grand plan to turn us from a small, struggling club into an ultra-competitive one that could generate millions. This led to the involvement of a company called Investors In Cricket, a group of businessmen whose stated aim was to put the game on a more commercial footing. It was presented as a ground-breaking partnership with some potentially lucrative links to the Asian market.

Neil was very bright and articulate, and certainly talked an impressive game. If his big vision came off, it was going to bring about a sea-change in the way things were done at the club. But I did wonder, as he laid the scheme out for all the players and staff, whether he was aiming too high. It sounded big and bold, but maybe a little too bold for its own good?

That summer of 2003 had seen a fundamental shift behind the scenes at Grace Road. By the time I returned from Kent, Kevin Hill – who had worked for the club for donkey's years – had at last risen to the chief executive position he had always aspired to. Along with Brian Groves, the then chairman, Kevin drove forward the idea that the club's members should vote in a board of directors, rather than be ruled by a traditional committee who were rarely inclined to rock the boat or push through dramatic change as the years went by.

It was a leap into the future, or perhaps the present, and this is where Neil Davidson came in. He was a successful businessman, heading up the Cravendale milk company – one of our shirt sponsors – and had led a big renovation and development at the nearby Loughborough Town Cricket Club. I didn't know a great deal else about his background, but it was Davidson who soon emerged as the head of this new board of business brains who would replace the old regime at Grace Road. In the beginning, it all seemed quite calm and smooth.

Well, you know by now what comes after calm. Before long, Kevin Hill was on his way out. So too was Brian Groves. A pair of club stalwarts, who had Leicestershire running through them like sticks of Blackpool rock – suddenly gone. Those were the first signs that things were starting to alter in a big way. The next sign was the appointment of a host of new staff in order to support the ambitious new marketing plans. Suddenly a lot more people were appearing around Grace Road, and I wondered what they could all be doing.

One of the next significant developments was the return of Jimmy Whitaker, when Davidson appointed our former captain as director of cricket. Jimmy, who had left the club fourteen months earlier in the wake of the Burns-Crowe court case, was a great planner, magnificent at understanding cricketers, one of the greatest allies I had ever known and had Leicestershire in his blood. So it felt like a no-brainer to have him back at the core of the club.

First rule of Grace Road during this period: never assume. The Jimmy Whitaker I thought I knew was a different animal to the new version. From an early stage in his new job he seemed a bit distant. One of the hallmarks of Jimmy's captaincy was that he was always in perfect control of himself and his environment. Now, you could see the bags under his eyes. He began to look like a man who hadn't slept for days. Then there was the issue with my contract.

My struggles for form over the years were often to do with what was happening in my head, but in 2003 the problems were mainly physical. My knee was niggling and I was having fresh problems with my eyes, which were watering a lot and swelling up, making it hard to see under bright sun or in fading light. I had tried to soldier on, but I knew I wasn't right. My scores and performances gave away the fact I wasn't playing to my potential.

But, still, when my appraisal came around, I didn't expect the club to go for me quite so intently. Years ago, if I had been having a difficult time, Jimmy would have approached me and asked how I was feeling, how he could help. Now, there was nothing. Just cold questions. It was all a bit frosty, and it left me wondering what they were driving at. Were Leicestershire actually not keen on the idea of renewing my contract? Did they want me out?

It was an anxious time and I didn't feel that Jimmy was sticking up for me anything like the way he used to. And this was someone who knew me inside-out. Why be so aloof? But the more I thought about it, and the more I stood back and considered the changes I had observed in Jimmy, the more I came to conclude that something else must be going on. Had he really changed of his own accord, or was he being subjected to the kind of pressure he had never experienced before? When I think back, now, it was almost like he was being operated by remote control.

I became increasingly insecure about my place in the team and after a while started to grow resentful. It didn't feel like the right way to be treating a senior player who had won trophies for the club, put everything on the line and never said no to any commercial duty, dinner, sponsors' appearance or anything else that was asked of me.

In the event, I went away, had a knee operation, got my eyes lasered, saw Wynford, engaged with Snapper, and *I* came back a different animal. My performances went skyward and the idea that I wouldn't be around at Grace Road for the foreseeable was quickly shoved off the agenda. But it didn't kill the growing sense of unease around the club.

As players, you tend to get on with life regardless of what your club's directors are up to. They have their domain and we have ours. On a daily basis there isn't much crossover. As the months passed, though, the lines started to be blurred at Grace Road. For one thing, the team had to get used to the experience of the chairman popping his head into the dressing room. Let me tell you, players never get used to the sight of the chairman in the dressing room. In the past, when a chairman wanted to talk to the coach or a player, a memo would be sent out and you would head for a meeting room. So when Davidson started coming into our domain and talking to Tim, it felt like our haven had been invaded.

Why he did that, I don't know. What I do know is that the players didn't like it. And when players don't like something, their default response is usually to mock.

As Davidson's appearances became more frequent, he steadily acquired a new name.

'Here comes Jim Davidson,' announced Player X, spotting the chairman making his way towards us.

'What does Jim want now?' enquired Player Y.

'Jim's on his way, does anyone want any more milk in his tea?' asked Player Z, just out of Davidson's earshot.

The head of our cricket club became the subject of an occasional piss-take. But there were serious questions behind the piss-take. We didn't really know where he was coming from. What was he all about? As much as he seemed to like being around the players, he always seemed quite cold and guarded. We knew he was in charge, we knew he had authority, but was he spreading his influence into one or two places where it wasn't wanted?

After what happened in the gym, my opinion started to set.

Leicester is a wonderful sporting city, and has never felt more wonderful than during the 1990s, when the place was flushed with success. Martin O'Neill led Leicester City Football Club to the Premiership and the Coca-Cola Cup, Leicester Tigers dominated the new professional rugby union scene with titles in 1995 and 1999, and Leicestershire were two-time County Champions. It was a feel-good city, and players from all three clubs – though mainly rugby and cricket – often mixed together.

The Tigers lads were first-rate, men like Martin Corry, Austin Healey, Martin Johnson and the big Aussie Pat Howard, who once memorably answered the call for an emergency fielder when he emerged from the crowd at Grace Road and took up position at third man. We frequently teamed up on nights out, and those of us who were stupid enough would often take them on at daft challenges, which would see us hanging from rafters in nightclubs, doing chin-ups and other contests we were second-favourites to win. We drank and had fun together and I always enjoyed their attitude to their sport, which seemed to be 'play hard, but have a beer afterwards' – the Aussie cricket mentality, more or less.

The connection endured down the years and was not just a social one. Along with Darren Maddy and Jon Dakin, I had began training with a man called Steve Long, an ex-bodybuilder who got us super-fit in the Tigers' spit-and-sawdust gym during the winters. The rugby players would often come in and see the three of us training like madmen, and we would sometimes have duels to the death on the machines with the academy boys. A couple of times I got stuck in with the first team, too – Austin Healey was one who couldn't resist a contest, while the great Martin Johnson mainly watched on with curiosity – and I enjoyed every second. It got me out of my comfort zone.

One man at the Tigers I got on particularly well with was Darren Grewcock, the former scrum-half who was later appointed the club's strength and conditioning coach. Grewy being a big fitness expert, we developed an obvious rapport, and he could often be spotted flogging himself silly in the David Lloyd gym in Leicester – another place I often frequented. These gym visits had become ever more necessary once Davidson had employed Susie Woolmer as our strength and conditioning coach. Susie, a personal trainer, was a great girl who put her heart and soul into everything she did, but a lot of the regimes she gave us were not what I felt I needed. That winter, for instance, I was asked to row. Nothing else – just row. It was the most basic fitness I had ever done in my life and it was never going to get me into the right sort of shape. So when Maddy and me bumped into Grewcock one day in the David Lloyd, we started talking about different regimes and techniques. He knew his onions and we left with a few useful ideas.

Not long after this, I was on a rare trip back to Cumbria when Davidson called.

'I want to see you tomorrow morning.'

No explanation, just an instruction.

I wondered what it was about, until Maddy called not long afterwards.

'Nico, Davidson has just been on. He's not happy. He saw us talking to Grewy in the gym and he wants a meeting with us.'

The next day, I packed up my things and drove back down to Grace Road to meet him. When I walked through the door, he was red-faced and looked on edge.

'I don't want you speaking to Darren Grewcock,' he said, abruptly. 'Susie is your trainer, not Darren Grewcock. If it happens again you will be severely reprimanded.'

The long drive had allowed me time to prepare my argument. 'Hold on a minute, Neil,' I replied. 'I'm a big boy now. I know my body. I've played 276 First Class games on the trot and my injury record is better than anyone's. I train my socks off. Do you not think I know what I need?'

No dice. He maintained his stance: I was not to train with Grewy, and that was that. I couldn't believe what I was hearing and I actually burst out laughing. It was ridiculous – utter bollocks.

Davidson then did the same with Maddy, who is a bit more sensitive than me and was quite stressed about it. Me – I gave it some thought but then decided to dismiss it. 'Fuck you', I thought. 'You're a successful businessman, and fair enough, but I'm a successful cricketer. The two shouldn't meet. Not about things like this.' I walked out of the room and shook my head at the thought that I had left my friends and family, and driven 200 miles, for *that*. Twenty minutes of my life, gone forever. And from that point onwards, I never felt that we were going to see eye-to-eye.

At the end of the 2005 season, the club went for me again. Jimmy, with Davidson's consent, slashed my wages and put me on a one-day contract worth £25,000. Bearing in mind that at Kent five years earlier my package had been worth about £90,000 with bonuses, it was another blatant piss-take and the club knew it. Kids were now being paid more than me!

The trigger had been a problem with my knee. It had been niggling for a while during the 2005 season and affecting my game, and towards the end of the summer I suffered a meniscus tear during a game of football in a pre-match warm-up. On the back of this big frustration, Jimmy then called me in and told me that the club didn't see me playing Championship cricket the following summer.

The new deal being tabled would restrict my earnings to limited-overs matches, with anything else only being added if I managed to force my way back into the four-day side. £25,000, plus £500 per Championship appearance, basically.

It was a total nonsense. The suggestion was that I was going downhill, which was bollocks. I knew I was as fit and strong as I had ever been. But I had little choice other than to stick it out, hold my nose and sign the contract, and work my nuts off to prove them wrong.

As it happened, things came back in my favour. I had a great pre-season, started the campaign in the team and didn't miss a game. But I spent the rest of the summer with a sour feeling about how I had been treated, and often batted with one eye on the boardroom. Sometimes, in the corner of my eye, I would see Davidson hovering around the balcony when I was out in the middle. A distraction? No – the opposite. 'Don't get out,' I kept telling myself. 'Don't play a high-risk shot here. Don't give him an excuse.'

Another out-of-the-blue development had, though, helped my cause. Just before the season had started, Jimmy's position had been made redundant as Davidson declared his wish for a more 'hands-on' approach at the head of the coaching team. It was probably for the best on all sides, in truth, and when Tim Boon was then appointed as coach it went down well with players and supporters.

Boony had been a popular player at Grace Road and I had always got on with him, so there were no grumbles from me on that score – and certainly none when he took one look at my contract, frowned, and made sure I was back on a proper deal for the following season. Then came my England call-up, after which Davidson was all over me like a rash. Well, relatively speaking. When I came back from the World Cup he would suddenly nod and smile at me, where before there had mostly been coldness. But I never thought those smiles were genuine.

In 2007, Davidson researched and wrote a big report on the state of the county game, its finances and its impact on the England team. It was wide-ranging, detailed, looked very impressive and earned him a lot of approving press. In the background, though, his own club was starting to get itself in a low way, and over the next couple of years the questions started to mount. The issues with my captaincy – the wrong pitches, the players departing under a cloud. Why? The sliding results, the dwindling membership. Why? Other stalwarts like Claude, who was suddenly feeling pissed off after being pulled up about his overseas coaching on the day before he was due to fly home with his pregnant wife.

Why?

The answers weren't clear, but there was no way it could carry on in that direction without some kind of reckoning, somewhere down the line.

Had Matthew Hoggard been privy to every detail of this history lesson before he signed for Leicestershire, the club would surely have been hard pressed to get him through the door. By the end of the 2009 season, he had fallen out of favour with England and left his beloved Yorkshire on not very satisfactory terms. He was entitled to feel that life was dealing him a dodgy hand. So what on earth was he doing coming to Grace Road?

And yet, he seemed to have a genuine belief that the club could go places, and in many ways he was the kind of person and personality the dressing room needed. Despite our brief disagreement in Pakistan, I always admired Hoggy as a player and a bloke. The club, though, was not a pleasant place to be and it was going to take a lot for one man to change everything.

When the new campaign started, the disquiet was still there. People didn't seem to be enjoying coming to work – I know I wasn't – and even our opponents were starting to ask about the rumblings behind the scenes. How had we lost all those good players? Why were we anything but a happy camp?

There was also a growing feeling that Tim Boon was coming under heavy pressure from above. Like Jimmy, it was starting to show on his face. There were signs of strain, too, in David Smith, who had been appointed by Davidson two years earlier. Results were still poor and the club was doing little better on the balance sheet.

Then, in June 2010, Smith resigned. It was a bombshell announcement and the fall-out was long and grim. Smith's opening salvo was to go on the record to accuse Davidson of 'interfering in team affairs'. The *Leicester Mercury* then carried a report of an e-mail, supposedly sent by Davidson to Smith and Boon, which contained a strong suggestion that Jigar Naik should play in a Twenty20 game at Yorkshire – something which went against the coach's wishes. Jigar was not 100 per cent fit, Tim said, but the thinly-veiled advice appeared to have come down strongly from above.

I can't say I was Smith's biggest fan, but the fact he had fallen out with Davidson to the point of quitting meant that things were finally coming to a head – and if the contents of that e-mail were true, it was a million miles out of order.

Davidson shot back. He contested Smith's version of events, denied the accusation of interference and things got increasingly bitter. The chairman made no secret of where he felt the blame should be laid for the club's increasingly poor health. Our failure to win a single Twenty20 match at home had led to slipping attendances and an inability to meet the chairman's financial targets. 'You cannot divorce performance on the pitch from the economics of the business,' he said, pointedly, as the crisis rumbled on. The obvious reading was that the team had struggled, Davidson had started putting heavy pressure on Smith as a result, and their views had diverged to the point where Smith could take no more.

Like a tennis match, the accusations came back and forth, over the net. One side blamed the other for not meeting the targets; the other felt that the targets were over-ambitious and putting a strain on resources.

It was then made public that Davidson had loaned the club more than £100,000 to get by. Hoggy, meanwhile, became concerned that the strife was having a damaging effect on an already low dressing room. He called meetings, asked for our opinions and was left under no illusion as to where the players pointed the finger. The outpouring of anger towards Davidson seemed to open his eyes.

'Lads, if you feel this badly, I'm with you,' he said.

He was as good as his word and took our views to the top. Naturally, this did not please Davidson, who felt Hoggy was misguided in his approach, but the man was not for budging. He spoke to the Professional Cricketers' Association's legal team, and the result was the drawing up of a letter, on our behalf, which officially expressed our dismay at the chairman. The word 'interference' again featured prominently. Hoggy and, significantly, Boony, signed it. The groundstaff were also with us. Here, then, was our stance. And then, lo and behold, the letter was leaked. No sooner had we delivered it, through the right channels, it came out on the Cricinfo website and was swiftly all over the press.

Who leaked it I have no idea, but as players we had nothing to gain by bringing our internal dispute out into the open. We were all suspicious that it had been sneaked out by someone in an attempt to make us look bad.

Davidson, again, continued to dispute our version and pressed Hoggy to change his stance. Then, during a game at Grace Road, a mass of cameras suddenly appeared beyond the boundary rope. We all turned our eyes to the swarm of lenses and saw that Davidson appeared to be holding court, giving the world his side of the story. The war was now being waged in public, but there was no ceasefire in sight.

As we wondered about our next move, there was some talk about staging a sit-down protest during a televised game. In the end, we decided that would be a step too far. Still – we were considering a sit-down protest against our chairman! Things had become very bad, very quickly. But we had 100 per cent faith in our course of action.

In September, another bombshell: Tim Boon's resignation. We had hoped he would stay with us throughout the fight, but amid the strife he was offered a job with the ECB, coaching England's Under-19s, and accepted. It was security for him, the ideal position for a bloke of his attributes and, by extension, great news for English cricket. Boony's passion was for getting the lads right in the nets, honing their techniques, developing them as cricketers. He was up there with the very best as a coach. What he was not built for was the hard world of decision-making, boardroom pressure and the vagaries of committees.

Next to go was Paul Haywood, one of the directors. The other four – Tony Hill, Mike Siddall, Andrew York and John Allen – backed Davidson at a board meeting, but Paul stood up and resigned in protest against the chairman.

There were petitions, aimed at forcing further meetings that could unseat Davidson, but to no avail. He then tried, again, to get Hoggy to retract our letter, but Hoggy refused to buckle. It felt like the whole thing was going nowhere. It dragged on and on, and got more complicated and messy with each day.

By the end of the season I was absolutely desperate to get away on holiday with Jen and Izzy and empty my head of all the nonsense that was going on. When October came around, we packed our cases and drove to Manchester, to stay with Jen's cousin. The following day we would fly to Spain and escape from all the crap for a couple of precious weeks.

That afternoon in Manchester I had agreed to do a live interview on BBC Radio Leicester. I sat in Paul and Carol's converted attic, took the call from the studio and pressed my phone to my ear. There was a news bulletin being read in the moments before my slot.

When I heard the top story, I nearly dropped my phone.

'The chairman of Leicestershire County Cricket Club, Neil Davidson, has today resigned . . .'

I sat with my mouth open. I recited that line over in my head. *Resigned!* Then, in a flash, it was my turn to go live. The presenter came on the line and I answered his questions, but I can't honestly remember what I was talking about. My head was buzzing and I was jumping around and punching the air like I had just scored the winner in a World Cup final.

He had gone! I could barely believe it.

It transpired that things had finally come to a head with a telephone call. Hoggy had been in the process of selling his house, and was back in Yorkshire when Davidson rang and demanded a meeting, in Leicester, the next day. Hoggy explained that he was up to his eyes with the move and wouldn't be able to meet for a few more days. Davidson insisted tomorrow; Hoggy steadfastly refused. It got increasingly heated, to the point where Hoggy put his phone on loudspeaker and took notes as the chairman continued to vent. The upshot of it all, it seemed, was an ultimatum – 'it's you or me' – but our captain was unwilling to follow the chief executive and the coach out of the door.

Hoggy refused to back down, and when word of their telephone chat reached the rest of the board, Davidson finally conceded he 'could no longer continue in these circumstances' and declared his position untenable. He left with a parting shot at Hoggy, maintaining the captain's words and actions were misguided. But . . . he had gone!

I enjoyed the Spanish sun more than usual that time. And when I returned, it felt the clouds had scattered. Davidson was replaced as chairman by Paul Haywood, who had never rocked the boat in more than twenty years on the committee but had stuck his head above the parapet when we most needed an ally. The way he acted gave the players great comfort in times of doubt. Once the dust settled we made it clear how much we appreciated what he did.

The club felt a better place with Paul at the helm. A few things changed on the marketing side, and some disaffected former members were invited to come back and rejoin. Hoggy, myself and a few more senior players took to the phones ourselves to try to stress that the club was going in a new, positive direction.

Many people had felt let down by what had developed at Grace Road over the years. It was going to be a hard sell, but a few said 'Yes' and pledged themselves to the cause. It was a start.

It was a shame we couldn't go forward with Boony, whose farewell speech at the end of the season was a classic. It was full of honesty and dignity and, in its own way, probably opened a few eyes on the board as to where the problems lay. I suppose, looking back, the way he left did us a favour in the long run. But, at the time, we still had to be led. We still had to be guided until the storm had passed. The Indians still needed a chief.

Matthew Hoggard is as daft as a brush. He is actually crackers. Becoming a dad to Ernie in 2007 clearly didn't change him one bit. For some, fatherhood brings wisdom and maturity; for Hoggy, it means you get to recite lines from *The Gruffalo* while fielding at mid-off during a Championship game. The sad thing is, when he did that, mine was one of the only faces that wasn't creased with confusion. I knew just about every word myself.

The man will always be nuts, but when he switches on and gets his head right, he is a very bright bloke. He's not the best communicator in the world, and once admitted that he actually doesn't like talking, which is an unusual thing for a captain to confess. We are different animals in terms of how we express ourselves, and I suppose we have had our moments. But he does everything from the heart and with all the right intentions, and is as straight as an arrow. He treats everyone equally and will talk to you in exactly the same way, whether you are a peasant in India or the King of England. And the way he led us into the light that summer was inspirational.

Realistically, he was the only one who could have ousted Davidson. He was the new arrival, the captain, the senior figure that the chairman had brought in himself before it had started turning sour. He held his dignity right the way through, kept us in the loop of everything that was happening, stood strong when we needed him to, rose immeasurably in my estimation as a leader and as a man, and this love letter to the big galoot from Pudsey concludes the story of the second most interesting thing that happened to me in that strange, strange summer of 2010.

twenty

THE OFFER

May 2010.

Leicester's plush Marriott hotel on a bright spring afternoon. Two men sit at a table in a discreet corner of the bar. One is in his early forties, Indian, suited and confident. The other is a veteran English sportsman in a state of shock.

'So . . . what sort of money are you talking about here?' the sportsman enquires.

'Name your price,' the businessman calmly replies.

'Go on, how much?'

'You tell me.'

'Well, I don't know . . . a million?'

This is clearly an absurd suggestion. The Indian laughs.

'More.'

'More?!'

'More.'

'OK . . . Three million?'

Another grin. 'More.'

'Five million?'

A beaming smile. 'No problem. Absolutely, no problem.'

A little later, the meeting ends politely; with a firm handshake and a promise to meet again in the near future. The sportsman strides to his car with his head in a fuzz, and wonders: did that just happen?

Some years ago I became involved in a big property development in the Bahamas. Port St George is a major project on a 900-acre site on Long Island, a luxury development that will include a marina, golf course, hotel and apartments and hundreds of homes. It's a big deal and an exciting investment.

I've always been fascinated by property – I like the challenge of knowing when and where to invest. To this day I curse not buying a place in South Africa when I had the chance. We went for our place in Spain instead and then, lo and behold, South Africa's housing market went berserk. That was a missed opportunity. I don't like missing opportunities.

During my time in the ICL, a common pastime was to open the laptop in my hotel room, dial up the internet and look at Indian property websites, just out of curiosity. I sent off a few e-mails to different companies and thought little more about it until one morning in 2009 when I checked my inbox and found a message from an old sparring partner from a Championship game many moons ago.

'Nico, is that you?' it began.

He explained that he was involved with one of the Indian property companies I had contacted, and his antennae had twitched when he saw my e-mail. He urged me to hook up with his company. I happily agreed. This led to a meeting in a London hotel involving me, a friend from the Port St George project, and an Indian man, K.

K could not have been more enthusiastic about our Bahamas scheme and declared his interest in buying a hundred plots to add to his portfolio. A hundred! But he was affable and relaxed, and appeared to know what he was talking about. As we kept talking, over a period of weeks and months, always in London but in different hotels, K's interest never faded, and a friendly, working rapport was established.

It was that October, while driving with Jen to London, for Mark Ealham's fortieth birthday and the wedding of a friend, Sam Davis, that the first surprise was sprung. K called my mobile and declared he had something to give us.

'It's a wedding anniversary gift,' he announced.

'Ah, don't be daft,' I replied. 'You don't need to do that.'

'Please, I insist. I am in India, but my brother has it. He will give you a call.'

We pulled off the M1 and met K's brother in the Holiday Inn at Brent Cross. He presented me with a beautiful, large gift-wrapped box which I was instructed to handle with care. It was a strange gesture from a man I hardly knew, but not an unpleasant one, and it seemed harmless enough.

I placed the box in the boot and continued the trip. When we returned home a couple of days later we unwrapped the gift to find a pristine collection of Vera Wang champagne flutes.

'Bloody hell,' I said. 'How nice are they?'

Happy Anniversary indeed.

Autumn and winter drifted by – more meetings, sporadic contact with K – and then, in May, my phone trilled again.

'I'd love to have a chat with you about a new business idea.'

'Sure,' I replied, and offered to meet in the Leicester Marriott.

On 21 May, I strolled through the hotel's big glass doors, passed through the large reception area and was swiftly greeted by K. We shook hands, traded pleasantries, sat down with drinks and then he briefed me about his business idea.

'You know, Paul, a lot of people have made a lot of money in India,' he began. 'And you – you could make a lot of money in England also.'

'How do you mean?'

With relish, K filled in the gaps. He wasn't talking about property at all; he was talking about cricket matches. Cricket matches in India. Cricket matches in India that were rigged. Dozens of them, he claimed. He then explained how I could become a very rich man if I was prepared to help throw a Twenty20 game in England.

'You have a couple of TV games coming up, yes?'

We did – a Sky Sports match at Durham on 14 June was one.

'That is the time to make it work.'

He then made it plain: if I could help things go a certain way in that game, I could make myself very wealthy indeed. All English televised games are beamed back to India, he explained, fuelling an underground betting market worth billions. If I was able to arrange it so that we lost the first six overs, I would be quids in. If I could influence the coin toss, all the better. And should I manage to fix the result, I could very quickly become stupidly rich.

Well, this was a first.

'Right . . . are you serious?' I enquired.

He was either deadly serious or the best actor Bollywood never had. By the time he had made it calmly clear that I could access five million pounds for myself and my team if I was able to organise a Twenty20 game to his wishes, my head was swirling. It was the most surreal conversation I have ever had. And if I had gone higher in my bizarre haggling game, I got the feeling he would have come with me. He was completely nonchalant all the way through it, despite the crazy sums we were discussing.

My next thought: *Christ, what am I doing here?*

My next thought: *I don't want to be here.*

My next thought, same as the last: *I want out of here. This isn't for me.*

But I stayed. I wanted to know more. Who, exactly, was K? Where was he coming from? What were his connections? I was shocked by his offer but addicted to its detail.

He went on to observe that Leicestershire were in poor form on TV, and that this was key to his scheme. Well, I gave him this: he had clearly done his homework. The sight of the television cameras being lugged into Grace Road had become an increasingly unwelcome one for us, once our early Twenty20 successes had passed and the rest had caught up. In 2010 the club was not exactly a happy place and results were following accordingly; especially, it seemed, when Sky Sports showed up. So the theory that Leicestershire losing an apparently random game on TV wouldn't arouse any suspicion was pretty sound. Any tracks could be covered by our mediocrity.

'This property arrangement of yours in the Bahamas,' K said, reclining in his chair and smiling. 'What a great way of hiding your money.'

'How do you mean, hiding?

'Well,' he continued. 'Every player who has been involved in this type of thing has a nice place in India, or maybe Dubai. And the Indian property market is driven by cash. Let's say a house is on the market there for £100,000. If you offer £100,000, but only £20,000 is in cash, and someone else offers only £90,000 for the house but that is entirely in cash, they will get the house, not you. That is how it works. There is always a way of hiding money over there.'

He was opening a door to a very unfamiliar world. Then, when it was nearly time to leave, there was one more request.

To do what he wanted me to do, I would need the team on board. The openers would have to 'lose' the first six overs, and the bowlers would have to send down an allotted amount of rubbish in order to squander the game. It would have to be a group effort.

'So will you talk to the team?'

'Yeah . . . I'm not sure . . . We'll see how it goes.'

I knew with 100 per cent certainty that I wasn't going to accept the offer, but I couldn't help bouncing the possibilities around in my head during the drive home.

Five million pounds? It could transform Leicestershire beyond all recognition! We could buy the best overseas players! Grace Road could be improved to Test standard! We could even cut a deal with Durham – we could lose the game, they could lose the rematch, neither team suffers and nobody suspects a thing! And we could get our hands on a phenomenal amount of money! Life- and career-changing money!

It seemed so easy. All they needed was the right man for their job.

I've never been happier to be the wrong man for a job.

The idea that we could go through with it was crazy.

My thoughts turned to Hansie. Had he started out like this, allowing himself to be lured in by the simplicity of it all? Had he presumed it would all end happily?

When I got home, I told Jen.

'You can't get involved in that,' she said.

I spent the next few hours on the phone ticking the main boxes: Tim Boon, the PCA, the International Cricket Council's Anti-Corruption and Security Unit, Matthew Hoggard and, for an extra ladling of advice, Michael Vaughan.

It was Vaughany who was the most animated. I'm not sure I have ever known him so angry. 'Nico, you've got to mention this in the papers,' he urged. 'I hate this stuff with a passion. We have to stop this crap coming into English cricket. It absolutely sickens me.' I took his advice and spoke to a *Daily Telegraph* journalist, on the condition that my identity wouldn't be revealed.

Tim and the others were all very supportive and assured me I was going down the correct channels, which was comforting to know. Hoggy was the same, once he had digested the tale with his unique sense of humour:

'Right, well, you can count me in. Nobody would suspect me of bowling badly on purpose anyway – I'm going for ten an over as it is!'

I called Dad next and his advice was the same as Jen's; Don't, Touch and Bargepole being the main words.

That evening I continued to toss everything around in my head. There were, obviously, a thousand reasons why I physically couldn't take money to fix a cricket match, but what remained in the mind most clearly was Mum and Dad, the sacrifices they had made for me, the way they had worked so hard all their lives and the way the family name was respected. The way Granddad never had a single bad word said against him. Could I honestly risk ruining all that by being forever known as 'Paul Nixon, disgraced cricketer', or, at best, spend the rest of my life looking over my shoulder? No, the idea was crackers. But what to do next?

An Anti-Corruption officer then made contact and flew over from Dubai. We met in – where else? – the Marriott, but this time in one of the hotel's bedrooms. He explained he had been involved with Hansie's case and also some of the Bob Woolmer investigations, and then asked me to explain what had happened. I answered as fully as I could. 'We'll be in touch if we need anything more,' he said at the end.

And that was that, the end of it, but only for a couple more days. When K next called again, he informed me he was on his way from London to Leicester, and could we meet again?

Scene two of the strange movie, on 26 May, saw the sportsman sitting in the passenger seat of a car in Grace Road's car park as the Indian businessman tried to close the dodgy deal.

'You know, there are four other counties who are involved in this,' K said.

'Really?' I enquired.

'Yes, I promise you.'

'I doubt that.'

'Trust me.'

'Well, who are they?'

'I can't say.'

He then mentioned the IPL and described what was happening in that competition, claiming it wasn't as sweet and innocent as it looked.

'Look,' he said. 'We would love you to come on board with this. I have some money with me, in the boot, just as a thank-you at this stage . . .' He reached to open his door.

'No,' I stopped him. 'You don't have to do that.'

'Please, just . . .'

'Look, it's early days, yeah? Let's just wait and see how it goes.'

The truth is that I was feeling quite vulnerable at this stage. I still had no idea, really, about who I was dealing with, and what was the right thing to say in order to get this to a conclusion. I did my best to stall K, to keep him at arm's length, and we ended much as we had in the Marriott:

'Look, let me talk to the lads. I'll come back to you.'

The mood, again, was never less than friendly, but I was relieved to get out of his car and head for home.

For the next few days I chewed things over with Jen and lost sleep wondering if I had done the right things, talked to the right people, and said the right words to keep myself safe from whoever might be behind all this. That week I chatted to some of the players and put the dressing room in the picture. All responded with eyebrows raised. I also confided the car park meeting in Tim and Hoggy.

The next call was soon to follow, but this time it was from me to K.

'Look, K, I've talked to the lads . . . we're not interested. We can't get involved.'

I would like to report, for the sake of dramatic effect, that he responded by issuing dark threats and making dangerous demands. But that's not how it was.

'Well,' K said, calmly. 'If you know anyone who might be interested, you have my number.'

And that, this time, was definitely that. I never heard another peep from K, there was nothing more from the Anti-Corruption Unit, normal life resumed and I went off to Chester-le-Street as though nothing had ever happened.

Ross Taylor blasts Durham to easy t20 win over Leicestershire

Durham 225-2, Leicestershire 154
Durham won by 71 runs

David Hopps at Chester-le-Street
guardian.co.uk, Monday 14 June 2010 23.04 BST

Paul Collingwood, England's victorious captain in the World Twenty20, took four wickets as he made a brief return to Durham's ranks tonight and the trophy was also on display in a nearby marquee, but it was a destructive display of power hitting by the New Zealander Ross Taylor that warmed up a chill north-eastern night.

Taylor hit a stand-and-deliver 80 not out, nine of his 33 balls clearing the rope, as Durham piled up 225 for two, the highest score of the season in Friends Provident t20, and the sixth-highest total in domestic Twenty20. He was dropped once, in the last over at deep square-leg off Nadeem Malik, and finished it all off with a swivel six over long-on.

The artificially short boundaries at what is now cumbersomely known as the Emirates Durham International Cricket Ground (as the games get shorter the ground names get longer) were appealing, but not remotely appealing enough for Leicestershire, who fell 71 runs short. Nobody has ever scored more than 210 to win a match batting second.

Paul Nixon's slog-and-miss, as he became the fifth Leicestershire batsman out with the asking rate climbing above 14 an over, admitted the impossibility of the task. Only then did Collingwood get the chance to enjoy himself. Bowling his medium-paced cutters with a nous that had been beyond Leicestershire's support pace bowlers, he dismissed Wayne White second ball and made short work of the tail to take four for 13.

As I say, it was not exactly a good era for Leicestershire, and we were well and truly taken to the cleaners in the north-east. Durham had some proper heavyweights in their line-up in Colly, Benky, Plunkett, Steve Harmison, Phil Mustard and Ian Blackwell. They also had Ross Taylor, who batted us into tiny smithereens. His 80 from 33 balls was the most ferocious Twenty20 innings you could imagine. We limped home in second place, my contribution was a single run from three balls, and the bus journey back to Grace Road was full of gallows humour:

'Christ, boys, we could have made a fortune out of that game!'

'A few hundred grand down the drain there!'

'Went around the park there . . . next time tell him we'll do it!'

But it still felt good, better than the average thrashing is ever allowed to feel, because I was heading home with a clear conscience.

I have always liked money. I enjoy what it can do and like the way it opens doors. I have never been oblivious to the appeal of earning a nice quid and I feel no shame in saying that. I appreciate the good things in life, whether that's a car, an expensive watch, some sharp clothes, a business-class flight or some other luxuries for the family. But those comforts should be earned through hard work and fair play, not by cheating.

But was it easy to decline when that ridiculous money was being waved under my nose? Well, yes, and no. Yes, because it was clearly dodgy and I had no intention of heading towards retirement with such a dirty secret, and risk losing my reputation at a stroke. No, because the source of the offer was, and remains, a mystery. How far back into the underworld did it all snake? If you followed the money, where would it lead? For that reason, I had tried to keep it as friendly as I could with K. I felt I needed to let him down gently.

I thought about it a lot as the weeks went by, and for a while I couldn't help playing a regular, dark fantasy through my mind. It involved me taking a few quid up front, and then going to the team. A few of them said yes, but a few said no, so those of us who were 'in' tried to make it happen. Except it didn't happen. It went wrong. We tried to lose the game, but somehow contrived to win. Someone, somewhere along this mysterious web lost a fortune as a result of our cock-up. Then, a couple of weeks later, I am driving along the A46 at a decent lick when the car in front brakes sharply. I respond by slamming on the anchors. But the anchors! They're not working! I jab harder at the pedal. Still nothing. Suddenly frantic, I jab, and jab, and then . . .

That's where the daydream stopped. Thanks, but no thanks. I wanted Isabella to have a dad for a long time. I wanted to be able to look at myself in the mirror every morning and every night. I wanted to live life without fear and guilt.

Later that summer, as if by coincidence, the *News of the World* published its spot-fixing exposé which incriminated three Pakistan Test players and led to custodial terms for Salman Butt, Mohammad Asif, Mohammad Amir and their 'fixer', Mazhar Majeed. I followed the controversy with a cynical smile. I have always been a trusting person – sometimes too trusting, Jen would say – but my mindset changed as the year went on.

I looked at other games on TV and found myself wondering. I saw no-balls and wides which suddenly appeared very dubious. I watched the start of certain bowlers' spells, and saw certain batsmen play certain shots. Do I know that anyone in county cricket has spot-fixed? No, I don't – unless you count Mervyn Westfield, who was shopped by his Essex team-mates for a spot-fix against Durham and sent to prison. But I'm convinced I saw things that weren't right. And I have personal experience of the temptations that exist. It can't have started and finished with me. It just can't.

When the three Pakistanis were exposed, my heart sank; Amir had the world at his feet, Butt was supposed to be the captain and the respected leader, and Asif – he was an absolute genius with a cricket ball in his hand. During his brief spell at Grace Road in 2006 he had been one of the finest bowlers I have ever had the pleasure to keep to. Winston Benjamin was a master of his art but Asif was even more skilful. He could make the ball talk. He was good fun, too, with a mischievous sense of humour, and the impression was of a young guy who had been let out into the big, bad world and was going to enjoy every minute of it. I didn't really witness his dark side, other than a morning at Taunton when he was warned by the umpire for picking the seam in the third over. But now the world knows his secret.

How to eradicate the menace of fixing from cricket? It's one of the hardest questions, and I don't profess to have the answers. Legalising gambling on the subcontinent, the obvious solution, isn't going to happen any time soon, so good luck to the authorities in trying to root it out for good. But there are a few things that I would like to know. Why have more people not been exposed? Can the powers that be not tap into mobile phones? Don't they know the trails to follow? Could they do more to encourage whistleblowers to come forward – incentives, for instance? What did they do with the information I passed on to the Anti-Corruption Unit? And what on earth had been going on in the ICL? I would love to know.

In the years after Hansie's scandal broke, the PCA had increased its advice to county cricketers. Representatives spoke about the way fixers work, how they seek to befriend you, how they get you on-side with a gift and then go in for the kill later. It was good education and opened a lot of eyes.

The champagne flutes.

Of course, the champagne flutes. Very nice they were, too.

You live, and you learn.

That December, I headed north to the Queen Elizabeth Grammar School, in Penrith, to coach some of Cumbria's top kids during the school holidays. I taught them some of the warm-up routines I had learned with England, passed on a few Twenty20 techniques and then closed with a session on the bowling machine. It was a rewarding, fun day, after which the boys presented me with a beautiful, framed photograph of the Lake District by way of thanks. This was the kind of unsolicited gift I was more than happy to accept. The gesture had me feeling quite emotional.

And the best thing? I didn't need to run my mate out on TV to get it.

I said my goodbyes to the youngsters, put the picture on the back seat of my car, and drove home for Christmas. Cumbria was in the grip of the winter from hell and the roads were beneath a treacherous coating of ice, but my brakes? Worked like a dream.

twenty-one

LAST SUMMER

L et's play a little game. We'll call it 'Have you ever?' I'll start. Have you ever gone to bed wearing two pairs of tight compression garments on your legs and nothing covering your top half? Have you then been woken by the cold across your chest, and by the hard, squeezing sensation around your middle and your thighs? Have you then felt the intense pressure on your bladder that these garments have inevitably caused? Have you then swung your legs out of bed, walked to the bathroom, prised your manhood from your skin-hugging trousers with one hand, flicked open a pre-prepared protein drink with the other, and drank, and pissed, and then crammed everything away and climbed back into bed?

Have you then looked at the clock, observed that it was four in the morning, and wondered – 'for how much longer?'

I'm not done yet.

Have you ever kept a nutritional chart on your fridge so detailed that it looks like you're planning a military campaign? Have you drummed the routine of vitamins, minerals and supplements into your head so often that you start to take them without thinking? Have you learned to love things called Creatine, Beta-Alanine, Glucosamine and Dioralytes?

Have you sprinkled protein powder onto your morning Alpen, and later consumed further protein shakes, mixed with olive oil and peanut butter, to keep your joints in harmony and to chase away your chocolate cravings? Have you ever driven to a sports centre a few dozen miles away to give a coaching class, with two bottles of protein drink on the passenger seat, just to keep yourself topped up? Have you ever looked at your watch and realised that you're behind on your daily water intake and need to get another litre on board, pronto?

Have you ever got up at 7.00 a.m., driven to your old physio's house, climbed into a big compression sock which is attached to a little motor, and then felt your leg squeeze, relax, squeeze, relax? Have you spent time every day for a week with your lubricated leg on a steel slab so that the magic of ultrasound can do its thing? Have you put on a pair of cycling shorts, clamped yourself into a harness, gingerly mounted an Alter-G running machine which takes some of the weight off your feet, and felt the shorts squeeze you like a vice as the treadmill started to roll?

Have you ever spent day after day with ice on your knee, wrapped in a tight bandage, and then every twenty minutes unwrapped the bandage, replaced the ice, wrapped up again and repeated the process? Have you ever been to see a surgeon, asked for the prognosis, and heard the sincere reply: 'Well, Paul, put it this way. You have the heart of a 25-year-old and the ligaments of a 25-year-old, but the knees of a 65-year-old'?

Have you ever sat on the toilet, doing the world's most natural thing, except for you it isn't quite so natural, because how many people right now are unscrewing a protein drink and sliding the contents down their throats while their trousers are around their ankles?

If you can answer yes to all of the above, congratulations – you are Paul Nixon in the summer of 2011. And they say life begins at forty?

A month after the end of the 2010 season, I was invited to help coach the Kenya team in the following spring's World Cup. I weighed up the pros and cons and then politely declined. It was going to be a long time away from the family, the money wasn't sensational, and it was going to eat into pre-season at Grace Road. I wanted to hit the ground running that summer. I felt like it could be a good year for me.

Six months later, not long before the season was due to begin, my right knee started to nag. The nagging got worse and the outcome was inevitable: the fifth knee operation of my career. The timing was rotten but this was 2011 and, with the aid of modern rehab and the desire to work my bollocks off, I was playing again just ten days after surgery.

One of our last games in preparation for the Championship opener against Glamorgan was an in-house match. I made 58 not out against our first-team bowlers and felt that my game was in a good place. I was limping a bit, but that was to be expected. I was operating within myself, to look after the knee, and I knew the next four days before the Glamorgan match would help me no end.

Hoggy and Phil Whitticase (who had returned as coach after Boony's departure) didn't agree. When they told me they didn't think I was ready, I was absolutely gutted. The Grace Road pitch was a beauty, Glamorgan would be coming without their main pace weapon, the injured James Harris, and I had to sit it out. Not only that – I had to go to Durham with the seconds 'to prove my fitness'.

Fine. I knew my body and what I needed, but the captain and coach insisted that there could be no special cases. So I went up to Chester-le-Street and made 72 in a one-day game and then a hundred in a three-dayer. I regained my place for the Championship trip to Derbyshire on 14 April, making 46 and 10, and kept it for the return match a fortnight later.

At one stage during Derbyshire's first innings in that second game, Hoggy opted for a short leg. Nobody was keen, so I jogged forward, got the helmet on and squatted into position. Later, when the spinners came on, I had an extended spell at silly mid-on. Derbyshire made 305, Claude and Jigar got through 59 overs and I knew I had done too much when my knee flared up on the morning of the next one-day match at Durham. I tried to get by, but I was struggling. Later, with a trip to Surrey on the horizon, Hoggy and Phil walked over to talk to me. I could tell by the look in their eyes that they were ready for a fight, but I wasn't going to give them one. Not this time. I knew in my heart of hearts that I wasn't right. I needed more rehab on the old knee.

More rehab – more lunges, more hamstring curls, more work with the Swiss Ball, more nights of pain with the compression garments. More pain? Yes, but it was worth it; well, I thought it was. Hoggy then called to inform me that Tom New was going to get a run in the one-day side. I would remain first pick in the Twenty20 games (I was still keeping wicket in limited-overs cricket) but in the Championship they were also keen to 'look to the future', by making room in the batting order for Greg Smith when he returned from university. Making room for Greg meant closing the door on me.

'Fine,' I countered. 'But if I'm in the team and in good form, I shouldn't be dropped. If you're scoring runs, you should play regardless of age. Look at Mark Ramprakash.'

A month later, I returned to the team for the Championship matches at Northampton and then against my old friends at Kent. The latter game was not, this time, at the St Lawrence Ground, but at Tunbridge Wells, where my abiding memory was not of scoring hundreds and hearing the applause but of smashing my nose one time while keeping wicket. We lost the toss, bowled badly into a strong wind and allowed Kent to amass more than 500. I batted at three and had made eight when I hit a square cut off Matt Coles' medium pace like a dream. The fielder leapt in the air, got a hand to it, then tumbled back and completed a hell of a catch. *Lucky swine.* When we later followed on, I middled an early drive off the pacy but erratic Robbie Joseph. My shot cannoned into the bowler's arm and popped up to mid-on, where Rob Key slipped, fell onto his knees and watched the ball disappear into his hands. *Lucky swine.*

Two of the cleanest hits you could wish for, and two dismissals. Were the gods trying to tell me something?

At the end of the game, I caught up with Keysey and asked him what he thought about my batting. 'You're very sideways-on,' he observed. 'And you're leaving balls you would normally hit.' That gave me something to think about. I went straight to the artificial nets for half-an-hour of throwdowns. I opened up, let my hands do more of the work, and started nailing it again. In no time it felt like I was back in the groove.

Then I was dropped again. At a time when I needed just a bit of backing, they dispensed with me in the Championship. After the Kent game I detected a certain aloofness in Hoggy and Phil – always a tell-tale sign when managers are preparing to give you some bad news.

And the strangest thing? Again, I didn't fight. Inside I was spewing, upset that I had been axed when others – Tom, for example – had been indulged without scoring enough runs. I felt I still had heaps to offer as a senior, experienced player. And throughout my career I had always fought adversity, on or off the field. But now? It was, with a heavy heart, time to call off the battle.

When we spoke about my predicament at home, Jen said something wise. 'You're nearly 41,' she observed. 'You should just enjoy your cricket now. You've still got the Twenty20s. Why don't you just go for that?'

So I met Hoggy and Phil and talked about retirement. Just saying the word was odd, but, looking back, the events of Tunbridge Wells had forced me to accept that I couldn't go on forever. After some thought I concluded that it was better to call it a day sooner rather than later, instead of trying to drag things on for another summer and finding my career end on some hollow, empty ground while playing for the seconds.

After that meeting, I went into the nets and threw to Greg Smith for a couple of hours. I was still a bit irritated and disappointed, and Greg looked a bit embarrassed that he had taken my place. But he needed my help and I had not forgotten the time when, as I had walked off after my second dismissal against Derbyshire at Grace Road, I had looked up to the balcony to see Greg enthusiastically clapping me off. 'Top kid,' I thought.

The more I sat and reflected, the more I realised that helping lads like Greg might be my new role. I enjoyed coaching and looking at other people's games. I knew my future was there, not fighting against the pain and the frustration. But I also knew how I wanted to bow out. So when Hoggy collared me one morning and extended a special invitation . . .

'We want you to come back into the team for a swansong at the end of the year.'

. . . I could not have imagined anything worse.

So the Friends Life Twenty20 became my focus. I wanted to go out with a game that meant something, not a meaningless exhibition appearance, and, well, what could be bigger than a Finals Day at Edgbaston? I could tailor my life and my training around that goal. I could refocus and drive myself towards one last challenge.

Then, out of the blue, Hampshire called. They had spotted I was out of the Championship team and asked if I felt like going there on loan. A transfer target at 40! It was enormously flattering, but my brain, and my knees, advised against it. The temptation was strong, if only to show Leicestershire I could still do it. We had been rolled over for a record low score of 34 by Essex in July and I had received a load of texts from fans, and friends, asking what the hell was going on, and why wasn't I in the bloody team? But no. I couldn't. The risk of tweaking my knee again over four days of slog, and of letting Hampshire down at a time when they were desperate for points, stopped me from saying yes.

The plan was to announce my retirement later in the summer. In the meantime, our Twenty20 campaign was given the most incredible boost by Abdul Razzaq, who hopped off a flight from Pakistan and 24 hours later came to Old Trafford for a dark and drizzly floodlit game where he pulverised Lancashire's bowlers for 62 match-winning runs from 30 balls.

Once Razzaq came, I felt we had the makings of a decent side, provided we got our batting order right. Andrew McDonald was good up front, Josh was going well, James Taylor was a machine, I could work it around in the middle and Razza was world-class with bat and ball. Things clicked and we became quite a force. Every victory injected a little more belief into the team and our momentum carried us to the quarter-finals.

Shortly before that game, I made the retirement announcement. I was flooded with messages and well-wishes. That was nice. As a result, the quarter-final, against Kent, was built up twofold – because of its importance to the team, and because everyone now knew it was going to be my last competitive game at Grace Road.

What was also nice was the presentation the club made to me before the game – a silver salver with my name on it – a moment that hit me like a ton of bricks. The previous summer, when walking off a ground, I had told myself to have a good look around, because it might be the last time. It wasn't; I had battled on. This time, though, it was going to be final. *You're retiring. This is the last time you'll be excited for a game at Grace Road.* The end was nigh.

What wasn't so nice was the way Kent then smashed their way to 206-7 courtesy of some awesome hitting from Azhar Mahmood and Martin van

Jaarsveld. That wasn't in the script! But the pitch was a belter and we knew if we could start well, retain wickets and keep our target to no more than 100 from the last 60 balls, we could just about do it.

We started well – better than well. Macca led the charge with a fifty and we went past 100 in the ninth over. We were close to the rate and everyone had managed to contribute usefully, but by the time Macca fell, and it was my turn, we had dipped uncertainly to 128-5, the pressure was on, and this – this is another point where the mental film reel activates itself again, every time, without fail . . .

I shove on my helmet and reach for my bat. I am aware of the noise of the crowd as I start to stride, but there are other noises, which begin thirty yards before I reach the crease.

'Good luck, Badger.'

'Thanks, Geraint.'

Yeah, thanks Geraint. Now I've got a fucking tear in my eye. Come on, man, snap out of this shit! Save the tears for later! This is big-time. Your team needs you.

I get to the middle, greet Razza and go to scratch out my mark.

'Alright maaaate . . . game to win here maaaate . . . game on maaaate.'

Hello, Keysey.

I stifle a laugh, put my head down and walk down the track. I spend a bit longer than normal tapping down the wicket, blinking as fast as I can to get rid of the moisture in my eyes, breathing deeply. I return to my crease and start my self-talk.

'Come on, get going, look straight, watch the ball.'

But this time I am saying it out loud, rather than chanting it to myself.

I get my bearings, consider the Kent attack and remember what Razza had told me in the nets earlier in the week about Wahab Riaz, their left-arm Pakistani seamer. 'With Riaz, stay leg-side, give yourself room and hit him through the offside, or backward of square,' Razza had said. 'Don't go across your stumps, because he will get you lbw.' He then came round the wicket and gave me a series of top-quality Yorkers, to mimic Riaz's line of attack.

Razza is a genius. When Charl Langeveldt tries to target his supposed weakness against the short ball, our talisman is ready for him with a flat-batted baseball shot which tears off to the boundary. He is in awesome touch, and I'm at the other end, doing my bit, feeling fine.

Razza hits another mighty six but then perishes for 27 attempting a back-foot drive over extra cover. Wayne White comes in and we're still trying to get to the line, but I'm now in command. I hit four fours, including one cheeky Chinese cut, and then Azhar Mahmood puts one in the slot. I give myself room and send it high over his head for six.

The crowd is going nuts.

Bloody hell, this is a proper fairytale!

Chalky has a big whoosh off his first ball. He looks a bit flustered. Wayne is a talented lad with plenty of outward bravado, but is also a worrier who is prone to getting down on himself when things aren't going well. The rabbit-in-the headlights approach is not what we need here. I walk down the track and remind him of what we had practiced in the nets.

'You know your areas, bud. Just try to get across your stumps more.'

Then he calms down and gets one off the middle of the bat.

Good lad, Chalky.

We need two off the last over to win. I am on strike. Grace Road is in ferment.

Fuck me, you're going to hit the winning runs here! What a climax, Nico! Your last game at Grace Road and you're the man to get the boys to Finals Day! They'll be carrying you off here in a few minutes!

Riaz runs up and swings one in. I go back and connect with thin air as the ball swerves from the line of off stump and cleans up my middle pole.

So much for the fairytale. I turn and head off, out for 31, cursing myself for thinking about the glory and not the ball. One more kick up the arse from Mother Cricket.

I am still shaking my head when I look up and see the crowd. All around Grace Road, people are on their feet – in the crowd, on the balcony, down by the boundary. I force a smile and raise my bat. Twenty yards from the rope I feel a wave of sadness smash into me. I tuck myself into the dugout with the rest of the players and watch Matt Boyce cream the next ball for four.

We leap from our seats and charge back out onto the pitch. I offer handshakes to some of the Kent boys and then reach Boycey and the others in the middle. I sense a couple of cameras following me but I just feel like going barmy and leading a conga line, like I did fifteen years ago.

No chance. I make a few jaunty steps but the outfield is flooded with fans and most of them are swarming around me. I am grabbed and pulled and mobbed and then I hear my name being sung and then I am lifted up and plonked on someone's shoulder and then someone thrusts a plastic pint pot in my hand.

'Come on Nico, get it down you.'

I dispatch the half-pint of flat lager in one go. Another roar goes up. Eventually I am set down and the bodies disperse. I am ushered towards the Sky Sports section, which is roped off. I am named man-of-the-match and the crowd is still singing in my ear as I talk to Nasser and try to remember to thank everybody who deserves to be thanked. I try to remember not to swear on live television. I then arrive at the bottom of the pavilion, where Josh Cobb tips champagne down from the balcony. I tilt my head back and feel the cold splash before heading upstairs with my own bottle of bubbly. There, I do more interviews, including a nice chat with Charlie Dagnall, an old team-mate who now works for BBC Leicester. I then walk into a dressing room which is still going crackers. 'Right, we're all going out,' someone calls. I grab a white beaker of cheap fizz and glug it down, and then pick at some food.

I flop down on a chair and take a big, deep breath.

I won't do this any more – sit among the piles of kit and absorb the feeling of victory at Grace Road. I am the last out of the dressing room. I don't particularly want to leave. Eventually I get to my feet, shuffle downstairs, sign some autographs, do more interviews, chat to the family and chuckle at the sight of a few waifs and strays in the bar, pissed out of their skulls. I go home, get changed into the loudest shirt in my wardrobe, then head into Leicester, to The Terrace bar, where it is like 1996 and 1998 all over again as champagne is guzzled, trays of shooters are passed around, drinks are poured into my mouth, the froth from pints is flicked into faces and the wives and girlfriends are challenged to do down-downs, with varying degrees of success.

I'm not sure what time it is when Jen grabs my arm and says: 'Come on, it's time to go,' or when I am stopped in my tracks when yet another bottle of champagne is extended. I don't know what time it is when, after demolishing the drink, my attention is then caught by Jen, again, tilting her head to the door, urging me (successfully this time) to make a crafty exit. I don't know what time it is when we get home and we flop into bed.

But I do know what time it is when I am woken with a start by Izzy, who is leaping on the bed and demanding a game of football in the garden. It is 5.00 a.m.

I'm not sure it was wise to agree to commentate on the following day's quarter-final between Nottinghamshire and Somerset at Trent Bridge for the BBC. After Izzy's wake-up call, I lay in bed trying to sober up, then later drove to Nottingham with a can of Red Bull for company, hoping and praying the police didn't stop me. When I got to the ground and took up position in the commentary box with Kevin Howells, the Beeb journalist, everyone seemed to be having a good laugh at my expense. They could see I was in pieces, but they were quite understanding too and the commentary passed – I think – without any disasters.

The next day, I was due to be on air again, this time at Hove for Sussex v Lancashire. I went to bed desperate for a lie-in. Izzy woke me up again at the crack of dawn. I thought about trying to explain to my three-year-old daughter what a hangover meant, and why Daddy needed a little more sleep, but in the end I just gave her a tickle, lifted her into bed and then switched on the TV.

What next? Finals Day, the catch and the grand finale.

What next? The Twenty20 game against India, two days later – my last of any kind at Grace Road. Hoggy asked me if I wanted to be captain but I declined. I didn't feel it was right. I was persuaded to go out for the coin toss, but that was enough. It was nice to get handshakes, hugs and good wishes from Rahul Dravid and the rest of the Indian boys, and nice to walk out to a big reception from the Indian supporters who had queued down the street to come and watch their heroes. But everyone was still feeling sluggish after our celebrations at Edgbaston. I was nowhere. We lost by fifteen runs and my last dismissal on my home ground was carried out by the leg-spinner Amit Mishra, who bowled me as I attempted a reverse-sweep.

What next? The Champions League, in India, once I had hurriedly renewed my passport. One more grand finale? Well, the boys did say I was enjoying more comebacks than Joe Frazier.

But not all of Smokin' Joe's comebacks went to plan. My fairytale ended in England. Our preparations for India weren't great and we were bundled out of the tournament after losing our two matches against Trinidad & Tobago and Ruhunu Rhinos in Hyderabad. Some of the team went straight from a four-day Championship match into the Champions League with no more than three days' build-up. It wasn't nearly enough. Instead of flying out for a week to prepare, acclimatise, adjust and have some serious practice, we found ourselves still battling the effects of jet-lag on the bus to our first game. We were probably also guilty of over-confidence after the way Finals Day had gone. An altered batting order allowed panic to set in, we were on the back foot straight away and the defeats came as a predictable consequence. Game over.

After the Ruhunu loss, we were ushered out of the dressing room quickly, because the next match was due to start soon. Again, I was the last to leave. Partly because this was *definitely* it – the last goodbye – and partly because my big, leather chair was so comfortable. 'Just give me a minute,' I said, reclining in the seat as the other players made for the door.

I had a few seconds of solitude, and then the door opened. Jacques Kallis came in and nodded a greeting. Gautam Gambhir walked over and shook my hand. Soon the dressing room was full of stars – among them Brett Lee, Yusuf Pathan and Brad Haddin, the Aussie wicketkeeper who stopped me for a chat on my way out and seemed to know more about my career than I did.

That's what did it for me. Seeing all those boys made me realise the game was up and the journey was over.

It wasn't a sad feeling; just an acceptance that I had given it my all, and that it was now a game for fresher faces. As I looked at Gambhir and Haddin and all the bright, young Indian players who followed them into the room, I knew more clearly than ever that it was time to make way.

There is a great tradition in Australian Grade Cricket of team songs. When I played Down Under there was nothing more disheartening than hearing the sound of the other dressing room belting out their chosen words as you packed up your kit. And nothing more invigorating than standing in a circle and singing your own song after a big victory.

The team song has long been part of a club's identity in Australia, and the practice has more recently come into county cricket. Everyone is doing it now and at Leicestershire we have a beauty:

> I was born in a country where people admired
> Their great sporting heroes and how they aspired
> To stand up on mountains and always be with us,
> And never give less than their all.
>
> I once met an old man who told me great stories
> Of legends of old who played hard for the Foxes
> Of lifting the cup in the moment of triumph;
> These memories kept me enthralled.
>
> On the fields of Grace Road
> On the fields where boys become men,
> On the fields of Grace Road
> May the best team win – Leicestershire . . .

> LEICESTERSHIRE, LA, LA, LA, LEICESTERSHIRE, LA, LA, LA
> (repeat to fade)

In India, Hoggy was particularly adamant that we should know the words off by heart and be able to produce them at a moment's notice. He asked us to learn the lyrics and then, in a fines meeting, he would walk up to a player at random, recite a line of the song and order the player to give him the next line, there and then.

It was like being back at school. It just wouldn't sink in. In the space of four days I only memorised the first four lines. I got fined loads . . .

twenty-two

BAT ON

'What inspires you? What are the things and the people that get you going?'

I told my ghostwriter that he might need to double the size of the book to record all my answers.

'Just the main ones, then.'

Here goes.

1. John Holliday

You might recall that I always regarded myself as a bit tougher than John. I mean, come on – when we played cricket in his back garden he actually used to tell me to stop bowling too fast, because he didn't want his legs to get hurt! He was mentally quite sharp, but was never exactly full of life, or activity, or physical resolve. His response to a tricky situation was to think his way out of it rather than run or fight. When he was lucky enough to enjoy a brief career as a centre-half with Carlisle United, he often complained about pre-season training. He absolutely hated it. He later drifted out of football and became a journalist, which seemed to suit him better.

So that's John, then – not very tough, and lucky.

In November 2007, John returned from a jog to find a lump on the side of his neck. Two months later he was diagnosed with cancer of the tongue. The following twelve months were painful and gruelling, and during his illness I went to visit him at his home in Richmond near London. A couple of Irish girls, fellow television journalists, were visiting at the same time, and there was John, sat on his sofa with Beth, his wife, all chilled-out and chatty. It wasn't until he stood up to say goodbye to these girls that I saw the hole in his stomach and realised he was being fed from a tube. It really hit me then that John wasn't in great shape.

But he stayed remarkably positive and upbeat, wrote a diary of his illness to help keep himself focused, and in April 2009, having received the all-clear, ran the London Marathon. It was a truly amazing feat and I was in awe of the bloke.

Then, in 2010, fortune dealt John another shocker. He suffered a stroke and had to learn how to walk again. During this second struggle, I visited him in hospital and felt my heart sink when he came through the door to greet me. Here was this strapping, 6ft 4in ex-sportsman recast as an injured soldier with a series of shrapnel wounds. His hair was straggly and scruffy, his lips were chapped, his skin was grey, and he moved with his head bowed and his body stooped forward. When we went for a stroll around the block with his physio, he had to drag one leg along the ground and stop for regular rests. One of his arms didn't swing, and he couldn't turn his neck.

I tried to be cheerful and upbeat all the time I was there, but it wasn't easy. I remember heading home thinking, 'Poor lad – I'm walking away from this now, and he's not.'

On Monday 24 October 2011, John went back to work, as a business journalist for Bloomberg TV. Another battle has been won and he is now a more positive person than I have ever known him to be.

One of John's old sayings is 'Come on – bat on'. Get cracking, in other words. What he has been through, and the way he has dealt with it, makes me realise what is important in life.

2. James Taylor

James isn't the only modern young player I admire, but he's a classic case. It took me most of my career to realise that the mental side of sport is as important as the physical side, but Titch is there already. At Leicestershire I marvelled at how he always seemed in control of his mindset and his processes. He knew his game inside-out from day one and if he doesn't go on to score bucketloads of runs for Nottinghamshire and England, I will give up trying to judge a cricketer's potential. Someone who has already made it to that wonderful stage, Stuart Broad, is a shining example for Titch and all the others. He is a brilliant cricketer but also the most humble bloke.

3. Moeneeb Josephs

If you asked me to nominate one piece of correspondence that has made me smile more than any other, it wouldn't be a letter from a fan or a good-luck message from home – it would be an e-mail which came out of the blue during my benefit year.

From: Mark Davids
Sent: 15 February 2008 11:40
Subject: Cape Town Kids

To whom it may concern.

My name is Mark Davids and I've been trying to get in contact with Paul 'Nico' Nixon again. I was searching for some links related to Paul,

& a couple of friends & myself will never forget him for all the things he gave us.

He might not remember my name, but in 2007 he wrote a letter on the net (Bunbury cricket) containing information of the time he spent with us. He used to be our cricket coach in 1992/93 in Mitchell's Plain, Cape Town. He always believed that all of us could go very far. I'm sure as a coach, he will be very proud to know that most of the people he coached went much further (Provincial & National level even).

The others that never went as far are busy coaching cricket as well. Another guy that played with us was Moeneeb Josephs and at the time when Paul was at our club, lots of people wanted to become wicket-keepers. This particular guy played soccer in our winter as well & he is currently South Africa's national goal-keeper.

This is just one of the success stories fermenting the seeds that he planted over here in Cape Town. We are all playing and coaching kids to stay off the street & the drugs and it's all because of him.

If it's possible we would just all like to give tribute to him again.

Mark Davids.

In all my trips back to South Africa, whether with Leicestershire on pre-season tours or with Jen on holiday, I never heard from the people who first welcomed me to that wonderful country. My Mitchell's Plain tracksuit remained one of my most prized possessions, but memories fade and, if I'm honest, it wasn't exactly on my mind every day.

Then came that message from Mark, which I still cannot read without grinning from ear to ear.

Moeneeb Josephs . . . Moeneeb Josephs . . .

For months I struggled to fit a face to the name, but then it hit me: the inquisitive bundle of energy who couldn't wait to get the gloves on any time I showed up for practice? That was him! He must have been 12 years old at the time.

Well, he might not have made a wicketkeeper in the end, but the records show that he did play in a small event called the 2010 FIFA World Cup. Will we settle for that? Yes, I think so.

4. The rugby man

Many moons ago, there was another farmer's lad from Cumbria's Eden Valley who played schools cricket for his county. This one was a dogged opening batsman who valued his wicket like nothing else on earth. Like the farmer who has to be careful with his outgoings, he was never one to play an exuberant shot with his Gray-Nicolls Scoop when a more responsible option was available.

He had the solid technique to back up this approach, and that's basically how he was in life: just a rock-solid character, who commanded respect even from an early age. He lived 3 miles away from Langwathby in the village of Culgaith and if he didn't outstrip me as a cricketer, he did as a rugby player and was streets ahead of me academically.

Our paths crossed often, back then, and we kept in contact as time went by. And when the Rugby Football Union finally got round to appointing him as England's permanent head coach I only had one question: what took them so bloody long?

Stuart Lancaster has always been 100 per cent straight, someone who does things properly and the kind of person you turn to if you ever need advice. He has been successful everywhere he has been in his sport and absolutely deserves to be where he is now. A great man, and a leader.

5. Family

Jen Nixon. How can I do justice to my wife in a few words? I can't, not really, but I will say this: Jen has been an absolute rock for me ever since we met, there to enjoy the ups, there to help me during the downs, a calming influence when my mind has been up to its weird tricks, understanding with everything I have thrown at her, and the person whose opinion I value the most. She is a worrier by nature but she has an incredible knack of getting the measure of someone within a few minutes of meeting them, and has kept me right on more occasions than I can remember. She also runs the house like clockwork, ensures I'm organised (an unbelievable feat in itself) and is brilliant with Izzy, and does all this while keeping on top of her own business stuff. She likes to be in control of things, whereas I'm generally flitting from one idea to the next. She is perfect for me – there is nobody I will ever trust more than Jen and I wouldn't be half the person I am without her.

Paul McKeown, my brother-in-law. Macca is a handy bowler, who wins games for Workington in the Cumbria Cricket League, and is also what you might call a straight-talker. When I was battling Leicestershire over my contract, he urged me not to let the bastards get me down. He spoke common sense down the phone countless times and I listened to him. He is one of my biggest supporters, with everything that word entails. When I got picked for England, he was probably more thrilled than anyone. He has also collected more of my spare kit over the years than anyone else, and I'm sure his (5ft 6in) dad is still walking around West Cumbria wearing (6ft 4in) Michael Kasprowicz's tracksuit bottoms.

Ernie Nixon was my grandfather. In my mind I can see him now: a man of about 5ft 8in, with his white vest creeping out from underneath his shirt, his waistcoat and jacket buttoned up, his old pair of suit trousers covering his long-johns and tucked into his Wellingtons. I can see his red, cracked cheeks, glowing beneath his flat cap. I can see him feeding the calves and the sheep and then walking up to the gate, resting a foot on one of the bars, and watching the kids playing football down on the green.

Granddad was fundamentally a good bloke. He settled his bills on time and sometimes paid over the odds for things, just to help people out. There was a lot of warmth in his house, too, with Grandma always having the table laid out with cakes and biscuits and all kinds of other treats. It created a lovely atmosphere and it gives me a tingle to think about it now. It also gave Granddad sugar diabetes, which is hardly surprising.

When Ernie Nixon died, in 1998, the whole community came out to say goodbye. St Peter's Church was packed and his coffin was driven through Langwathby on a beautiful, horse-drawn hearse. When it stopped at his gate before carrying on to the church, I was bawling my eyes out, and I wasn't the only one.

There was so much respect for him, and I have always felt proud to be a Nixon; proud of that respect, proud of the way I am treated back home because of my family, because of the name, because of men like Granddad. I hope I have done something to make them proud of me, as well.

6. Teachers

(Yes, you read that correctly). Rick Martin at Ullswater School was like a second father when it came to sport. We were kindred spirits (he liked his rugby, but cricket was his first love) and he challenged me to improve every day. He recognised my passion because he had it himself.

Paul Leeming, a former goalkeeper and another Ullswater man, jokes to this day that I owe my career to him. The reason? A game against the Grammar School, when I was plumb lbw but he didn't give me out. I went on to score a hundred and won the match. Paul, I will buy you that pint soon.

Peter Kremer was sports master at Queen Elizabeth Grammar School, Penrith. He should have been the enemy, but he was also my county rugby coach and was more mentor than teacher. Every pupil who he took under his wing spoke glowingly about him. He died far too young, of cancer, at 44.

Mr Howarth. I'm not sure what to say about my spelling-test nemesis, who is sadly no longer with us, but I do wish he had lived to see the invitation I received in the post early in 2012:

Dear Mr Nixon

It is with great pleasure that I write to inform you that you have been nominated for the award of an Honorary Doctor of Letters of De Montfort University in recognition of your outstanding achievements in cricket.

The University awards honorary degrees upon individuals who have distinguished themselves in their professional lives and who have made outstanding contributions to the intellectual and cultural life of the nation and the region.

Your successful career is evidence that hard work, commitment and dedication will bring rewards at the highest possible level. This, coupled with your strong association with the county of Leicestershire, makes you an excellent role model for young people. The University would feel very proud if you would accept this award.

With best wishes,

Yours sincerely,

Professor Dominic Shellard
Vice-Chancellor

Paul Nixon, Doctor of Letters. Nobody saw that coming, it's safe to say.

I have never much been driven by statistics. For me, cricket and life shouldn't be all about numbers.

By all means, I can list a few. I can tell you my First Class average is 34 and a bit. I can tell you I made 99 stumpings in one-day cricket. I can tell you I did not miss a single Twenty20 game for Leicestershire. I can write down all my First Class wickets in one go (William Porterfield, lbw Nixon, Gloucestershire v Leicestershire, 10 May 2010). I can recite the number of times I have been dismissed for a 'pair' of ducks in the same match (zero) and I can inform you very modestly that my 2007 World Cup average (38.6) was higher than Brian Lara's (38.42).

I am also happy to produce my annual Championship averages from 2004 to 2008, to display how my form took off after meeting Wynford Dore:

2004 – 361 runs from 21 innings, average 20.05
2005 – 708 runs from 27 innings, average 35.40
2006 – 895 runs from 23 innings, average 59.66
2007 – 879 runs from 21 innings, average 48.83
2008 – 954 runs from 24 innings, average 53.00

I can, too, reel off some of the bests and worsts from a 22-year career, from the quickest bowlers I faced (Patrick Patterson and Shaun Tait) to the best delivery I ever received (Bravo's slower ball in the World Cup; as I've said before – I've sent search parties out looking for that one but I still can't find it).

I could nominate my greatest shot (Murali in the World Cup, although I reversed Monty for a bigger one in a county match before then) and my most memorable catch (bet you can't guess that one). But I don't want to be identified by facts and figures. I don't want my life and career to be measured by a chart, or noted down in a list.

When I take my last breath, I want to be remembered as a good bloke, someone who worked his bollocks off, played hard and was proud to wear that Leicestershire fox on his cap, but always made time for a drink with the other team at the end. I want to think of myself as someone who gave enjoyment. I want to recall the people who came up to me after the quarter-final against Kent and told me that their kids loved me now because they were allowed to stay up late to watch the cricket on TV.

I want to remember the goodwill I received from all corners, some of them surprising, like Don Wilson, who I never thought believed in me when I was on the Lord's groundstaff but who wrote me the nicest, most humble letter in the world after that Kent game. I want to remember how the national anthem always moved me to tears, how the biggest and the bravest stirred my blood (Goughie, Beefy, this means you), how the sight of a young rugby player or footballer or cricketer playing his heart out on TV got me going.

I want to be remembered as someone who was passionate for life, who liked to be around people, who liked to be happy around people, who didn't say no, who might have been 'mad as a badger' (copyright R.W.T. Key, 2000, in response to my nocturnal nature and my endurance on an average evening on the sambucas) but tried to use his energy in a positive way. I want to look back and know that yes, I made a couple of mistakes along the way, but mainly I didn't lose sight of the important stuff.

I want to reflect not only on how the six-year-old boy hitting the tennis ball onto the pavilion roof at Penrith Cricket Club went on to win trophies and play for his country, but also how he handled dyslexia and tackled his demons. I want to think about the relationships I struck up over the years, the mates I have been privileged to make in different countries, how I can call legends like Steve Waugh and Rahul Dravid friends, how Chris Adams and Ian Salisbury thought enough of me to try to get me on the coaching staff at Surrey last summer, all those years after we first played together for the Under-15s and groundstaff respectively.

I want to remember myself as someone who was generous and who tried to share, whether by saying hello to a kid in a school or by doing something much bigger. Yes, I want to do well in life after cricket; I want to be a successful coach, a highly rated media pundit, a winner in business and the best 'club ambassador' Leicestershire could possibly have. But I never want to forget that I came from a kind, hospitable background, and that life is essentially about giving.

I've seen a lot of hardship in the world. I have seen poverty in India and South Africa. I have seen children in cancer wards in England and been touched to the core. I have seen dying African kids on TV weighing no more than a candle, and thought, 'Right, Nixon, it's time to get your finger out'.

Once or twice in recent years Jen has given me a bit of grief about my benefit year, because I gave so much away. But why not? I want to do more, give more. I want to create a foundation, whether it's back in Cumbria, in Leicester or abroad. I want to be the ex-cricketer who does the most for the PCA Benevolent Fund. I want to be proactive in other cricket charities, like Chance to Shine and the Lord's Taverners. I want to do a big charity event myself, like running from John O'Groats to Land's End, although I'm not sure the knees could cope with that idea.

I want to do something. I want to make a difference.

There's something else about Granddad. One of his oldest friends and workers is a man called George Watson, who still lives in one of Granddad's houses in Langwathby. George always regarded Granddad as the world's hardest-working man. 'He nivver had time te' finish a piss,' he once said to me. I can see that trait in myself, at times, when I'm so busy that I start to forget things, and I also see it in Izzy, when my little daughter leaps off the loo without wiping her bum and charges off to do something else. I can hear George laughing in my ear: 'Aye, just like her great-grandfather . . . She's a bloody Nixon, lad.'

Ernie was a get-on-with-it kind of man, and when he needed to take on a new worker for the farm, he had a special criterion. He would judge the candidates based on how quickly they walked from the front gate to the house. 'If they've got a good, brisk walk,' I once heard him say, 'it means they're a worker.'

Years later, I received a letter from a Leicestershire supporter, who wanted to know about my walk from the pavilion to the wicket. He said it was the fastest walk he had seen, a walk that gave the impression I was heading off to do a job. A statement of intent, if you like. 'Where does that walk come from?' my correspondent asked. It wasn't a difficult question to answer.

EPILOGUE

Friday 3 February 2012.

I sit back down at the table, pausing to check the time on my phone; I will have to get changed soon. If I can scribble a few more lines down quickly, now, then I can set off happy and confident that I will be able to put all the pieces together and bring the house down.

He is at me the second I pick up my pen and try to focus on the page.

What are you writing here? Why are you doing it that way? That's no good. Call that a speech? That's rubbish! Now, make sure you get that joke right. Don't want to get the words in the wrong order now, do you? No, there's only one thing for it – you'll just have to start all over again . . .

I swat him aside and reach across the table for the ruler. The ruler, needless to say, isn't there. It is still in the office. I curse, shove my chair back and repeat the trip upstairs.

The war still has to be waged. I still do some of Wynford's exercises, but probably not enough of them. When I wake up in the morning I can rate myself out of ten as to how good I'm going to be feeling for the rest of the day, about how cluttered or how clear my mind will be. On a bad day I still feel like lying on the sofa and doing nothing. On a bad day, the little man still makes his presence felt. On a bad day, like this one, the distractions can still take over and make me a nightmare in conversation.

Look at him, through the window, crossing the road. Who's that, getting out of her car? Who is on Twitter? Who is on Skype? Who was that who just texted?

I'm sorry, what was the question?

On a bad day, my speech can be terrible. I stutter, um and er, lose track of my, er, line of thought, and, um, it's probably not ideal when you have to, er, speak at big dinners or corporate, you know, functions. But the good days tend to outweigh the bad. On a good day, I can write something down and it will instantly enter my head. I can then deliver it sharply and clearly. That's what I have to try to harness.

Sometimes, when I am home alone, I will listen to a relaxation CD before going to bed. Andy Whiteman, our groundsman at Leicestershire, made a few for me and it's good to hear some positive affirmations when the mind is going ten to the dozen.

On other days, I will involve Izzy in my little routines. She loves being spun around, and when I am rotating on one leg, with my daughter whizzing around me, giggling and laughing, she probably doesn't notice that I'm doing my eye exercises and going through a times table at the same time . . .

'One four is four
Two fours are eight
Three fours are twelve
Four fours are sixteen
Five fours are twenty
Six fours are twenty-four . . .'

. . . but I am. Now, how mad is that?

ACKNOWLEDGEMENTS

It was in January of 2007, just as Paul Nixon's cricketing dreams were about to come true, that we first talked about a book. Well, I did. The setting was the practice nets at Sydney Cricket Ground, the sun was purest Australian gold, and the man was cheerfully noncommittal.

'Yeah,' he said, eventually, when I suggested he should consider putting his story between hard covers. 'It's something I've thought about. I think I've got some tales to tell.'

I left, twenty minutes later, with a handshake and a lively interview on my notepad, but also a sense that he had been nothing more than incredibly polite to the impertinent journalist who had suggested he might be entrusted with the account of his life's work.

The idea was left to bake, slowly. In the shorter term, the fact that the conversation had taken place at all said something about Paul, who had persuaded the stadium's security staff to allow an optimistic, holidaying reporter he barely knew (and his friend, posing as a freelance photographer) into his working environment. That day he seemed to me as he appears to everyone: an open door, with a smiling attitude that says nothing is too much trouble. He seemed as happy as it was possible for a 36-year-old man to be and was keen to share his joy with anyone who crossed his path. Already, in his upbeat bearing, I felt I had the essence of the man.

By 2010, after many more calls and conversations, I had persuaded him to allow me to tell his tales. When, over coffee in the Leicester Marriott (where else?), he confided that he had recently been offered 'serious money' to fix a cricket match, I nearly launched my drink over him in excitement. I drove back to Carlisle that day convinced that the book had its headline-grabbing hook, and that the rest of the story would flow simply from there.

It was only when the interviews started in earnest that the real narrative began to unfold. I knew something of Paul's dyslexia and his commitment to sports psychology, not to mention his maverick nature, but there were further depths to the man I had not imagined. As a sportswriter you go into the trade expecting to describe goals and wickets, triumphs and failures, and perhaps to point the finger at a villain or two. What you do not anticipate is to sit in an international cricketer's kitchen and ask him some seriously strange questions . . .

'This might sound daft, but . . . do you think you could draw him?'

'Yeah, I can.'

I still don't know who the little negative man is, exactly, but I feel grateful to have been introduced.

Another thing Paul said in the Marriott that summer was that the book should be 'honest'. Throughout the last couple of years he has held onto that principle. Without his commitment to openness this book would be different and duller. Thanks, Paul, for *not* keeping quiet.

There are too many other people to thank than this space can possibly contain but some have gone above and beyond since the idea started to develop. Michelle Tilling at The History Press believed in the book from the outset and has been wonderfully supportive throughout. At some stage in the future I'll run out of questions to ask her, she probably hopes.

Before a word was written, Chris Bascombe of the *Daily Telegraph* gave me some useful pointers in the art of ghostwriting, while Roger Lytollis, at Cumbrian Newspapers, has offered invaluable help, support and advice at every painstaking stage. His brilliant book, *One Hit Wonder: The Jimmy Glass Story* is the best you will read about an accidental sporting hero.

Chris Goddard, doyen of the *Leicester Mercury* sportsdesk for many years, helped with the detail of Leicestershire's *annus horribilis;* his knowledge and time is appreciated. Thanks for memory-jogging and anecdote excavation are also due to Scott Boswell, Darren Maddy and James Whitaker.

John Holliday's guided tour of Langwathby in the wind and rain was better than any of his performances for Carlisle United (sorry, John, but it was either that or I called you an inspiration again), while I have lost count of the friends who have urged me along the way. I would love to name them all, but Phil Houghton and Paul Morris are two who have been there from start to finish. Thanks to them, to the good men of Ingol CC, and to the Bowland Old Boys.

I'm extremely grateful to my employers and colleagues at Cumbrian Newspapers for their understanding while this book has been in the making, and for permission to reproduce photos. Stewart Blair, the picture editor, has my thanks. Likewise Barry Hollis at the Kent Messenger Group, and the indefatigable Lynda Smart at the *Leicester Mercury*. Just one more request, Lynda . . .

Before the writing began in earnest, Brian Nixon was kind enough to throw some light on Paul's youth and in the process unearthed some fantastic memories. Sylvia Nixon and Christine Young helped immeasurably with family photos, while Jen Nixon's eagle eye at a late stage in the process helped keep this book off the fiction shelves; and her friendliness and warmth during my many visits, often at short notice, never wavered. And Izzy, the strange man with the silly hair won't be calling by so often now. You can have your old man back.

I have still yet to meet Marcus Charman but I can say for sure that the man is a marvel. Along with Ed Melia's superb photographic skills he has produced a wonderful jacket design, but that is only one part of his contribution. Along the way he has also been a priceless confidant, and possesses the precious skill of saying something encouraging when it is most needed. Thanks, mate.

Mam and Dad, Jeff and Noreen Colman, have tolerated my grumpiness and failures to answer the phone more than anyone over the past year, and in return I have received only love, encouragement and the best sanctuary for writing and relaxing in all of Cumbria. Clark Colman's spare bed and port supplies have been other essential features of the journey, and, more importantly, his brotherly advice and care have never wavered. I can't thank him, or his fiancée Claire, enough. Tess Worden, meanwhile, doesn't seem to appreciate how special she is, but now it's down in print she is just going to have to believe it.

Jon Colman, June 2012

*   *   *

Over recent years I have been fortunate to have several people chat to me about writing my book. They have all been wonderful people and quality writers, but happily one man stood out head and shoulders above everyone else. It's hard to do justice to the quality of the man, and that's not just because it takes me three weeks to type out a paragraph using modern technology, never mind several of them!

To make a dyslexic Cumbrian farmer's son enormously proud of writing an open, honest account of his life, all 41 years of it, is beyond belief and exceedingly heart-warming. Throughout our journey Jon Colman has been awesome. The drive, commitment, structure and sheer man-hours he has given to our cause have blown my mind. The late nights – many after long days away watching our beloved Carlisle United – must have pushed him to the edge, I'm sure.

Without Jon's passion and direction, this book would never have happened. The late-night chats, the tweets, the e-mails and the calls have all been worth it. At times it's been like finding that needle in a haystack, with my memory, but Jon really dug deep and has pulled out the stories from friends and colleagues far and wide across the globe. In fact, Jon should be a private detective. With that haircut and dodgy jacket, there's every chance he could be the new Sherlock Holmes!

It's been a pleasure getting to know you, Jon – you were the best man for the job and you deserve a bestseller, as good things happen to good people.

Thank you for everything, bud.

Nico